Praise for *Leading for Instructiona*

"Finding ways to increase the effectiveness of teac[...] most hotly debated policy issues of recent times. By focusing on the experience of educational leaders who have been successful in providing instructional leadership this book offers insights that are invaluable to educators who seek to enhance teacher effectiveness now. The ideas presented are practical and applicable to schools in a variety of settings."

—*Pedro A. Noguera, Ph.D., Peter L. Agnew Professor of Education, Steinhardt School of Culture, Education and Development and executive director, Metropolitan Center for Urban Education*

"In this age of intense focus on how we evaluate teachers, we have to remember that any evaluation is only as good as the evaluator. What Stephen Fink and Anneke Markholt have done with this extremely useful book is to provide an excellent roadmap for how principals can become more effective in the most important aspect of their work, instructional leadership. We cannot lose sight of the fact that if we want to improve teaching and learning, then we have to make all evaluations meaningful and a real tool for the professional growth of our teachers."

—*Jerry D. Weast, Ed.D., superintendent of schools, Montgomery County Public Schools, Maryland*

"Fink and Markholt provide a deep and thoughtful look at how the issue of expertise is cultivated in the complex world of teaching, learning, and instructional leadership. Seizing upon their Center's research-based instructional framework, they provide important insights and tools designed to develop the expertise of teachers, principals, and district leaders in their collective work to improve teaching practice."

—*Dr. Beverly Hall, superintendent, Atlanta Public Schools*

"Amid growing recognition that it is powerful and effective teaching that will advance the learning of every kind of student, Fink and Markholt bring us their field-tested framework for developing higher expertise, and therefore greater capacity, among teachers and school leaders. This well-crafted, thoughtful and pragmatic book shouldn't be filed in bookshelves — it should be open and in use on the desks of principals, teachers, and district leaders across the country who intend to drive better policy through better practice."

—Jill Powers Kirk, vice president,
Oregon Business Council

"As our nation faces the challenges of the 21st century, equal opportunity in education is an irreplaceable pillar of a just and stable society. The methods and strategies outlined in *Leading for Instructional Improvement* have the potential to raise the standards for both teaching and learning. The National Urban League has set a goal for 2025 that every American child is ready for college, work and life. Stephen Fink and Anneke Markholt can help set the nation on the path to empowerment by ensuring that every teacher is engaged, informed and aware."

—Marc H. Morial, president,
National Urban League

Leading for Instructional Improvement

How Successful Leaders Develop Teaching and Learning Expertise

Stephen Fink • Anneke Markholt

with Michael A. Copland • Joanna Michelson

Foreword by John Bransford

JOSSEY-BASS
A Wiley Imprint
www.josseybass.com

Published by Jossey-Bass
A Wiley Imprint
One Montgomery Street, Suite 1000, San Francisco, CA, 94104-4594—www.josseybass.com

Jossey-Bass books and products are available through most bookstores. To contact Jossey-Bass directly
call our Customer Care Department within the U.S. at 800-956-7739, outside the U.S. at 317-572-3986,
or fax 317-572-4002.

Jossey-Bass also publishes its books in a variety of electronic formats. Some content that appears in print
may not be available in electronic books.

Library of Congress Cataloging-in-Publication Data

Fink, Stephen L.
   Leading for instructional improvement : how successful leaders develop teaching and learning
expertise / Stephen Fink, Anneke Markolt; foreword by John Bransford.
     p. cm.
   Includes bibliographical references and index.
   ISBN 978-0-470-54275-0 (pbk.); 978-1-118-03174-2 (ebk.); 978-1-118-03175-9 (ebk.);
978-1-118-03176-6 (ebk.)
  1. Educational leadership–United States. 2. School administrators–United States.
3. School management and organization–United States. 4. Teacher effectiveness–United States.
5. Effective teaching–United States. 6. Educational change–United States.
I. Markolt, Anneke. II. Title.
  LB2805.F456 2011
  371.2–dc22

                                   2010049430

Printed in the United States of America

FIRST EDITION

PB Printing 10 9

CONTENTS

FOREWORD

Reading this book activated a range of emotions—from exhilaration to frustration. The exhilaration comes from reading the critical assumptions and insights about teaching and learning that the authors discuss based on many hours spent in classrooms and districts. I've seen CEL's work in action and I know that they truly "walk their talk." Especially noteworthy is the respect they show for teachers and schools that are working mightily to help all students succeed. They understand the complexity of learning to teach and to lead well and understand that the development of expertise is necessary and doable. As learners, we are always on the edge of our own expertise. The authors illustrate how instructional leaders lead while in the midst of learning and developing adaptive expertise.

My frustration stems from two things: (1) wishing I had seen a book like this twenty or so years ago as I was beginning my career as a learning scientist and (2) wishing our current policy makers, documentary filmmakers, and talk show hosts, who in their effort to bring more attention to the current state of public education continue to promote a national discourse that is troublingly superficial in terms of what is needed to ensure quality learning for all students.

First in terms of my own practice, I had the great privilege of being one of the first students to attend the Center for the Study of Human Learning, directed by James Jenkins at the University of Minnesota. It was a fabulous experience and one that I appreciate more and more as I continue to study processes of human learning. Our work in Minnesota started at the cusp of what has been called *The Cognitive Revolution.* We did laboratory experiments on processes that affected attention, memory, retrieval, problem solving, transfer, and other important phenomena but almost all of this work was in laboratories that used college sophomores as participants and experimenters as the ones leading the "intervention" or instruction. We constantly discussed and worried about the "ecological validity" of our research but the prevailing paradigms for most of us were still one-to-one sessions (one experimenter and one participant) that could be easily managed and controlled in order to ensure "treatment fidelity."

Many of my cognitive friends were trained in a similar way in labs across the country, and eventually a number of us decided to move at least some of our work from pristine laboratory settings to actual classrooms. We were in for a shock. Teachers were dealing with twenty or more students simultaneously and that was a far cry from our one-on-one laboratory experiences. Teachers also had to be accountable to a number of different people including each of their individual students, along with other teachers, principals, superintendents, parents, school boards, state tests, and so forth.

As we worked in schools, we saw many of our laboratory-based research projects crash and burn because of the complexity and other priorities that teachers and schools had to meet. In looking back on this era of our early school-based research, I realize that work in the schools involved experimenters teaching some small lesson while teachers took on the role of saving us from our lack of classroom management skills, but they never had to learn to change their own instruction. Helping teachers improve their instruction never appeared on our to-do list. Discussions in this book advance many of the findings from laboratory research on learning and I am still an extremely strong advocate for laboratory experiments that allow people to carefully study important phenomena, but more is needed, and this is where the wisdom from this book kicks in.

The authors clearly respect the deep expertise needed for effective teaching and learning. Perhaps more important, the authors are fully aware that simply asking teachers and educational leaders to learn to change their practices by attending a professional development session or reading a book or article is not sufficient to support a trajectory of improvement. Schools need to create communities of learners that continually help one another improve. The authors not only cite important general principles for teacher and organizational change, they also give many specific examples—including tools and procedures for self-assessments of teaching and leadership proficiency.

It is precisely because of the authors' deep and insightful treatment of teaching and learning that my frustration continues when I see those who are quick to offer the next most-important fix to public education, all the while remaining ignorant to the core issue facing public education in America, which is the issue of expertise—an argument the authors advance with eloquence.

Just recently, I was asked to suggest a team to work with a school district that is doing well but wants to do much better. My first step was to call Stephen Fink and Anneke Markholt and ask if they would join the team. The insights they provided in just a short amount of telephone time were invaluable and the insights in this book are even more impressive. I'm going to make sure that my learning science students read this book so that, unlike me and my early graduate school colleagues, my students will get a clearer picture of the complexities of initiating and sustaining successful organizational change that enhances learning for educational leaders and teachers (including parents) so that they can better help their students learn.

It is a great privilege and honor to know the authors of this book, work with them, and see the key ideas from their work that this book communicates with such clarity. There are a lot of pieces to the educational puzzle and this book represents a huge advance in identifying and providing tools to manage the inherent complexity of instructional improvement. I read it and wept a bit because this book was not around when I started my career. I hope you can read it and enjoy.

John Bransford
Shauna C. Larson Professor of Education and
Professor of Psychology at the University of Washington in Seattle

For my father, Bob Markholt, whose life work inspired my own.
—Anneke

To my parents, whose early lessons on leadership somehow instilled in me the strong sense that it is better to be the sheepherder than the sheep. And to my wife, Debbie, who long ago recognized my sheepherding tendencies and has never wavered in her support as I continually seek new land on which to graze.
—Steve

ACKNOWLEDGMENTS

This book has been years in the making. Since our beginning at the Center for Educational Leadership, we have been honored and humbled to work and learn alongside many educators. The ideas and tools found in this book are the result of our collective efforts and learning with our colleagues and district partners. We have been fortunate to work and learn with people who are willing to put towering ideas, scholarly research, and theory into practice. They pushed our thinking and allowed us to push theirs. We are indebted and grateful for their willingness to partner with us to bushwhack through uncharted terrain until we arrived at plans, strategies, and qualities of professional learning that worked in their unique district context.

Our colleagues at CEL have been our thought partners and have taught us much about the development of instructional leadership. The Five Dimensions (5D) of Teaching and Learning is the brainchild of Dina Blum and we are fortunate that for over a year she spearheaded our meetings where we hunkered down with the 5D framework, deliberated, argued, and wordsmithed. Dina and Mike Copland took our collective thinking and created a tool that has helped us and our partners get smarter about the definition of high-quality teaching and learning and understand just how sophisticated teaching can be. Our colleagues who spend their time in our partnership districts work hard to put compelling theory into practice and we have been privileged to work alongside them since 2003. Wilma Kozai, who had just retired from San Diego Unified School District before joining CEL, has taught us how to *teach* instructional leadership. Wilma is a consummate learner and her passion for equity fuels a fire deep within her that is contagious. The intellect and energy that Sandy Austin brings to CEL and to the partnerships with which she works is inspiring. A number of the tools and protocols throughout this book are Sandy's brainchild. Sandy is the epitome of one who practices a work ethic with pizzazz. Max Silverman recently joined CEL, although we worked with him in one of our district partnerships beginning in 2003. We are fortunate to have his smarts and sensibilities and you will see examples of his work throughout this book in the form of instructional letters and other tools. Lara Lyons has performed multiple roles at CEL, always providing a keen eye to ensure that our materials speak to our audience. You will see examples of Lara's thinking in several chapters. Since 2007 Rita Lowy has been CEL's lead project director for the 5D assessment. Her thinking and the rest of our CEL directors' thoughts can be seen in the latest edition of the 5D framework (Version 3.0). We also appreciate her thorough review of Chapter Three, where the 5D framework is applied to classroom practice.

We want to acknowledge the superintendents, executive directors, principals, coaches, and teacher leaders from our district partnerships who have allowed us to learn with and from them. These district leaders have been courageous enough to invest in the long-term proposition of developing teaching and leadership expertise. In the face of pressure for quick test score gains, these districts recognize that although they need to address the urgency of adequate yearly progress (AYP) demands, they also need to invest in building their district's capacity.

We have also been fortunate to have several consultants who have worked steadily with us since 2004. Jenn McDermott's brilliant thinking is exemplified in Chapter Seven on coaching and in the discussions and examples of separating observation from interpretation. She has taught many of us about how to avoid conflating our observations with our interpretations and how to coach in ways that honor the extant knowledge of our learners while pushing their practice. Since the beginning of our school district partnership work in 2003 Katherine Casey has taught us how to study instruction while understanding the strengths and needs of teachers. Early in our work, Lesley Gordon reminded us that we should help our district partners learn to be "hard on the work, gentle with one another." Her wisdom has become part of the bedrock of our efforts and you will see Lesley's words repeated throughout this book.

The fact is, each time we have the opportunity for a conversation, a classroom visit, a study session, a think-tank gathering, or the privilege to be invited into a school to coach, we learn something from the experience and from our peers. The nature of constant learning, of still trying to "get it right" urges us to continuously learn and to continue to grow our own expertise. We are indebted to the many people who continue to work alongside us and help us figure it out along the way!

Every year we spend many hours in classrooms teaching leaders how to observe and analyze teaching and learning and how to help teachers improve their instructional practice. In fact, along with our colleagues at the Center for Educational Leadership (CEL) at the University of Washington, we spend thousands of hours in hundreds of classrooms each year. We are in schools and school districts—dozens of them each year as well. We are not at all surprised that too many of our students are still not learning at high levels and that long-standing academic achievement gaps that divide our nation's children along lines of race, class, language, and disability continue to persist. In fact, we believe that any astute observer of teaching, learning, and school leadership who spends ample time observing classroom teaching and talking with school and district leaders about their leadership strategies and actions would come to the same, inescapable, two conclusions:

1. The quality of teaching in the vast majority of our schools is inadequate to ensure quality learning for *all* students. By *quality learning*, we mean not only what is measured on a standardized test, but also learning that is reflected by students' access and opportunity to engage deeply in the sciences, language arts, and the arts, which is manifested in ways of thinking and communicating. By *all students* we mean just that—*each* and *every* student, including students academically behind, students still developing the English language to make sense of their academic

subjects, and students who have adapted some form of behavior to cope but not learn.

2. The prevailing leadership strategies and actions employed in many districts and schools across the country are inadequate to improve teaching practices at the scale necessary to ensure quality learning for all students.

It is important to state at the outset that the inadequacy of teaching and leadership practices we observe is not due to uncaring, unmotivated, lazy teachers and school leaders who weren't smart enough to be doctors and lawyers. In fact, nothing could be further from the truth. We stand in awe and admiration of just how hard teachers and leaders work every day on behalf of the students in their care. The problem—as we will illuminate further during the course of this book—is that the art and science of teaching is far more complex and sophisticated than our lay public and policy makers realize. As such, the requisite school leadership to improve teaching practice is also far more complex and sophisticated than most people realize. In addition, as we discuss teaching and learning throughout this book, we are setting a very high bar for what we mean by quality teaching practices designed to promote quality learning for all students.

Again, quality learning is much more than what is measured on the typical annual state achievement test, the usual marker for our pernicious achievement gap. As long as tests serve as any kind of gatekeeping mechanism, performance judged by these tests is an equity issue—we do not advocate ignoring this fact. But when we refer to quality learning, we are talking about students using their minds well—how well they can reason, synthesize, evaluate, design, innovate, and create; how students take ownership of their own learning; how they develop agency and advocacy for themselves and others as learners; and the very premium students place on their own learning in the service of humanity. It is important to note that achieving quality learning for all is not simply an economic argument. It is *the* equity and social justice issue of our time. At the end of the day, a rigorous, high-level curriculum and quality teaching for every student is an equity issue. The fact that not one of the approximately fifteen thousand public school districts across the country has been able to realize the dream of quality learning for each and every student should underscore the depth of this challenge. Although this seems like an intractable problem of insurmountable proportions, in the ensuing chapters we will provide an insightful perspective, examples, and useful tools for leaders committed to a theory that the road to improved learning for all students lies in improving the quality of teaching.

This brings us to six foundational ideas that guide our theory of action and work at CEL and serve as a subtext for this book:

1. If students are not learning, they are not being afforded powerful learning opportunities.

2. Teaching is a highly complex and sophisticated endeavor.

3. Practice of sophisticated endeavors only improves when it is open for public scrutiny.

4. Improving practice in a culture of public scrutiny requires reciprocal accountability.

5. Reciprocal accountability implies a particular kind of leadership to improve teaching and learning.

6. Leaders cannot lead what they don't know.

IF STUDENTS ARE NOT LEARNING, THEY ARE NOT BEING AFFORDED POWERFUL LEARNING OPPORTUNITIES.

The research on teacher quality as the primary correlate for student achievement is unequivocal—teaching matters above all else, including family income and education—reasons often cited by educators as the reason their students are not learning (Haycock, 1998; Peske & Haycock, 2006). In fact, there is a common mythology that the type or quality of schools matter most for student learning, which sends hundreds of thousands of parents scurrying every year in a quest to find the "right" school for their child. However, a closer examination of variance in student achievement across the country yields once again that differences among students, as well as schools, are but a small factor compared to differences in the quality of teaching from classroom to classroom (Rowan, Correnti, & Miller, 2002). In short, parents would be better served to ensure their child has the most highly qualified teacher rather than search for the right school. Of course this is easier said than done considering that the kind of high-quality teaching practice necessary to guarantee quality learning for all students is still in short supply in schools across the country.

TEACHING IS A HIGHLY COMPLEX AND SOPHISTICATED ENDEAVOR.

As we will see in later chapters, teaching is a highly sophisticated endeavor—much more so than the public, policy makers, and many educational leaders understand. To underscore this point, log on to any state Department of Education Web site and take a look at the array of grade-level subject matter content standards prescribed for school districts within that particular state. Examine the sophistication and complexity of these standards. Now (hypothetically) imagine yourself as the teacher, tasked with ensuring each of the thirty students in your class meet these standards despite the fact many students are already performing far below these grade level standards, despite the fact that perhaps eight of your thirty students are newly immigrated English language learners with minimal English language proficiency, and despite the fact that a number of your students are living with daily violence—either in their homes or community. This picture is not intended as an excuse for chronically under-performing schools. However, it is intended to illustrate the complexity of the challenge, understanding that at any given point in time teachers are working to the limits of their subject matter knowledge and pedagogical skills. In testimony to the U.S. House of Representatives, Deborah Ball (2010) said it best:

> . . . despite how commonplace it may seem, teaching is far from simple work. Doing it well requires detailed knowledge of the domain being taught and a great deal of skill in making it learnable. It also requires good judgment and a tremendous capacity to relate to a wide range of young people, understand culture, context, and community, and manage a classroom. It requires interpreting and using data to improve the effectiveness of instruction. And as we seek to increase the academic standards and demands that we want our young people to meet, the challenges of good teaching will only escalate. Teaching complex academic skills and knowledge, not to mention skills of collaboration, interaction, and resourcefulness in an increasingly networked world, is still more difficult than teaching more basic skills.

The good news is that with appropriate, sustained, and robust professional learning and support, teachers will improve their subject matter content knowledge and instructional craft expertise and will make the very sophisticated kinds of instructional decisions necessary to ensure high levels of student learning given these seemingly intractable challenges.

PRACTICE ON SOPHISTICATED ENDEAVORS ONLY IMPROVES WHEN IT IS OPEN FOR PUBLIC SCRUTINY.

If teacher practice is to improve to the level required for quality learning for all students, schools can no longer be places for the private practice of teaching. Teaching must move from a historic and inherently private endeavor to public practice. We know that just-in-time feedback and coaching is the way that any of us improve our practice, whatever that practice may be. However, unlike all other respected professions in which practice is indeed a public endeavor, teaching (and for that matter leading) has been a very isolated process. Can you imagine doctors, lawyers, writers, musicians, artists, and athletes improving their practice in isolation? Of course not. Yet every day in thousands of schools across this country teachers engage in what might be called a quasi-practice in the privacy of their own classroom.

IMPROVING PRACTICE IN A CULTURE OF PUBLIC SCRUTINY REQUIRES RECIPROCAL ACCOUNTABILITY.

Although this book focuses squarely on what it will take to improve the quality of teaching and student learning, it is ultimately about leadership, which moves us to the fourth of our big ideas. That is, in order to move teaching from a private to public practice, and to create a truly professional body of practice in the first place, we must make certain that accountability is characterized by a series of reciprocal relationships from the classroom to the district office (Elmore, 2000; Resnick & Glennan, 2002). Reciprocal accountability simply means that if we are going to hold teachers or school leaders accountable for something, we have an equal and commensurate responsibility to verify that they know how to do what we are expecting them to do. In practicality it means that district leaders must ensure that they are building the capacity of their principals, and that principals must ensure they are building the capacity of their teachers. This is not some kind of hierarchical model of leadership. It is, however, a recognition that the core challenge of improving the quality of teaching is one of expertise and that leaders play a critical role in supporting the building of that expertise.

RECIPROCAL ACCOUNTABILITY IMPLIES A PARTICULAR KIND OF LEADERSHIP TO IMPROVE TEACHING AND LEARNING.

If teachers are not providing powerful learning opportunities for all students, then it ultimately becomes a leadership issue—for principals and district leaders in particular. Here again there is a growing body of research evidence that leadership is only second to teaching as the highest correlate to student achievement (Leithwood, Louis, Anderson, & Wahlstrom, 2004). If teachers are not providing powerful learning opportunities for all students, then leaders are not doing what they need to in order to create conditions for teacher learning as a public practice and to guide, support, and nurture teachers in the improvement of their teaching practice. This expectation requires leaders to learn how to navigate and manage the complexity of the instructional improvement endeavor and to remain open to their own learning along the way.

LEADERS CANNOT LEAD WHAT THEY DON'T KNOW.

We have a mantra at the Center for Educational Leadership that happens to be our sixth and final big idea: you cannot lead what you don't know. If one assumes, as do we, that the purpose of leadership is the improvement of instruction—period—then it naturally follows that leaders charged with the task of leading the improvement of instruction must know what good teaching actually looks like. To the layperson—and to many educational leaders as well—there is a tacit assumption that school leaders know what good teaching looks like. This makes good sense—it is their profession after all. In our work at CEL we have run the following experiment dozens of times. We take leaders on a virtual classroom walkthrough. We spend approximately ten to fifteen minutes watching a classroom lesson. We have watched elementary, middle, and high school math and reading lessons. At the end of the lesson we ask the leaders to rate the quality of the teaching on a scale of 1 (low) to 5 (high.) In every case, the responses vary greatly with some rating the lesson high quality and some rating it low quality. In no instance has there been agreement about the quality of the lesson. In fact, there are usually as many high ratings as low ratings. The sad reality is that even among our school and district leaders, there is not a widely shared view of what constitutes quality teaching. Without a common language and shared understanding from which to anchor improvement efforts, it's no wonder that the quality of teaching in too many instances remains inadequate.

These six foundational ideas provide the context for the central focus of this book, which is that quality teaching along with quality leadership is ultimately a matter of expertise. If teachers knew how to teach more powerfully so that all students would learn at high levels, they would be doing it. If leaders knew how to design and deploy systems, structures, practices, routines, and rituals that actually support the improvement of teaching practice, they would be doing it. Teachers and leaders are doing the best they know how to do. At the end of the day it is all about expertise, not one's motivation, beliefs, and values. We are not saying that motivation, beliefs, and values do not play a critical role in professional practice, but as the reader will see throughout the ensuing chapters, entering the improvement process with a focus on building expertise is in fact the best way to simultaneously address deeper issues of beliefs and values.

With our six big ideas in mind, the following nine chapters are designed to take the reader on a journey into the more nuanced aspects of instructional leadership—all anchored to the central theme that the improvement of teaching practice and the leadership necessary to support this improvement process is an issue of expertise. We offer these chapters in four parts. Although we hope the reader finds the material compelling enough to read all four parts, we have structured the parts to stand alone for book study and discussion. At the end of each chapter we offer questions to prompt further thinking and discussion. In addition, many of the tools, protocols, and frameworks contained in this book can be accessed electronically by visiting the Center for Educational Leadership Web site at www.k-12leadership.org.

Part One: Making the Case for Instructional Expertise contains Chapter One, which focuses deeply on the leader's role in developing teacher expertise. We tap into a growing body of literature from the learning sciences to explore issues of learning and expertise. We discuss the leader's role in designing and supporting environments that nurture the development of expertise.

Part Two: Developing an Expert Instructional Eye contains Chapters Two and Three. Chapter Two introduces CEL's Five Dimensions of Teaching and

Learning, which is a comprehensive instructional framework designed to help school leaders build a common language and shared vision for high-quality instruction. This thoroughly researched framework is a valuable tool that helps leaders learn how to analyze the quality of instruction and provide meaningful feedback to teachers in support of their professional learning. Chapter Three takes the reader into a real classroom through a case study vignette to see how the Five Dimensions of Teaching and Learning can provide school leaders with a rich analysis of classroom instruction as they begin the process of growing teacher expertise.

Part Three: Leading for Instructional Improvement contains Chapters Four through Seven. Chapter Four focuses on how leaders (including teacher leaders) go about the business of observing classroom practice in the pursuit of deepening teacher expertise. This chapter provides useful information and tools for conducting learning walkthroughs and connecting classroom visits with wider school improvement goals. Chapter Five follows up with an examination of how effective instructional leaders provide constructive feedback. Readers will learn how to shape responses to their classroom observations and connect those responses with the broader educational improvement goals of their schools. Chapter Six provides concrete examples of how leaders can orchestrate and guide professional learning designed to improve teaching practice. We offer examples of how leaders draw on the extant expertise in their schools and districts and what professional supports actually look like when they are strategically placed. Chapter Seven focuses on instructional coaching. We address some of the typical coaching responsibilities in schools, typical challenges and dilemmas that coaches face in their role, and provide tools for leaders as they manage the most effective placement of coaches for developing teachers' expertise.

Part Four: Embracing New Opportunities for Leading and Learning contains Chapters Eight and Nine. Chapter Eight reintroduces the concept of reciprocal accountability, specifically tracing how teachers and leaders from the classroom to the boardroom can go about improving the quality of teaching and learning. It also introduces the concept of leading from an inquiry stance, highlighting CEL's Habits of Thinking for Instructional Leadership framework. In the context of accountability we provide a look at the latest instructional expertise data highlighting nationwide results from CEL's Five Dimensions of Teaching and Learning assessment. Chapter Nine serves as a concluding chapter and offers a new vision for improving teaching and learning. It explores some of the economic and structural issues we face in our effort to develop instructional expertise. It lays out the challenge ahead of us as we grapple with improving the quality of teaching. This is not just an academic challenge. It is a very real and frankly high-stakes challenge that has students' lives—particularly students of color and students living in poverty—hanging in the balance. It is a challenge compelling enough to warrant yet one more book focused on leadership. We trust the following chapters will serve to provoke teachers' and leaders' deep thought and reflection and provide useful tools that can be applied immediately in the service of improving teaching and leadership practice.

THE AUTHORS

Stephen Fink, EdD, is the executive director of the Center for Educational Leadership (CEL) and affiliate associate professor of Educational Leadership and Policy Studies in the College of Education, University of Washington. Stephen has worked for many years with school district leaders focusing on the school district as the "unit of change"—particularly on developing the systems-level leadership capacity for eliminating the achievement gap. In pursuit of this seemingly elusive goal, his particular interest and expertise is in helping school district leaders dramatically improve the quality of instruction in every school and in every classroom. In addition to directing CEL, Stephen provides facilitation and executive coaching for superintendents and district-level leaders in a number of CEL partnerships. He has also been affiliated since 1989 as a senior consultant for the Panasonic Foundation's urban school district partnership program focusing on school district reform in numerous medium and large urban school districts across the country. Prior to coming to the University of Washington Stephen spent twelve years as an assistant superintendent in the Edmonds School District (WA) and was a principal and special education teacher in Idaho and Los Angeles.

Anneke Markholt, PhD, is an associate director for the Center for Educational Leadership and an affiliate faculty member in Educational Leadership and Policy Studies in the College of Education at the University of Washington. Anneke designs and directs CEL's district partnerships focused on the development of instructional leadership. She is particularly interested in the intersection of teaching, learning, and the leadership capacity necessary for school and district systems to engage in instructional improvement, especially for linguistically diverse students. Prior to her work with CEL, Anneke spent five years as an associate researcher for the Center for the Study of Teaching and Policy at the University of Washington. She began her career as an English as a Second Language specialist for Tacoma Public Schools, where she taught for ten years.

Michael A. Copland, PhD, is currently associate professor and chair of Educational Leadership and Policy Studies in the College of Education at the University of Washington. Dr. Copland has extensive experience with the preparation and professional development of prospective and practicing school and district leaders. Currently, he works with the University of Washington Danforth Educational Leadership program, the Center for Educational Leadership, and directs the Leadership for Learning EdD program. His research interests lie at the intersection of education policy and leadership, focusing on various ways leaders and leadership matter for policy initiatives and processes and how policies influence aspects of leadership work in schools and school systems. His specific research interests include learning-focused practices of central office leaders, the preparation and professional development of school and district leaders, transformation of comprehensive high schools, and distributed leadership in the context of education reform.

Joanna Michelson is a secondary literacy specialist in the Highline School District in the Seattle area. In collaboration with principals, she supports and helps shape the instructional improvement work of middle and high school teachers and coaches. She is also a PhD student in Educational Leadership and Policy Studies in the College of Education at the University of Washington with a focus on adolescent literacy learning, teacher learning, and organizational culture in diverse districts. In the past, Joanna has taught sixth grade and secondary-level English language arts.

ABOUT THE CENTER FOR EDUCATIONAL LEADERSHIP

The Center for Educational Leadership (CEL) at the University of Washington was founded in 2001. As an integral part of the College of Education, CEL's mission is dedicated to eliminating the achievement gap that continues to divide our nation's children along the lines of race, class, language, and disability. CEL believes the nexus for eliminating the gap lies in the development of leadership capacity—specifically, nurturing the will to act on behalf of the most underserved students while increasing leadership knowledge and skill to dramatically improve the quality of instruction.

CEL has partnered with dozens of school districts across the United States with a focus on building the instructional leadership expertise of school and district leaders as well as the instructional expertise of teachers and coaches. CEL employs a two-part leadership theory in all of its work with school leaders:

1. *Developing a common language and shared vision for high-quality instruction.* With the mantra *the better we see, the better we are able to lead* CEL believes that deep instructional improvement can take place only when school leaders have a shared vision for and understanding of high-quality instruction. This vision and understanding serve as their "north star" to guide improvement efforts.

2. *Developing greater expertise in leading for instructional improvement.* Although a shared vision of high-quality instruction is critical for instructional improvement, simply having this vision does not guarantee that teachers will in fact improve their practice. Leaders still must go about the very challenging and complex work of leading this improvement effort. To accomplish this, CEL faculty work closely with school and district leaders to use their growing instructional knowledge to lead for systemwide improvement.

CEL faculty are continually developing new tools, protocols, and other resources to support school and district leaders in their work to improve the quality of teaching. To learn more about CEL's work and to sign up for their quarterly newsletter that features some of these tools, please visit www.k-12leadership.org.

Leading for Instructional Improvement

PART ONE

Making the Case for Instructional Expertise

The Leader's Role in Developing Teacher Expertise

The visitor strolling through an herb garden sees what looks like a large-leafed weed. The herbalist sees comfrey, a remedy for burns. The patient can read only the second row on the eye chart. The eye doctor sees 20/100 vision and knows that glasses are needed. The teacher explains the rotation of the earth, sun, and moon. What do the principals observing that classroom lesson see? In our experience, not enough. At least not enough to inform the one most important aspect of their job as instructional leader, which is to provide useful, just-in-time feedback to the teacher and even more important, support the teacher's further professional learning guided by a clear picture of the teacher's strengths and weaknesses and grounded to a deep understanding of quality instruction.

Although the idea of teacher quality has received much greater recognition in recent years as the number one correlate of student achievement (Haycock, 1998; Peske & Haycock, 2006), the concept of teaching and instructional leadership expertise—particularly how one develops expertise—has received scant attention in educational policy and leadership circles. We take for granted that somehow teachers have acquired the deep subject matter and pedagogical expertise required to provide high-quality teaching for all students. Or, worse yet, that great teachers are born with this amorphous "gift" for high-quality teaching without understanding and acknowledging how professionals deepen their practice over time. Furthermore, we too often fail to consider that even the best university teacher-preparation programs cannot cultivate the kind of deep expertise necessary to teach all students well in a one- or two-year program. Keeping in mind the big idea that teaching is a complex and sophisticated endeavor, school district leaders, principals, and teacher leaders must play a critical role in developing and cultivating the expertise necessary for high-quality teaching. This warrants a brief discussion of the expertise literature, particularly what we mean by *expertise* and how one goes about acquiring it.

The National Research Council's seminal work on how people learn presents a useful distinction between experts and novices in given disciplines that we see playing out every day in school leadership (Bransford, Brown, & Cocking, 2000). By studying the differences between experts and novices in a variety of disciplines, Bransford and his colleagues found that experts ". . . have acquired extensive knowledge that affects what they notice and how they organize, represent, and interpret information in their environment" (p. 31). This deeper level of seeing and understanding enables experts to think more effectively about problems of practice within their specific discipline. And because a school leader's primary problem of leadership practice is how to improve the quality of teaching, the idea of expertise is particularly germane.

Although Bransford and colleagues' initial research on expertise was in disciplines other than school leadership, for example, physics, mathematics, history, and so on, our work with school and district leaders is completely consistent with their findings. If we start from the premise that extensive background knowledge affects what one notices and that the act of "noticing" is indeed an important skill for school leaders intent on improving instruction, then it begs the question of just how much school leaders notice when they go into a classroom. We have led hundreds of school and district leaders on classroom walk-throughs. We have found that there is a vast difference between expert observers and novices in terms of what they notice about the quality of instruction. Specifically we have found that

- Novice instructional leaders do not notice or think about key elements of instruction and often convey obvious misconceptions about or misuses of those key elements. However, leaders with greater expertise can identify and discuss key elements with specificity; elaborate on what they see with specific examples, that is, evidence from the observed lesson; express wonder or questions about observations (for example, what is behind teaching decisions); and offer alternatives to teaching decisions or suggest ways to improve the lesson with specificity.

- Novices tend to make evaluative judgments more quickly based on superficial understanding. By contrast, experts tend to withhold judgment until they can describe in evidentiary terms what they are noticing along with important questions they may have that will guide further leadership actions.

- There is a vast difference between experts and novices in terms of what they wonder about and how they go about posing relevant problems of leadership practice based on what they did or did not notice. Experts in particular tend to be much more metacognitive in their formulation of next steps or specific leadership actions.

We know from experience there is not a widely shared view of what constitutes quality instruction—not among teachers, principals, or school district leaders. We think this poses a fundamental and challenging issue for educational leaders and policy makers. Without a shared understanding of what we mean by quality instruction, we have no basis from which to mount an improvement effort. This is an issue of expertise or in our case a lack of sufficient expertise necessary to improve the quality of teaching in every school and every classroom. The anecdotal observations that lead us to this conclusion also have been corroborated by extensive research by our colleagues at the University of Washington. Chapter Eight will offer a deeper look into this research, so for now we will assume prima facie that the expertise necessary to improve teaching practice is in short supply. This means the primary role of school and district leaders must be the cultivation of expertise to improve practice, including both teaching and leadership practice.

IT TAKES EXPERTISE TO MAKE EXPERTISE

In various presentations to school district leaders we like to show a slide with pictures of well-known people (athletes, actors, musicians, doctors, scientists, and so on) who are the very best in their field. After displaying their images, we ask the following question: what do these people have in common?

Truthfully, these people may have many things in common but our particular teaching points are threefold:

1. These people all represent professions that have clear and accepted standards for professional practice. There is shared understanding among all in their profession (and often outside their profession as well) about what constitutes quality performance.

2. All of these professionals have improved their given craft with public scrutiny and feedback. Not one of these professionals practices his or her craft in isolation.

3. All of these professionals have had or continue to have extensive coaching. It is understood and accepted that the most powerful way to improve one's craft is through coaching by someone with high expertise.

We believe that K–12 education as often practiced is a quasi-profession at best because we do not in fact have common standards of professional practice. City, Elmore, and colleagues (2009) frame this best in a chapter titled "A Profession in Search of a Practice":

> We tolerate a kind of benign vagueness in how we talk about the core functions of teaching and learning that privileges good intentions over demonstrable effectiveness in our practice. We sanction unacceptably large variations in teaching from one classroom to another with rhetoric about teaching as "style," "art," or "craft." And we reinforce the public's stereotype of teaching and learning as a knowledge-weak practice by largely refusing to exercise anything but perfunctory control over who gets to practice in classrooms and what happens to people who are demonstrably incompetent. (p. 188)

Whether under the guise of academic freedom, local control, or perhaps just simply doing what we have always done, millions of students are taught every day by hundreds of thousands of teachers, supported by thousands of school and district leaders without a clear understanding and agreement on quality practice. Frankly, this is shocking to consider. Can you imagine leading a team of surgeons in a complex organ transplant without common, accepted, and well-understood standards of surgical practice? We have heard some argue that teaching is different because it's so individual and cannot be measured by the kind of quantitative metrics we use for our athletes such as the lowest round of golf, final score of a basketball game, or by how many seconds by which one wins a swimming competition. However, even in professions in which subjectivity plays into the definition of quality, there are still common accepted standards of practice. The Nobel Prize for scientists, the Pulitzer Prize for writers and journalists, and the Academy Awards for actors have a subjective element of measurement, but make no mistake, each of these awards are based on common, accepted standards of professional practice.

In most other professions than teaching, one thing clearly stands out—expertise is understood and valued. There is complete acceptance that the way to become the best in your field is to nourish and nurture the development of expertise. In the 2009 Los Angeles Open golf tournament Phil Mickelson was the leader after the first round, posting a score well below par. In the second round he posted a score above par and fell out of first place. After his disappointing round, he placed a call to his coach who was living in Las Vegas at the time. His coach flew to Los Angeles and they worked together for hours on the driving range. Mickelson went on to win the golf tournament. What is accepted as standard operating procedure in most professions has been anathema in public education. Can you imagine a teacher, who after struggling with a particular lesson, calling his or her instructional coach to do some work on the "driving range"? Actually we can imagine this same kind of public coaching cycle taking place in our schools because we are in fact doing this kind of work every day with teachers and principals in schools across the country. However, it is still the very rare exception, not the norm. In far too many cases teachers have no access to coaching, and in cases when they do have access the coach does not have sufficient expertise to help grow the teacher's expertise. In too many other cases the conditions—structural, cultural, political, and so on—preclude a successful coaching relationship between coach and teacher. In all cases it goes back to the leaders' own expertise and their conception of how to grow theirs and others' expertise.

One effort to address professional practice that has swept schools across the country is the creation of professional learning communities (PLCs). Most everywhere we visit, there is a major PLC initiative underway. The concept of professional learning communities popularized by Richard DuFour is sound (Dufour & Eaker; 1998). Implicit in the creation of professional learning communities is the idea that continued learning is key to improving practice; that learning is inherently a social process; and that learning can be facilitated—in fact accelerated—through well-developed and supported organizational structures. We believe that the idea of expertise is still not well acknowledged and explicated in the PLC literature but nonetheless the concept of adults studying practice together as a way of improving practice makes sense. Yet in school after school we visit, we see PLCs that have little influence on improving teaching practice, and in some cases the PLC is a structure that ultimately reinforces the current state of teaching. Because schools and school districts are in fact complex organizations, we need to be cautious about attributing one causal factor for the ineffectiveness we see when observing PLCs across the country. The truth is that there are many factors at play that ultimately lie at the heart of leadership. Yet one idea in particular that is worthy of deeper consideration is the idea of expertise. Before school leaders consider forming professional learning communities, there are two important questions to consider:

1. What role does expertise play in promoting group and individual learning?

2. How much internal expertise—in terms of internal to the group—is necessary to accelerate group and individual learning?

From our observations at least one factor limiting the effectiveness of PLCs is an insufficient level of expertise within the group necessary to advance the learning of that group. Let's think about this in another context. Suppose a group of eight snow skiers come together as a learning community to study skiing with the expressed purpose of improving their skill level. This, of course, is step one—actually coming together with the expressed purpose of improving their knowledge and skills versus attending to their other adult needs. As it turns out, the skill level of the group ranges from novice to perhaps a beginning intermediate level. The group meets on the ski slopes every weekend during the ski season to ski together, watch each other ski, and offer tips for improvement as necessary. In between they read books on skiing and watch videos of expert skiers tackling challenging terrain. It is not unreasonable to assume that over time individual group members could improve their skills. Much of this would depend on how well the group functions, adherence to agreed-on norms, the amount of time dedicated to study and practice, and so on. There are indeed important organizational and sociocultural aspects of learning that play out within and among group members. Suppose, however, that this group of skiers had access to at least one expert skier—whether within the group itself or as an outside coach to the group. There is no question this one change *could* accelerate the group's learning along with the skill development of each individual group member. This idea of access to expertise—either internally or externally—is a fundamental challenge for leaders interested in creating professional learning communities.

Notice we say that access to expertise—whether inside or outside—*could* accelerate group learning. Whether or not this acceleration actually takes place leads to another important idea: it *takes expertise to make expertise.* Bransford and Schwartz (2008) posit that there are two kinds of expertise involved in the idea that it takes expertise to make expertise. The first is *learning* expertise, which "... involves the degree to which would-be experts continually attempt to refine their skills and attitudes toward learning—skills and attitudes that include practicing, self-monitoring, and finding ways to avoid plateaus and move to the next level" (p. 3). Inherent in the concept of learning expertise is the idea of how coachable one is as a learner. The extent to which one can move more quickly along the continuum of novice to expert depends in part on how open one is to the kind of public scrutiny and critical feedback necessary in a coaching relationship. We will talk more about this in a moment because it has tremendous implications for leaders as they address their school or district culture.

Bransford and Schwartz call the second kind of expertise *teaching expertise,* which involves a variety of forms including but not limited to coaching. The key argument here is that simply being an expert in something does not guarantee that one is also good at teaching that expertise to others. The idea of two integral kinds of expertise—learner and teacher—significantly increases the level of complexity for school and district leaders. Not only do they need to consider how to nurture the learner's role in the acquisition of expertise, but they also need to find or develop experts—either internally or externally—who can actually teach others. This is complex and sophisticated leadership work whether one is a teacher leader, school principal, or district leader. If leaders do not understand this level of complexity, they run the risk of glomming onto structures and processes such as PLCs without giving careful consideration to the role of expertise—and more important, not knowing how to create conditions so that group and individual expertise can be developed in the service of improved teaching practice. In ensuing chapters we will provide some tools to support leaders in this work, but first we want to go back to the idea of critical feedback and public practice—both essential concepts for the development of learner expertise.

If we accept the argument that public practice and critical feedback are essential components and catalysts for the development of expertise, then the culture of schooling—at least how it manifests every day in most American public schools—stands in stark contrast to the conditions necessary to grow expertise. Although most professions are characterized in part by public practice and scrutiny, American public education is epitomized by privacy and isolation. This phenomenon is widely recognized, has been talked about for many years, and has been great subject matter for researchers and reformers. Yet this inherent and historical way of doing business persists. There have been varied attempts at breaking through this isolation including the aforementioned professional learning communities and other like structures and processes. Still, the unfortunate reality is that in the vast majority of schools across the country today, public practice, scrutiny, and feedback remain anathema to the culture of schooling.

In our view this presents a major leadership challenge for school leaders who are intent on improving teaching practice. Although we hear leaders lament about this challenge time and again, there is often a troubling disconnect. We often hear leaders wish that their teachers were more willing to open their classrooms, invite feedback, and work together to improve practice. It is in this state of wishful thinking that school leaders search for structures and processes such as PLCs, all the while neglecting to understand that their instructional leadership plays a fundamental role in this work. Too many school leaders see their role as being the purveyor, supporter, and cheerleader for new structures and processes without understanding their more integral role in the improvement process. In subsequent chapters we will explore this integral role in depth but for now we want to discuss the leader's role in creating a culture of public practice. Simply stated, the extent to which leaders make their own practice public is the extent to which they can help teachers confront their own vulnerabilities, which is a necessary prerequisite to making one's practice public.

Let's examine how school district leaders can do this. As an example, let's explore Public Practice School District (PPS), an urban school district of twenty-five thousand students that shares a contiguous boundary with one of the larger urban school districts in the country. The majority of the students are Hispanic with large numbers of English language learners (ELLs). PPS had a history of poor student performance with approximately five out of ten students reading at grade level according to their reading achievement scores on the state-administered assessment. District and school leaders tried a number of different programs and approaches but were missing a systemic effort, rooted in a clear theory of action, and supported by well-developed strategies and actions. The superintendent and his executive staff understood that the only way to improve reading achievement was to improve the quality of teaching, and that meant teachers had to be open and willing to examine their own practice, learn new strategies, and incorporate those new strategies into their existing practice. In fact, in some cases teachers had to be willing to completely overhaul their previous practice for a new and improved practice—much like professional baseball players and golfers must do when their swings are no longer sufficient to perform at the highest level. The superintendent and his staff could have outsourced this improvement effort to principals but they recognized that as district leaders they were responsible for modeling the kind of practice they wished to see in schools. By practice in this case we are not referring to the actual quality of teaching but to the process of making one's practice public. The superintendent understood that many teachers were never going to invite coaches into their classrooms to work on teaching practice until the principal was able to create the conditions necessary for self- and public reflection. This meant that principals had to make their practice public as well.

For the first year of the reading improvement effort district leaders, principals, and newly identified K–12 literacy coaches met monthly to learn new reading strategies from leading outside experts. What happened in between these monthly meetings was most important. The district leaders, including the superintendent, the assistant superintendents, and other central office staff, went to schools to teach reading lessons, employing one or more of newly learned reading strategies. These reading lessons were not meant to be exemplars nor were they. The idea of the superintendent and assistant superintendents teaching lessons was meant to model what we mean by making practice public, by exposing and being willing to talk about their own practice, and being metacognitive about what they were doing in terms of specific teaching moves and inviting teachers and principals into the observation and analysis. As we will discuss in later chapters, this co-inquiry and co-learning stance on the part of district leaders is most critical for leaders who want to create a culture of public practice.

Throughout the course of the year the large group studied together and after much district leader modeling, principals were expected to teach reading lessons in their own schools as a way of modeling how professionals come together to study and improve practice. The superintendent understood the concept of reciprocal accountability, which meant that first and foremost district leaders had to build the capacity of principals and literacy coaches and tackle the pervasive culture of privacy and isolation. This is akin to the work farmers and gardeners do all of the time as they tirelessly ready the soil for planting. They understand the importance of soil preparation.

After a period of "soil preparation," the PPS reading improvement effort moved to a more embedded professional development model with literacy coaches working actively in teachers' classrooms, with teachers and coaches coming together in what we call *studio classrooms* to study and model practice, and with principals and district leaders continuing to model, monitor, and lead. (We provide a much deeper look at this type of professional development in Chapters Five, Six, and Seven.) Eventually the PPS district also formalized a *professional learning community* strategy; however, this strategy was an outgrowth of a culture that had already (1) made a fundamental shift from private to public and (2) developed a strong foundation of expertise among many teachers, coaches, and principals. In an already established culture of public practice PLCs can more easily serve the intended purpose of improving practice.

It is clear that leaders who are intent on improving teaching practice must be mindful of *learning expertise* and all that is required to nourish and support its development. At the same time they must pay equal attention to Bransford and Schwartz's notion of *teaching expertise*. In fact, the same thoughtful consideration that should be paid to the recruitment, assignment, induction, and ongoing support for teachers of children should be given to teachers of adults. In far too many school districts there is no systemic and strategic approach to developing the expertise necessary to be effective teachers of adults. It is no wonder that professional development for teachers in these districts is often isolated, episodic, and disconnected from teachers' daily practice. Even in school districts where district leaders have acknowledged the need for coaches to embed professional development into daily practice, there often is still a disturbing lack of foresight in terms of the recruitment, assignment, induction, and ongoing support necessary to ensure an effective coaching model.

Here is a typical example. We'll call this district Chance Public Schools, which is a medium-sized school district with an enrollment of nineteen thousand students. The district has three comprehensive high schools, four middle schools, and nineteen elementary schools. Chance School District leaders came to the conclusion that instructional coaching for teachers is a worthwhile investment. Rather than basing the size of the investment on a thoughtful plan, grounded to a clear theory of action and long-term strategy for the development of expertise, district leaders based this investment solely on a recently identified pot of available dollars. District leaders determined in April that they had enough funding to hire thirteen coaches for the following school year. With no thoughtful plan in place and guided by a prevailing mental model that school allocations must be equal, district leaders decided to hire a half-time coach for each school. Chance principals were all notified of this decision at a district meeting with the superintendent. They were told that the human resources department would work out a selection process after deliberations and a memorandum of understanding was put in place with the local teachers' association.

In May, the principals were notified that they could create their own internal process to select the instructional coach. They could involve other teachers in that process but ultimately they had the authority to make the appointment. Assuming that most principals would appoint an existing teacher to that role, principals were reminded that this would be a half-time appointment only, which meant that the teacher-coach would have to continue with a 50-percent teaching assignment. Principals went about making these individual decisions during the rush of end-of-school-year activities and with the pressure to have their teacher assignments and master schedule all completed before they went on vacation at the end of June.

Because no forethought was given to the expertise required to be an effective coach, principals were given no guidance in terms of subject matter expertise. In other words it didn't matter whether a teacher (soon to be coach) had a particular content expertise. Principals were told to identify a strong teacher who was well respected. Because Chance leaders had no widely shared understanding of what they meant by quality instruction, their individual conception of a "strong teacher" was not necessarily shared by other principals across the district. By the close of the school year in June, most of the principals had made their appointments. Several principals had to wait due to impending retirements, teacher leave issues, and other factors that affect the timing of human resource decisions. In all cases a half-time coach was identified before the start of school in September. When teachers came back to work in August they were notified by the principals that they would have an instructional coach supporting their efforts during the upcoming school year.

The Chance Public Schools coaching investment totaled a million dollars based on an average annual teacher cost of $77,000 including benefits. This large sum of money was invested without any thought given to the issues of learner and teacher expertise discussed in this chapter. There were several middle and high schools in which the coach had a language arts background and was asked to support all of the teachers regardless of their subject area. In several other secondary schools principals made the determination that the coach should at least focus his or her efforts with like–subject area teachers. In one high school the coach also taught Advanced Placement Calculus so she worked only with the math teachers throughout the year. Because the only guidance principals received was to select a strong teacher, and because *strong* was not defined in terms of subject matter expertise and the expertise necessary to be an effective teacher of adults, the quality of the coaches varied greatly. Because nothing was done to create the prerequisite conditions for instructional improvement of the kind that occurred in our prior example, Chance School District leaders were essentially rolling the dice on a one-million-dollar investment. Contrast the Chance District leaders' strategy—or lack thereof—with what occurred in our Public Practice School District at the inception of their reading improvement effort. We have already discussed how the PPS leaders went about creating the conditions necessary to grow learner expertise. However, prior to the official kick-off of the reading improvement effort the PPS district had assigned a group of coaches called TOSAs (teachers on special assignment) to the curriculum and staff development department while some individual schools purchased their own TOSAs. There was no single job description or training focus for the TOSAs. Consequently, they were used in a variety of capacities with most assuming administrative duties. There was absolutely no strategy for how the TOSAs would actually improve teaching practice. This was before they began the reading improvement effort. When PPS launched this effort—unlike the Chance School District—their leaders did have a specific focus, guided by a clear theory of action and concomitant strategies to improve the quality of reading instruction. A strong, sustainable, and embedded instructional coaching model was one of those strategies. Consequently, the district sent all of the TOSAs back to the classroom prior to beginning their improvement effort in order to free up funding to hire a very different kind of instructional coach.

The superintendent and his key leaders then determined how much they could invest in the coaching model. However, that specific determination was predicated on the larger investment decision necessary to launch and sustain a multiyear commitment to improve the quality of reading instruction. In other words, the amount the district could invest in hiring instructional coaches was directly related to the amount they could invest in the overall effort, understanding that a successful effort required simultaneous investments such as bringing in outside experts and coaches and purchasing instructional materials, classroom libraries and substitute teachers to cover classes while teachers studied together. Guided by examples of the very best instructional coaching models across the country, Public Practice leaders developed a comprehensive job description that paid particular attention to the kind of expertise necessary to be a successful coach. They advertised the coaching positions inside and outside of the district. Prospective candidates had to teach a lesson so that district leaders could assess the level of subject matter expertise—in this case, reading. Prospective candidates also had to go through an extensive interview process so that PPS leaders could ascertain their level of *teacher expertise* in terms of supporting adult learning. Because they had only enough money to hire nine coaches initially, they assigned those coaches directly to the assistant superintendents instead of having the school principals hire their own part-time coach, as in the case of the Chance School District. This allowed the assistant superintendents to deploy coaches thoughtfully and strategically with the sole intent on developing teacher expertise in reading instruction. Without being conscious of the expertise literature per se, the PPS superintendent and his executive leaders certainly understood the concept that it *takes expertise to make expertise.*

BUILDING SHARED UNDERSTANDING

In the truest spirit of *you cannot lead what you do not know,* it is incumbent on school leaders to develop their own expertise about quality instruction. Leaders charged with the improvement of teaching practice must understand and be able to explicate what good practice looks like in order to lead and guide professional development, target and align resources, and engage in ongoing problem solving and long-range capacity building. This is part one of a two-part instructional leadership equation. It is foundational and sequential. Without developing this expertise school leaders can struggle to provide the leadership necessary to improve teaching practice.

The challenge for school leaders lies in the fact that simply developing a more expert understanding of high-quality teaching doesn't mean they can successfully lead the improvement process. This brings us to the second part of the leadership equation, which is still about expertise, but a very different kind of expertise. Successful school leaders have to develop their expertise in multiple disciplines. They must have enough expertise to recognize quality instruction. This provides the guidepost—the "north star" so to speak—for their leadership efforts. They must also develop the leadership expertise necessary to influence and mobilize action within complex organizations amidst a prevailing culture designed to blunt most attempts to improve individual and collective practice. This is akin to effective classroom teachers who must have both content and pedagogical expertise in order to successfully educate all students. In the case of the leadership discipline, leaders' content expertise is their deep understanding of quality instruction, and their pedagogical expertise is in knowing how to guide, support, nourish, and nurture teachers in their own improvement effort.

Since the mid 1990s there have been a number of emergent structures and processes designed to develop this kind of leadership learning. One of the first such structures and processes was the learning walkthrough. The learning walkthrough grew out of the work of Community School District 2 in New York City under the leadership of Anthony Alvarado. Much has been written about District 2 that documents what is arguably one of the most successful school district improvement efforts to date (Elmore & Burney, 1997; Fink & Resnick, 2001; Stein & D'Amico, 1999). One hallmark of the District 2 improvement strategy was the very public nature of teaching. District leaders routinely spent time in classrooms with school principals observing instruction and mapping out specific improvement efforts that were then linked to carefully developed and implemented professional development for teachers and principals. The premise behind the learning walkthroughs was to make teaching a public practice, develop a deepened and shared understanding of that practice, and use this emerging knowledge to implement specific improvement efforts.

Since the beginning of our work at CEL in 2001 we have seen as many locally developed variations of learning walkthroughs as there are butterflies. The only common denominator is a leadership decision (typically at the district level) that having administrators in groups going into classrooms is a good thing. And in the spirit of deprivatizing teaching practice, having other adults in classrooms on a regular basis can be a good thing. However, the expectations for what these walkthroughs are supposed to accomplish—including the set-up, delivery, and follow-up—vary significantly from district to district. Accordingly, in many cases these locally designed walkthrough processes do little to improve leaders' expertise and as a result do little to improve teaching practice. We will delve much deeper into the walkthrough process in Chapter Four.

Over the last several years City, Elmore, and colleagues (2009) have addressed the expertise issue through a structure called *instructional rounds*, in which leaders are afforded opportunities to increase their knowledge of instruction and their expertise in terms of how to lead for the improvement of that instruction. In terms of developing a common language and a shared understanding of quality instruction, leaders are taught how to stay in the descriptive versus evaluative mode as they observe classroom teaching. This is premised on the concept of medical rounds, in which over 90 percent of the doctors' conversations are descriptive (describing the patient symptoms) versus evaluative (making a specific diagnosis). As we have already mentioned, one of the differences between novice and expert observers of instruction is the ability to withhold judgment until they can describe fully in evidentiary terms what they are seeing. As City, Elmore, and colleagues (2009) assert, this ability to stay in the descriptive mode is the way to develop shared understanding and separate the observation from the person. This is indeed a powerful way to deepen leaders' knowledge of quality teaching.

Elmore's instructional rounds model also addresses the second part of our leadership equation, which is how to seize on a deepened understanding of instruction to actually lead for instructional improvement. This is facilitated in part by learning how to construct a viable theory of action that forces leaders to think about how their specific strategies and actions are going to result in accomplishing their vision for improvement. In our work with networks of superintendents and principals, we, too, have found that attention to theory of action is an important starting point in leading for instructional improvement. We found that all school districts—even very small ones—all suffer from what Elmore calls *organizational clutter*. Our like phrase is MIS—multiple initiative syndrome. We are amazed at how many school district initiatives are operating at any given point in time, often on separate tracks, administered from deeply entrenched organizational silos, and with no relationship to a single improvement effort. And this isn't just the province of large urban school districts. We see this in suburban and rural districts as well. A strong theory of action can serve as a filter from which to develop specific strategies and actions. In our superintendent and principals networks we tackle the theory of action work by learning how to engage and sustain an ongoing cycle of inquiry with real leadership problems of practice. We will discuss this work in greater depth in the ensuing chapters but first we want to conclude this chapter by going back once more to part one of our leadership equation—how to help leaders develop a deeper understanding of high-quality instruction—because this expertise remains foundational for improved teaching and learning.

In our work with school and district leaders—in formal, informal, and ad hoc networks—we have learned the importance of teaching them how to describe what they are seeing in classrooms. The skill of noticing and wondering precedes analysis, theorizing, and evaluating. It is a prerequisite knowledge and skill and in too short supply across the national school leadership ranks. We teach leaders how to script lessons as a starting place in this process. Similar to Elmore and his colleagues' networks, we encourage leaders to stay in the descriptive mode as a way of building a common language, shared understanding, and separating the observation from the person. That said, we have been searching along the way for how to accelerate this foundational learning, knowing (as per our two-part leadership equation) that developing expertise in the observation and analysis of instruction doesn't mean leaders can actually lead for instructional improvement. And given the urgency to eliminate long-standing academic achievement gaps, we don't have years to wait while leaders slowly accrue this important foundational learning. We grappled with the following question: by providing an instructional framework that clearly identifies quality teaching practice, is it possible to accelerate leaders' learning of quality instruction while still fostering the critical elements of individual and group learning involved in the instructional rounds process? In other words, is it possible to teach leaders how to stay in the descriptive mode while using a lens to help them focus their observations?

The answer to these questions has been a resounding yes. In fact, we now argue that just like an astronomer who uses a telescope to see the planets and constellations in greater detail and sharper focus, a quality instructional framework can help leaders sharpen their lens in terms of what they notice and wonder about when they walk into classrooms. Chapter Two will offer an in-depth examination of our Five Dimensions of Teaching and Learning framework. In the spirit of the astronomer, we offer this framework as a way of helping school leaders see more. In and of itself it won't help them reach the stars but at least they will know in which direction to shoot.

CONCLUSION

In this chapter we introduced the concept of expertise drawn from extensive research in the learning sciences. We discussed the difference between *learner expertise* and *teacher expertise* and argued that school district leaders who are intent on improving instructional practice must address both of these important concepts in their strategic planning. We introduced an argument that *it takes expertise to make expertise* and provided examples of how school district leaders can nurture and then seize on the development of internal expertise. We argued at length the importance of making our *practice public* as a starting place for significant improvement efforts. We also introduced our two-part instructional leadership equation that first places great importance on developing a shared vision and common language for high-quality teaching and then focuses on how leaders can use that emerging picture of high-quality teaching to lead for instructional improvement. The ensuing chapters will build and expand on this leadership equation by providing a clear picture of what we mean by high-quality teaching and then provide numerous examples, tools, and protocols for leaders engaged in the daily practice of instructional improvement.

DISCUSSION QUESTIONS

- How does the idea of "expertise" fit with improvement efforts in your school or district?

- In your role as a district, school, or teacher leader, how do you currently develop your own and others' "learner expertise" and "teacher expertise"?

- How are you developing a shared vision and understanding of quality instruction in your school or district?

PART TWO

Developing an Expert
Instructional Eye

The Five Dimensions of Teaching and Learning

The question, "How will we define 'quality' instruction?" forms the basis for Chapter Two. In answering this question we introduce a new framework that defines what expert observers of teaching and learning look for when observing in classrooms. The Five Dimensions of Teaching and Learning introduced here, or 5D framework, was derived from an extensive four- to five-year effort to mine research on what constitutes quality instruction, informed by the experiences of practitioners we identified who possessed demonstrated expertise with observing in classrooms and providing feedback to teachers. This chapter summarizes the findings from that effort and develops a supporting rationale for including each of the five dimensions of teaching and learning as the foundation of what expert observers pay attention to in classrooms.

In defining this expertise base, we've drawn together material from three sources: (1) empirically based studies of teaching and coaching practice, (2) practitioner-oriented prescriptions and frameworks for instructional and coaching practice, and (3) descriptions of practice from an identified panel of expert observers who included instructional coaches and school administrators hired as consultants or project managers for CEL and who work daily with teachers to improve instructional practice. Specifically, we paid attention to the kinds of questions our panelists asked about what they observed and combined those with findings from the research and practice literature. Taken together, analysis of information gathered from these three sources enabled us to form a framework for differentiating expert observers of instruction from those who are more novice. Our framework addresses these key questions regarding the nature of expertise in the practice of observing instruction and providing feedback to teachers:

- What do expert observers of instruction pay attention to in classrooms?
- How do experts make sense of what they observe?
- How do experts use what they see in classrooms to craft feedback to teachers?

In answering these questions, we present the scholarly basis of the five broad dimensions of instructional practice (Figures 2.1) in our framework and

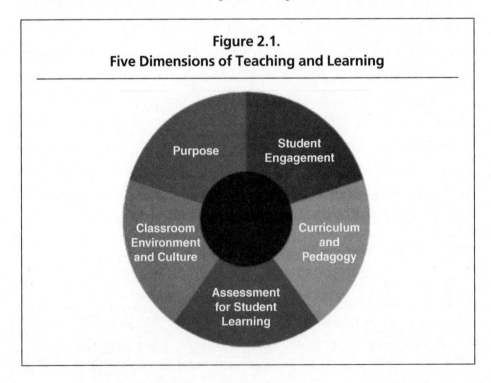

Figure 2.1.
Five Dimensions of Teaching and Learning

corresponding thirteen subdimensions (Figure 2.2) and make a case for the nature of expertise that observers need. Please refer to Appendix A for a complete copy of the Five Dimensions of Teaching and Learning framework (Version 3.0).

The graphical representation in Figure 2.1 of an eye is meant to symbolize the expertise required to *see* deeply into the craft of teaching and learning. Just as movie goers don special glasses to take in the wonders of 3D movies, the idea behind CEL's 5D framework is similar. However, in this case the "glasses" one wears to see all five dimensions of teaching and learning in their full interactive depth and breadth is instructional expertise.

The remainder of the chapter explains each one of the five dimensions and the thirteen subdimensions in depth. While you are reading this—and staying with our metaphor of "seeing" the five dimensions—we invite you to think about your own instructional visual acuity. In other words, how much expertise will you need to develop to be able to see all five dimensions and thirteen subdimensions with 20/20 (or better) vision?

Figure 2.2.
Five Dimensions and Thirteen Subdimensions of Teaching and Learning

Purpose	1. Standards
	2. Teaching Point
Student Engagement	3. Intellectual Work
	4. Engagement Strategies
	5. Talk
Curriculum & Pedagogy	6. Curriculum
	7. Teaching Approaches and Strategies
	8. Scaffolds for Learning
Assessment for Student Learning	9. Assessment
	10. Adjustments
Classroom Environment and Culture	11. Use of Physical Environment
	12. Classroom Routines and Rituals
	13. Classroom Culture

PURPOSE

Expert observers of instruction pay attention to ways that the lesson purpose is made clear in the context of the lesson and the extent to which the purpose is meaningful and relevant through these measures:

- Standards—how does the lesson purpose connect to external standards for what students should know and be able to do at this age or grade level?

- Teaching point—what are the specific learning goals that students are expected to accomplish for this particular lesson?

Standards

In observing for standards in the classroom, an expert instructional leader first identifies the extent to which the lesson purpose is clearly articulated, connected to standards, embedded in instruction, and understood by students. Expert observers "examine the explicit nature of a teacher's communication of expectations in terms of its being direct, specific, repeated, positive, and tenacious for different tasks in different cases—and then look at the standards implicit in those expectations" (Saphier & Gower, 1997, p. 330). Panelists raised questions such as "How is the purpose of this lesson connected to external standards for what student should know and be able to do at this age or grade level?" and "What do students understand about what they are learning and why they are learning it?"

Along with simply paying attention to whether and how standards are communicated, the expert observer of instruction critically analyzes lessons and raises questions about teacher decision making based on evidence of student learning. Schmoker (2001) notes that when trying to understand a lesson's appropriate connection to standards, it is important to remember that standards, particularly explicit ones, are more about what students should be able to achieve rather than what teachers, parents, and the community think they can achieve. The latter is often a level of mastery far lower than what a student can and should be pushed to reach. Expert observers therefore ask questions such as "are [the standards] high enough, reasonable, and appropriate as we look at a teacher dealing with different groups and different individuals?" (Saphier & Gower, 1997). Our panelists reinforced these ideas by relating the types of questions they would typically focus on in observations such as "Does the lesson match the purpose?"

and "How does what students are actually engaged in doing help them to achieve the desired outcomes?" Panelists also reinforced the importance of observing not just for the presence or absence of a reference to standards in any given lesson, but also for the crucial next step of ascertaining whether those are appropriate standards for students to attain and how the standard connects to meaningful learning.

From this process, CEL faculty identified vision statements that define high-quality instruction related to standards. These vision statements can be found in the actual 5D framework as well (Appendix A), but for ease of reading, we will provide these vision statements in the form of a summary at the end of each subdimension.

VISION OF HIGH-QUALITY INSTRUCTION RELATED TO *STANDARDS*

- The lesson is based on standard(s) that are meaningful and relevant beyond the task at hand (for example, relate to a broader purpose or context such as problem solving, citizenship, and so on) and helps students learn and apply transferable knowledge and skills.

- The lesson is intentionally linked to other lessons (previous and future) in support of students meeting standard(s).

Teaching Point

Expert instructional leaders also pay attention to the teaching point of the lesson. Sometimes called the *lesson objective,* the *learning target,* or the *lesson purpose,* the teaching point establishes the specific learning goals for the lesson. These goals should be linked in key ways to help students meet identified standards. As Danielson (1996) points out, teaching "is a purposeful activity—it is goal directed, designed to achieve certain well-defined purposes. These purposes should be clear" (p. 68). Experts are able to identify whether the teaching point is clearly articulated, connected to standards, derived from specific content demands, embedded in instruction, and understood by students.

The teaching point can be observed in various ways and focuses on what students are expected to know and be able to do. Perhaps the simplest and most direct communication can be observed when teachers write the teaching point or objective for the lesson on the board or state it explicitly for students. However, as our expert panel was quick to point out, observers may find evidence of the teaching point of a lesson in the ways effective teachers, for example, "target questions to lesson objectives" (Stronge, 2002, p. 76) or how the teacher talks with students about the expectations for learning or the relevance of what is to be learned. Expert observers also recognize instances when teachers fail to connect narrowly stated behavioral objectives with a deeper trajectory of learning that is meaningful and relevant. For example, a more expert observer would notice the difference between a stated objective that asks students to learn three facts about the Boston Tea Party and one that connects the events of the Tea Party with an understanding that revolutions such as the American Revolution occur as a result of social, political, and economic upheaval. An expert observer is able to critically analyze the content and delivery of a lesson in relation to the teaching point and raises questions about teacher decision making based on evidence of student learning. How teachers connect the teaching point of a given lesson to prior learning, for example, is critical for bridging students' understanding. As Bransford, Brown, and Cocking (2000) suggest, "a logical extension of the view that new knowledge must be constructed from existing knowledge is that teachers need to pay attention to the incomplete understandings" (p. 10). Expert observers notice whether and how teachers connect the teaching point to what students already know and are able to do.

We have learned that expert observers also consider whether and how the teaching point helps students to meet grade-level standards and content demands. Eighty percent of teachers polled in an early validation study of the parameters [of teaching] thought the most important parameter of teaching was having a clear objective for what is to be taught and learned. In explanation they said, "if you don't know where you're going, you can't get there" (Saphier & Gower, 1997, p. 397). Moreover, the issue of relevance answers why the objective or teaching point is something worth learning, whether it is meaningful and relevant beyond the task at hand—in other words, what is the transferable skill? This is what Saphier and Gower (1997) call the "who cares" question (p. 212).

VISION OF HIGH-QUALITY INSTRUCTION RELATED TO *TEACHING POINT*

- The teaching point is based on knowledge of students' learning needs in relation to standard(s).

- The teaching point is clearly articulated, linked to standard(s), embedded in instruction, and understood by students.

- The teaching point is measurable. The criteria for success are clear to students and the performance tasks provide evidence that students are able to understand and apply learning in context.

STUDENT ENGAGEMENT

The second broad dimension of the framework focuses on student engagement. Expert observers move well beyond simple time-on-task checks in observing for student engagement and focus on

- Intellectual work—who is doing the work and what is the nature of that work?

- Engagement strategies—what are the particular structures, strategies, and approaches teachers use to elicit student engagement in learning?

- Talk—what is the substance of student engagement as embodied in communication between and among students and between teacher and students?

Intellectual Work

Experts observe for student engagement in terms of the nature of intellectual, academic work and critically analyze the substance of that work in support of student learning. Our panelists pointed out the importance of observing for the relationship between assigned tasks and specific content demands. They ask questions of the lesson such as "What is the level and quality of intellectual work in which students are engaged?" and "Does the work focus on factual recall? On making inferences? On analysis? Metacognition? Based on what evidence?"

Experts also critically analyze who is doing what work in the classroom, when and how this work occurs, and whether it connects to or directly fosters student learning. For example, our panelists reinforced the importance of paying attention to the frequency of teacher talk versus student talk and the kinds of questions teachers and students ask during the course of learning. This reinforced the importance of considering the question, "Where is the locus of control over learning in the classroom?" and assessing the extent to which control resides primarily with the teacher, with students, or whether it is shared in key ways.

Expert observers consider the role of students in their learning, which could include paying attention to how students "own" the content—how the processes of engagement reflect efforts to help students to engage in making meaning. The nature of questions students ask of the teacher or of each other can reveal the extent to which tasks are aimed at moving beyond basic factual recall to more sophisticated forms of understanding. To this end, experts notice the nature of students' participation in constructing meaning, not just what the teacher does to foster this. This is consistent with Danielson's (1996) characterization of the classroom as a "community of learners," where "a teacher is not the sole source of knowledge; students also participate in generating and sharing understanding" (p. 26).

Our panelists further suggest that expert observers raise questions about teacher decision making about planning for engagement in intellectually challenging work and the rationale for choices the teacher makes about which tasks to provide for students. Experts also consider and discuss alternative tasks that could assist students with meaning making, grounded in evidence from the observed lesson, knowledge of content, and pedagogy.

VISION OF HIGH-QUALITY INSTRUCTION RELATED TO *INTELLECTUAL WORK*

- Students' classroom work embodies substantive intellectual engagement (reading, thinking, writing, problem solving, and meaning making).
- Students take ownership of their learning to develop, test, and refine their thinking.

Engagement Strategies

Expert instructional leaders critically analyze the efficacy of strategies teachers use to ensure that all students have access to and are expected to participate in learning, including how strategies serve to engage students in learning within particular content areas and how to use the academic language associated with those content areas. Panelist's comments about what they look for in terms of access to content included questions such as "Do all students have access to participation in the work of the group? Why or why not?" And simply, "How is participation distributed?"

Experts also consider how the use of strategies encourages equitable and purposeful student participation in talk, in their own learning and meaning making, and in informing teaching decisions. Such strategies can vary but they are well described in the literature. For example, Danielson (1996) notes, "instructional techniques that enhance student engagement and achievement include frequent review, multiple learning tasks, engaging and appropriate material, and clear explanations that highlight key concepts and make use of appropriate metaphors" (p. 126). Our expert panelists described a number of engagement strategies or structures they look for, including small-group work, partner talk (when students are engaged in group work with an assigned partner), turn and talk (when students quickly turn to a partner to share their thinking as the teacher listens in), and think-pair-share (when students spend a few minutes of individual think time in response to a teacher's question or prompt, share their thinking with an assigned partner, and then share their thoughts with the class and others).

Expert observers further consider how the teacher takes into account student needs and interests to foster active engagement in learning. Such observations range from simple attention to the ways in which lessons are structured to including necessary breaks and changes in activity in order to (Yatvin, 2004) avoid boredom that invites "daydreaming or engaging in disruptive behavior" (Saphier & Gower, 1997, p. 31) to activities that are "guided by the students' interests and strengths" (Danielson, 1996, p. 26). Our panelists suggested expert observers further consider teacher moves with regard to engagement in the ways that teacher's questions reflect knowledge of content, pedagogy, and student learning and how the teacher capitalizes on student responses in order to extend conversation and learning as evidence of strategies for engagement. As Danielson (1996) further notes, "what is required is *mental engagement*, which may or may not involve physical activity. Hands-on activity is not enough; it must also be 'minds-on'" (p. 95).

Finally, in following up from a lesson observation, expert observers may raise questions about the teacher's decision to use particular engagement strategies and the rationale for those choices, while at the same time considering alternative strategies that could be helpful, grounded in evidence from the observed lesson, knowledge of content and pedagogy, and a vision for student engagement.

VISION OF HIGH-QUALITY INSTRUCTION RELATED TO *ENGAGEMENT STRATEGIES*

- Engagement strategies capitalize and build on students' background knowledge, experience, and responses to support rigorous and culturally relevant learning.
- Engagement strategies encourage equitable and purposeful student participation and ensure that all students have access to, and are expected to participate in, learning.

Talk

Attention to the nature of talk, whether teacher initiated or student initiated, also offers insight into student engagement in learning. An expert observer critically analyzes the rigor of student and teacher discourse, including the use of academic language, content knowledge, construction of new meaning, metacognition, and the nature of questions raised. The importance of talk in making meaning is well supported by learning theory. As Bransford, Brown, and Cocking (2000) note, "because metacognition often takes the form of an internal dialogue, many students may be unaware of its importance unless the processes are explicitly emphasized by teachers" (p. 21). Expert observers, therefore, pay close attention to the substance of what is said in classrooms and how the dialogue prompts deeper learning processes of various kinds.

Part of the rationale for a focus on talk when observing teaching and learning stems from the need to reveal students' prior knowledge in order to connect new learning and to create accountability for that learning. The expert observer considers how talk connects student background knowledge and experience to discipline-specific ways of thinking and communicating through, for example, brainstorming activities that "activate prior knowledge and allow students to be introduced to concepts in an accessible manner" (Wiske, 1998, p. 128). Furthermore, the nature of student talk reveals ways they are accountable for learning habits of thinking (both individually and collectively) within the particular discipline and to the content or concept under consideration. Experts consider the teacher's language in facilitating accountable student talk, raising questions such as "What questions does the teacher use to encourage students to share their thinking with each other?" and "How are students asked to build on each others' ideas and assess their understanding of each others' ideas?"

Expert observers also demonstrate the ability to raise and consider alternative ways to promote substantive student talk. For example, experts recognize that for some students, engaging in talk may be culturally discouraged. As Bransford, Brown, and Cocking (2000) note, "norms [about classroom talk] can also encourage modes of participation that may be unfamiliar to some students. . . . Expert observers pay attention to how teachers use knowledge of students' cultural norms to encourage authentic engagement" (p. 146).

Although experts use evidence they gather from the observed lesson, and link to a vision of what high-quality talk sounds like, they also recognize the importance of talking with the teacher to examine the teacher's understanding of the role of student talk in a given lesson.

VISION OF HIGH-QUALITY INSTRUCTION RELATED TO *TALK*

- Student talk reflects discipline-specific habits of thinking and ways of communicating.
- Student talk embodies substantive and intellectual thinking.

CURRICULUM AND PEDAGOGY

Curriculum and pedagogy form the third broad dimension of focus for expert observers of instruction and includes experts' emphasis on the following:

- Curriculum—assessing the instructional materials (for example, texts, tasks, and so on) used in the lesson and the extent to which these are aligned with the lesson purpose and appropriately challenging and supportive for all students
- Teaching approaches and strategies—identifying what pedagogies are used and how instruction reflects pedagogical content knowledge
- Scaffolds for learning—observing how the teacher balances the interplay of explicit teaching, scaffolding for the gradual release of responsibility

Curriculum

Expert observers focus attention on the content of the lesson and how it links to lesson purpose. They analyze choices of curriculum materials such as texts or tasks, asking whether the materials are appropriately challenging and supportive for students and evaluating the extent to which the materials are aligned with the lesson purpose and content area standards. Our expert panelists raised questions such as "How does the content of the lesson, such as the text being read or the task that is assigned, influence intellectual demand, such as the thinking or the reasoning that students are required to do?"

Experts also analyze the use of curriculum materials to support student learning of content area knowledge and skills and how this knowledge builds over time. Panelists raised questions linked to the development of conceptual understanding, for example, "How does the content actually reflect what mathematicians do and how they think?" This emphasis highlights teacher decision making

VISION OF HIGH-QUALITY INSTRUCTION RELATED TO *CURRICULUM*

- Instructional materials (e.g., texts, resources, etc.) and tasks are appropriately challenging and supportive for all students, are aligned with the teaching point and content area standards, and are culturally and academically relevant.

- The lesson materials and tasks are related to a larger unit and to the sequence and development of conceptual understanding over time.

regarding choice of materials and use for promoting particular aspects of learning. Expert observers also wonder about the relationship of the observed lesson to the larger unit of study and to the sequence and development of conceptual understanding over time.

Teaching Approaches and Strategies

Expert observers also pay attention to the particular instructional strategies or teaching approaches (methods) used in the context of a given lesson. As Stigler and Hiebert (1999) note, "challenging content alone does not lead to high achievement. The same content can be taught deeply or superficially" (p. 58). We found that expert observers of instruction analyze both the rationale and use of instructional approaches and strategies for the particular purpose of the observed lesson. Our expert panelists raised questions for consideration about teaching strategies such as "How does the particular set of strategies used in the lesson serve the identified purpose of learning or the teaching point?" and "To what extent do the teacher's choices of instructional strategies support student learning of particular content or development of specific transferable skills?"

Expert observers also pay attention to the ways that teachers gradually release responsibility for learning to students so as to foster independent use of transferable skills. We heard our expert panel reference the "to, with, and by" approach to literacy learning, which involves a gradual shifting of responsibility for the demonstration of learning from the teacher to the student (Mooney, 1990). This is consistent with a more general focus experts bring to evaluating teacher decision making in the ways that pedagogies support specific aspects of learning.

Experts are also able to suggest alternative pedagogical strategies grounded in evidence of student learning, knowledge of content and pedagogy, and a vision of effective, powerful instruction. This ability is consistent with Danielson's (1996) notion that "no one [pedagogical] approach is a 'one size fits all.' But some approaches will be better suited to certain purposes than others. Making good and defensible choices is the hallmark of a professional educator" (p. 19).

VISION OF HIGH-QUALITY INSTRUCTION RELATED TO *TEACHING APPROACHES AND STRATEGIES*

- The teacher makes decisions and uses instructional approaches in ways that intentionally support the instructional purposes.

- Instruction reflects and is consistent with pedagogical content knowledge and is culturally responsive in order to engage students in disciplinary habits of thinking.

Scaffolds for Learning

Finally, expert observers of instruction focus on analyzing planned teacher moves to provide scaffolding and support of student learning. Scaffolding involves the specific ways teachers provide assistance to students to take ownership of their learning and aids the gradual release of responsibility. Teachers' scaffolding of learning may occur in various ways, for example, through the use of co-constructed charts (between the teacher and students) in literacy or by the introduction of strategies for guided practice on key concepts.

Experts look for both planned methods to scaffold for students and the identification and discussion of in-the-moment teacher decisions to support student learning. Teachers can change lessons in the moment to assist with learning. As Stronge (2002) notes, "effective teachers think through likely misconceptions that may occur during instruction and monitor students for signs of these misconceptions" (p. 57). This is consistent with Saphier and Gower's (1997) comment that "many teachers . . . pursue personalized objectives for particular students . . . outside the formal boundaries of their academic agendas. . . . For many teachers these moves are quick and spontaneous" (p. 558).

Ultimately, scaffolding should help move students toward independence. As Saphier and Gower (1997) suggest "guidance should be high with new tasks and withdrawn gradually with demonstrated student proficiency" (p. 249). Experts who pay attention to scaffolding analyze if and how teacher support is strategic and intentional in moving students toward increasing independence with a transferable skill. Experts also raise questions about teacher decision making regarding how the sequence of learning experiences supports each student in reaching the learning objective(s) and grade-level standards.

Experts recognize that scaffolding of learning may be assisted by technology-based tools, which can enhance student performance when they are integrated into the curriculum and used in accordance with knowledge about learning. But as Bransford, Brown, and Cocking (2000) note, "the mere existence of these tools in the classroom provides no guarantee that student learning will improve; they have to be part of a coherent education approach" (p. 216). Expert observers pay attention to the subtleties associated with using technology as an aid for learning not as an end in itself.

Finally, expert observers recognize the importance of feedback about ways to adjust the instructional strategies observed in classrooms for the benefit of student learning. Experts possess pedagogical content knowledge that enables them to pose alternative suggestions to teachers for how to scaffold student learning, grounded in evidence from observation and their knowledge of content and pedagogy (Stein & Nelson, 2003).

VISION OF HIGH-QUALITY INSTRUCTION RELATED TO *SCAFFOLDS FOR LEARNING*

- The teacher's use of instructional approaches balances the interplay of explicit teaching, scaffolding for the gradual release of teacher responsibility, and for student choice and ownership.

- The teacher uses different instructional strategies based on planned and in-the-moment decisions to address individual learning needs.

ASSESSMENT FOR STUDENT LEARNING

The fourth broad dimension of instructional practice that experts observe for in classrooms is assessment for student learning. Expert observers pay attention to how teachers determine and help ensure student success through

- Assessments—ways teachers expect students to demonstrate learning in relation to the lesson objectives, specific content demands, and transferable skills

- Adjustments—instructional decisions or moves made in the moment to better support student learning based on evidence of progress gleaned during the course of the lesson

Assessment

Planful assessment of student learning feeds information back to the instructional process and allows teachers the opportunity to refine and redirect strategies for improving learning. Danielson (1996) posits that assessments should be congruent with the instructional goals, have clear criteria and standards, and be used in planning the next steps of instruction. Expert observers should analyze how the classroom teacher uses multiple forms of assessment to understand the learning of each student within the observed lesson and over time. Our expert panelists made clear their emphasis on assessment of learning, raising questions for focus in observations such as "How does the teacher gather information about student learning in the lesson?" and "How comprehensive are the data sources used to inform instruction and decision making?"

Expert observers also analyze the quality of assessment tools and strategies the teacher uses and how these inform lesson objectives and higher-level thinking skills. As Bransford, Brown, and Cocking (2000) note, "assessment should reflect the *quality* of students' thinking, as well as what specific content they have learned" (p. 244). Our expert panel pointed out that assessment should include a variety of tools and approaches to gather comprehensive and quality data and that these tools should include efforts to understand evidence such as anecdotal notes from student-teacher conferences and student work samples among other sources.

Expert observers also look for teacher decisions that are assessment driven and consider multiple ways teachers can help students to demonstrate and represent their learning in context. As Wiske (1998) suggests, experts ask "What might students do to develop and demonstrate their understanding?" (p. 73). Answering this question reminds teachers that students can undertake a much more varied range of activities as part of their schoolwork than is encompassed by typical assignments. Experts pay attention to what is guiding the teacher's assessment of student learning, for example, ways that assessment efforts connect to benchmark standards or reflect on professional development efforts to improve particular aspects of the teaching and learning process. This process is consistent with Saphier and Gower's (1997) notion that "the act of assessment should be an act of learning too" (p. 480). Connecting assessments to expectations for learning and then using this connection to drive changes in instruction completes the cycle of teaching and learning improvement. As Stigler and Hiebert (1999) note, "the true meaning of learning goals becomes apparent only as teachers link them to assessments and weave them into a coherent curriculum and use them to guide their teaching decisions" (p. 142).

Beyond a focus on teacher decision making and instructional improvement, expert observers also analyze opportunities for student self-assessment and reflection in lesson observations, which is consistent with Wiske's (1998) notion that "teachers should encourage students to reflect on their learning by having a clear ongoing assessment plan" (p. 311).

Experts also pay attention to ways assessment(s) could be used for future planning and pose alternative methods or strategies for assessing learning based on knowledge of content and pedagogy and a vision for powerful instruction, about what is being assessed, how it is being assessed, and how evidence of student learning will be used to shape future teaching decisions.

Such a focus is consistent with the way Marzano, Pickering, and Pollock (2001) emphasize the importance of early planful assessment in the process of defining goals and expectations for student learning, noting that "at the beginning of each unit, one should define learning goals for the students. The middle of the unit will contain strategies for monitoring progress as

VISION OF HIGH-QUALITY INSTRUCTION RELATED TO *ASSESSMENT*

- Students are able to assess their own learning in relation to the teaching point.
- The teacher creates multiple assessment opportunities and expects all students to demonstrate learning.
- Assessment methods include a variety of tools and approaches to gather comprehensive and quality information about the learning styles and needs of each student (for example, anecdotal notes, conferring, student work samples, and so on).
- The teacher uses observable systems and routines for recording and using student assessment data (for example, charts, conferring records, portfolios, and rubrics).
- Assessment criteria, methods, and purposes are transparent and students have a role in their own assessment to promote learning.

well as introducing new knowledge. The end of the unit comes back to the learning goals, where teachers and students measure their success in meeting their goals" (p. 146).

Adjustments

Schmoker (2001) argues that there is a great value in brief and frequent assessments, both formal and in the moment, while teaching is in process. Clearly, creating and carrying out best-laid plans for assessing learning is critically important, yet we also agree with Danielson (1996) that "the most difficult [teaching] decisions have to do with adjusting a lesson plan in midstream, when it is apparent that such adjustments will improve students' experience" (p. 103). With regard to observing for adjustments in the moment during a lesson, an expert observer analyzes how teachers assess student learning—understandings, confusions, and so on—based on students' performance throughout the lesson.

These in-the-moment assessments should relate directly to progress made toward lesson objectives. As Wiske (1998) reminds us, "goals not only serve as endpoints, but as constant reminders during a lesson of how far the class still needs to go" (p. 138). Progress in the moment can be assessed in relation to specific content demands or in relation to helping students achieve and demonstrate transferable skills. In operationalizing the issues of in-the-moment assessment, our panel of experts raised questions such as "How does assessment inform the teacher's instruction right now as well as decisions about what to do next?" and "How does the teacher's understanding of each student as a learner inform how that teacher pushes for depth and stretches boundaries of student thinking?"

Recognizing the importance of adjusting instruction in the moment is only the first step. Expert observers also analyze how the teacher actually adjusts his or her own teaching based on evidence of student learning in the moment. Evidence of this can be observed in whether the teacher persists with premade plans in spite of evidence of student misunderstanding or confusion or chooses to modify both expectations and pedagogy based on evidence that students need more instruction on a key idea.

Part of this adjustment lies in the teacher's ability to diagnose the reasons why students may not be able to demonstrate understanding(s) and how the teacher responds. Expert observers pay attention to the ways in which teachers talk about their decisions to adjust instruction post-lesson, and offer feedback that is sensitive to expressed teacher decisions and may raise questions about teacher decision making or pose alternatives grounded in evidence from the lesson.

Finally, expert observers of instruction are able to pose alternative ideas about both formal and in-the-moment assessments to help inform teaching decisions based on evidence from the observed lesson, knowledge of content and pedagogy, and a vision for the role of assessment in powerful instruction.

VISION OF HIGH-QUALITY INSTRUCTION RELATED TO *ADJUSTMENTS*

- The teacher plans instruction based on ongoing assessment and an understanding of students, standards, texts, tasks, and pedagogical content knowledge.
- The teacher makes in-the-moment instructional adjustments based on student understanding.

CLASSROOM ENVIRONMENT AND CULTURE

How teachers structure the classroom environment and create cultures that are inviting and respectful of student learning efforts form the final broad dimension for focus by the expert observer. Specifically, expert observers pay attention to the following:

- The physical environment—how teachers use resources and space to purposefully support and scaffold student learning
- Routines and rituals that support learning—how systems and routines of the classroom facilitate student ownership of learning and independence as well as reflect values of community, inclusivity, equity, and accountability for learning
- Classroom culture and climate—what discourse and interactions reveal about what is valued in the classroom

Use of Physical Environment

How the physical environment serves learning is an important aspect of the instructional process. An expert observer of instruction pays attention to how the physical arrangement of the room (for example, meeting area, resources, student seating, technology, and so on) is conducive to student learning and how the physical environment (for example, libraries, materials, charts, technology, and so on) is used to assess student understanding and to support learning. Experts pay attention to ways in which the physical environment of the classroom shifts to correspond to the particular instructional focus and how these shifts occur in the context of instruction (Saphier & Gower, 1997).

Attention to the physical environment also involves observing for whether and how materials and resources are accessible to all students, and how teachers use resources in the physical environment to scaffold student learning (for example, whether the teacher listens to student talk, moves around the room to observe and confer with students, and so on). As Danielson (1996) notes, "organization of space sends signals to students about how teachers view learning: 'centers' for exploration, desks facing forward for a presentation, chairs in a circle for a group discussion, or a science lab organized in a businesslike manner" (p. 88).

Experts observe for teacher behavior and decisions regarding physical space and also watch for how students use resources in the physical environment to support learning and independence. Members of our expert practitioner group, for example, observed for whether students refer to instructional charts posted around the room during independent work time and whether it is apparent that students know how to access the appropriate materials in the rooms, independently, to support their learning.

Observers recognize the importance of the physical arrangement of space in support of helping students concentrate on tasks of various kinds, particularly when multiple modes of learning are occurring inside one physical classroom space. As Yatvin (2004) notes, "when large numbers of students are engaged in different types of work at the same time—some of it interactive and noisy, and some of it solitary and quiet—they need elbow room, boundaries, and neutral passing zones to minimize distractions" (p. 14).

Expert observers also focus on how student learning is physically represented and accessed in the classroom. They pay attention to how student work is posted for viewing in the classroom and how this work reflects student critical thinking and ownership of learning. Our expert observer panel highlighted a number of kinds of student work examples they look for in classrooms, including co-constructed charts that focus on key learning and concepts, assignments that provide evidence of student reasoning or critical thinking, and examples that show various facets of student writing ability.

Finally, in conversations with teachers, expert observers may raise questions about teacher decisions regarding the use of physical space or suggest alternative ways for the teacher to reconsider the use of space. These reflections on practice should be based on specific evidence from the observed lesson, knowledge of content and pedagogy, and an articulated vision for how physical space in or around the classroom can be used to effectively support student learning.

VISION OF HIGH-QUALITY INSTRUCTION RELATED TO *USE OF PHYSICAL ENVIRONMENT*

- The physical arrangement of the room (for example, meeting area, resources, student seating, and so on) is conducive to student learning.

- The teacher uses the physical space of the classroom to assess student understanding and support learning (for example, teacher moves around the room to observe and confer with students).

- Students have access to resources in the physical environment to support learning and independence (for example, libraries, materials, charts, technology, and so on).

Classroom Routines and Rituals

A second aspect of the classroom environment and culture that expert observers pay attention to is analysis of the routines and rituals used to facilitate learning in the classroom. Our panel of experts noted transitions between lesson segments and the kind of processes for management and collaboration used and how they appear to be engrained in student routines to maximize student learning time. This focus is consistent with Danielson's (1996) comments about non-instructional routines: "experienced teachers devise routine techniques for expediting the myriad non-instructional duties for which they are responsible, leaving maximum time for instruction" (p. 83).

But rituals and routines are not just about maximizing learning time, although that is an important focus. Experts also pay attention to how classroom routines and rituals facilitate student ownership and learning and foster inclusive and respectful relationships in building a community of learners to make students "feel like useful, confident, and successful members of the classroom community" (Yatvin, 2004, p. 25). Our panel of experts noted rituals such as greeting one another by name and ways teachers identify and highlight the specific intellectual contributions of all students as key aspects of building community in the classroom. Further, student ownership of classroom rules and norms forms an important focus for the expert observer, consistent with Saphier and Gower's (1997) emphasis on "opportunities students have to influence the rules of the classroom game, to shape the form and dynamics of interaction and operation" (p. 377).

The expert observer further examines student work habits and how these reflect responsibility for their own learning as shown by coming prepared to class, using time productively, and participating in small- and large-group learning experiences. This focus on work habits is consistent with Marzano, Pickering, and Pollock (2001), who note that "effort itself is a primary indicator of [learning] success; those students and teachers who exhibit a belief in its importance demonstrate high levels of achievement" (pp. 50–51). As our expert panel pointed out, routines also focus on procedures and processes for entering class and getting to work, for accessing tools and resources students need to work independently, and for functioning within a collaborative learning community.

VISION OF HIGH-QUALITY INSTRUCTION RELATED TO *CLASSROOM ROUTINES AND RITUALS*

- Classroom systems and routines facilitate student responsibility, ownership, and independence.
- Available time is maximized in service of learning.

Classroom Culture

The culture and climate of the classroom create the needed conditions for student learning. Expert instructional leaders analyze how the importance of the learning is conveyed through time on task, expectations, accountability, language, and actions.

When it comes to creating a culture of learning, Danielson (1996) highlights the responsibilities teachers have in creating such an atmosphere in their classroom. How teachers convey messages about the value of learning matters a great deal. Expert observers focus on how language and interactions (teacher-student, student-student) reflect belief about whether all students are valued, respected, and viewed as intellectually capable. Expert observers pay attention to how teachers emphasize beliefs in their students' abilities and "expect all of them to learn, regardless of their skill levels and starting points" (Stronge, 2002, p. 36).

Expert observers also pay attention to participation, communication, and interaction patterns to assess intentional efforts toward creating a culture of equity and learning (for example, explicitly addressing issues of power and inequity, including and valuing all voices). Such a focus is consistent with Yatvin (2004), who argues that "children learn best in a community of equals where they continually teach and learn from each other and produce in concert what no one of them could produce alone" (p. 13). Experts take note of routines that support a culture of risk taking, academic press (how students clarify and elaborate their thinking, how they challenge each other's ideas and premises, and so on), and collective ownership and accountability for learning in the classroom. Routines can also be supportive of the development of what Saphier and Gower (1997) call a "psychological climate of safety" and, in fact, esteem for students who need and seek assistance.

Expert observers further consider the extent to which the work of the classroom is intellectually rich and reflects the lives, interests, and culture(s) of students as shown in opportunities for student choice in selection of tasks and initiative for learning. As Wiske (1998) notes, "students must construct their own understanding. Identifying one's own interests, developing one's own arguments, discerning the new layers of questions beneath every provisional set of answers are all concomitant with constructing one's own understanding rather than merely absorbing knowledge made by others" (p. 36).

Experts also consider evidence and raise questions about the extent to which classroom culture reveals opportunities for strong, ongoing development of relationships. Stronge (2002) asserts that effective teachers are "caring, outwardly so; demonstrate fairness and respect; are able to interact with their students in ways appropriate to any given situation, varying their stance from highly professional to informal or even joking; show enthusiasm for both the material and the act of teaching itself; and cultivate high levels of motivation in their students" (p. 71). Experts also consider the ways in which student-student interaction embodies relationship building and supports learning.

VISION OF HIGH-QUALITY INSTRUCTION RELATED TO *CLASSROOM CULTURE*

- Classroom discourse and interactions reflect high expectations and beliefs about all students' intellectual capabilities and create a culture of inclusivity, equity, and accountability for learning.
- Classroom norms encourage risk taking, collaboration, and respect for thinking.

CONCLUSION

The framework described in this chapter rests on a synthesis of research, policy prescriptions, and practitioner wisdom that is well established. The framework we've articulated focuses on five broad dimensions of instructional practice that form the basis of what "experts" pay attention to when observing in classrooms: (1) purpose, (2) student engagement, (3) curriculum and pedagogy, (4) assessment for student learning, and (5) classroom environment and culture.

We suggest that effective instructional leaders at a minimum need to embrace these five broad dimensions in their classroom observations and begin to specify the more fine-grained thirteen subdimensions associated with these five dimensions. In Chapter Three, we elaborate on the initial descriptions of how to put into practice each of these dimensions with an example that reveals how expert observation of instruction plays out in real time.

DISCUSSION QUESTIONS

- To what extent does your vision of high-quality teaching and learning align with the five broad dimensions explained in this chapter?
- Which of these dimensions require more attention and study on your part or the part of school leaders in your district?

chapter THREE

Applying the Five Dimensions of Teaching and Learning

In Chapter Two, we introduced the Five Dimensions of Teaching and Learning, including the genesis of this framework. We explained the five dimensions and thirteen subdimensions that define what expert observers of teaching and learning look for when observing in classrooms. The purpose of this chapter is to bring the Five Dimensions of Teaching and Learning framework to life by applying it to an actual classroom setting. We illustrate how the five dimensions can help a classroom observer navigate the complicated terrain of teaching and learning by taking the reader into a third-grade classroom where the students are in the middle of a mathematics lesson and see how the observer of instruction, in this case the principal, applies the 5D framework in her lesson analysis. You will note that the principal is guided by her deep expertise and the fine-grained detail provided by the 5D framework. We recognize that most instructional leaders will not yet have developed this level of expertise but this deep expertise can be learned. Our purpose in this chapter is not to discourage the reader by illustrating how much more there is to learn. Our intent is to portray the depth of expertise necessary to fully understand that quality teaching is a most sophisticated and complex endeavor. We will show how this principal uses the framework as she thinks about guiding the professional learning of the classroom teacher and her staff.

This fictional vignette takes place in Jacob White's classroom. Jacob is an enthusiastic third-year, third-grade teacher who is well respected by parents, students, and colleagues alike. In fact, his grade-level colleagues often look to him for lesson ideas. After a leader's observation, Jacob always requests feedback and listens carefully to what he hears. Jacob's students are quite diverse: 70 percent receive free or reduced lunch and roughly half are English language learners (ELLs) with varying levels of formal schooling in their numerous countries of origin. His students struggle on state mathematics and reading tests.

The vignette uses second person narration ("you enter the room . . .") in attempt to draw *you,* the reader, into the experience of the classroom observation, which begins at the start of a mathematics lesson. You might place the 5D framework from Appendix A beside you and refer to it throughout your reading. Imagine you are conducting a routine, informal classroom visit as a principal and are watching the lesson in real time. Do not worry if you do not yet consider yourself an "expert" in the content area or grade level being described. This vignette is not intended to represent an ideal state of instruction or to exemplify ideas from the five dimensions of teaching learning. We do not intend for the vignette to represent a particular philosophy of teaching. We include the vignette as an example of the type of classroom that might exist in your school(s).

After the vignette, you will find 5D analysis of the imagined classroom lesson. We provide this analysis in first person ("I noticed that Jacob . . . "). The principal already has a relationship with the teacher and is committed to his development. In italics, we (the authors of this chapter) offer commentary on the 5D analysis to guide your reading and interpretation of the principal's comments. You may wish to read the vignette and try to analyze it yourself using the 5D framework first, then read the analysis.

JACOB WHITE'S THIRD-GRADE MATHEMATICS CLASSROOM

As you enter the classroom and close the door quietly, thirty sets of eyes greet you. The students sit in five rows of six students each, all desks facing the front of the room. The students all turn back to face you with curiosity. The room is silent except for one boy who shouts, "Hi!" You nod at him and glance at the board in the front. Jacob White, a young third-year teacher from the local neighborhood, waves at you. He is holding a meter stick and is pointing at a large rectangle drawn on the board.

"Class? Eyes up here," he commands in a soft but certain voice and all students turn back to the front. "Like I was saying, what is the perimeter of this rectangle?" he asks the students, pointing at the sides of the shape. You notice that he also has written "Purpose = using toothpicks to find the perimeter of rectangles, pages 15–18, lesson five" in large print on the left side of the board above the daily schedule.

As you make your way into the classroom weaving through the rows of student desks you notice that students have their math textbooks open to a page entitled "Calculating Perimeter." They also have stacks of graph paper, pencils, and lots of toothpicks. Some of the toothpicks are broken and a few litter the floor. "What's *perimeter* mean?" one student whispers to the student next to her. Her neighbor appears to ignore the question or simply does not hear her. The girl looks down and moves her toothpicks into a triangle.

"OK, class. Who remembers how we learned to find perimeter?"

Three boys and a girl raise their hands instantly, then, noting each other, start shouting out their answers.

"You add up the sides!"

"You put your toothpicks there and count how many there are!"

"You plus the length and width!"

"You use a ruler!" Two students make this last comment in unison.

"OK! One at a time," interjects Jacob. "Hillary, would you come up and show us how you would find the perimeter of this rectangle?"

(continued)

Hillary nods and pushes back her chair. She is the student who had shouted about using toothpicks. She walks directly up her row to the white board. Most of the class looks at her. The other students who had shouted out answers look down at their desks and busy themselves with calculating the rectangle's perimeter on their own. When she gets to the front, Jacob taps her on the shoulder and shows her the pile of drinking straws on a rolling cart. "Pretend these straws are your toothpicks," Jacob instructs the class. He glances out at the students. "Tomas and Peter? Look up here!" he prompts two boys seated in the back. They had started whispering when Hillary picked up a straw.

Hillary silently stares at the giant rectangle on the board. She holds her straw up to the bottom of the rectangle. "One . . . " she counts aloud. She tries to hold that straw while picking up the next one and drops the first one. A student giggles. She tries again, this time dropping both straws and then stares at the floor.

"What should Hillary do now?" Jacob asks the class. A student shouts something that is hard to hear. No students seem to react to the in-audible answer. Jacob commands, "tell your partner what Hillary could do now to use the straws to find the perimeter of this rectangle. Make sure each partner talks. Start with the partner who is oldest first!"

The students turn to face the person who is sitting closest to them in the next row. The students in the fifth row turn to face the person either in front of or behind them. As soon as they are prompted, there is an animated buzz of young voices in the room. As you listen to the pair closest to you, you hear, "she should just hold the straw up there and mark where it ends!" Her partner replies, "I think she should for-get the straws and use the ruler." Jacob shouts over the noise from his spot at the front of the room, "OK, next partner should be talking now!"

Another student near you says, "She should get Mr. White to hold the straw for her while she gets the new one." His partner replies, "I don't know what she should do." The boy squints at her and says, "She could also use the straws to measure one side and add it by two. Or she should just measure one side and times it by two."

"One–two–three eyes on me!" shouts Jacob over the din. The students stop talking on cue, turning to face him. "OK, I heard lots of good ideas to help Hillary. Let's see some hands. Who has an idea?" Three students' hands shoot up.

"John?"

"She should just make a mark at the end of the straw. Then, she can move the straw and do it again," John replies.

Jacob responds, "Good. Who else has an idea? Jody?"

Jody replies, "She should just put a dot where the straw ends and then move the straw over."

"That's what I said," shouts John.

"I said it different," Jody adds quietly.

Before Jacob can respond, Hillary already has started using John and Jody's proposed strategy. She uses one straw to measure from the corner of the bottom of the rectangle, marking the end of the straw and then moving it over each time. Once she reaches the other side, she writes a big "7" at the bottom. Then, she starts using the straw to measure the height of the rectangle. "Watch Hillary now!" Jacob cuts in to interrupt the argument between John and Jody. Almost all of the students watch as Hillary writes "3" to indicate the height. She starts to repeat the process for the top of the rectangle.

"Wait!!!!" shouts John. "It's the same!!! You don't have to measure the top." There is a pause as the students all turn to look at their teacher.

Hillary freezes. Jacob White glances at John. "Hillary, John is right. You don't have to measure the top, too, because it's a rectangle. The top and bottom are the same, just like the two sides are the same. He takes the pen from Hillary and writes "7" on the top and "3" on the other side of the figure. "OK," Jacob says to the class, "thanks, Hillary, you did a nice job getting us started. Go and sit down." Hillary puts down the stack of straws and makes her way back to her seat. Her partner gives her a high five. The students clap for her as she sits down.

"Class," Jacob says, "we've been working on how to find perimeter. You have all the information you need now. Go ahead and practice your adding to find the perimeter of this shape. Remember to add all the numbers you see. Work by yourself this time."

The students stare at their graph paper and straws. Several students start scribbling numbers on their papers. A few students pick up their

(*continued*)

toothpicks. Jacob walks up and down the rows. He whispers to one stu-dent who sits with his head down, "go ahead and draw the rectangle just like it is up there . . . " The girl nearest to you is drawing tick marks on her paper and she counts each one. "14, 15, 16, 17 . . . " Her partner shouts at her, "this is easy! You don't have to write it out like that! Look, make tens!" You notice that the girl crouches closer to her paper to finish counting. Her partner shrugs and picks up a chapter book from his desk and starts reading it.

After about ten minutes of work time on this problem, Jacob returns to the front of the room. "OK, class, what is the perimeter of this rectan-gle? Hands please."

Almost all thirty students raise their hands. Jacob looks at Hillary, who is waving her hand triumphantly. "Yes, Hillary?"

"20! The answer is 20 straws!"

Jacob smiles at her and writes "P = 20" on the board. "Very good," he tells her. "Class, go ahead and do numbers one to fifteen in your book. You can use the strategy we learned together."

You stand up to exit the classroom, noticing that most students have shifted their attention to the textbook.

ANALYSIS

In this section we provide a written analysis of this lesson through the eyes of the principal. The principal use her deep knowledge of the 5D framework as the lens for analyzing the teaching and learning in this classroom. The principal has been at this school for three years so she has observed and supported Jacob's practice for this young teacher's entire career. You can use the italicized annotations interspersed in the analysis to guide your reading of it.

Purpose

We refer to *purpose* as the linchpin dimension because everything that tran-spires in a lesson must connect from and back to purpose. Purpose has two subdimensions. *Teaching point* refers to what the teacher intends the students will know and be able to do as a result of the lesson. *Standards* are what we call the "what for" subdimension in that teachers must always ask how their teaching point will help students transfer knowledge and skill in order to meet a rigorous and college-going standard over time.

Subdimension: Standards The white board in the classroom states that the purpose of the lesson is "using toothpicks to find the perimeter of rectangles, pages 15–18, lesson five." The students' district-adopted textbooks, opened to page 15, state "Lesson Five, Calculating Perimeter." *Note that the principal starts by stating what she sees. She uses two sources to identify the stated purpose. At this point there is no judgment on the part of the principal. She is simply jotting down what she notices.*

In relation to mathematics standards, this purpose statement confuses me. It seems the mathematical concept at play here is "calculating perimeter of rectangles." This purpose is reflected in the third-grade standards, though, it is articulated as "finding the perimeter of quadrilaterals." Jacob's substitution of "rectangles" for "quadrilaterals" might reflect his choice to simplify the lesson by focusing on one quadrilateral. The textbook designers made a similar decision. I know that subsequent lessons in the book include finding the perimeter of other four-sided shapes. Jacob might be scaffolding to support student understanding of what a quadrilateral is. I wonder why he made this decision, however. Does he know the students need this level of scaffolding? It seems it could limit student ability to generalize their definitions of four-sided shapes and the meaning of *perimeter*. They might walk away thinking that perimeter means different things with different shapes or that the process varies. *Note the principal's awareness of the district expectations, the standards, and the textbook. Note also that she is trying to figure out why Jacob made the decisions he made. She is moving from her noticing to now wondering about the teacher's teaching decision.*

In order to fully comment on the standards in this lesson, I need to know what Jacob has already taught the students about quadrilaterals and perimeter. At the end of the lesson, John seemed to be applying his knowledge of rectangles (two parallel sides the same length) to advise Hillary's measurement of the sides ("It's the same!!! You don't have to measure the top.") but it is unclear how the other students understood this concept. Furthermore, based on student comments, it seems that Jacob preceded this lesson with others that addressed perimeter. At least some students knew that perimeter had to do with the lengths of sides of a shape. I would predict that Jacob would follow up this lesson with lessons on finding the perimeter of other shapes, including ones with more than four sides and shapes with sides of all different lengths. *The principal is knowledgeable about the pacing guide and the order of lessons it recommends. She is also looking for evidence of the logical pacing of lessons and is seeking reasons for teacher decision making. She is making some inferences based on student comments.*

Additionally, I have some questions about the standards in the arithmetic portion of the lesson. When Jacob set the students loose to add up the lengths of the sides of the rectangle, they worked, to various degrees of success, for ten minutes. Some students completed this task quite rapidly; one started reading his chapter book. The adding of four one-digit numbers is actually a second-grade mathematics standard. By third grade, students should be able to mentally compute this sum, at least of two numbers at a time. In this case, because the figure is a rectangle, students only needed to add two numbers (length and height) and then add the sums together. The numbers were simple enough that I would expect this to be an easy calculation for third-grade students. I would like to talk with Jacob about this portion of the lesson. After he set them up with very clear expectations, "go ahead and practice your adding . . . ," he made the choice to give students total independence (they were to calculate on their own) and he circulated around to see how they were doing. Did he think they needed this amount of scaffolding to know which numbers to add? Was he assessing their computation? Did he believe that the mathematical work of the lesson was more about measuring the sides and that this part was just practice? What does he know about his students that contributed to his choice? What did he learn about them during this time? Why did he give them this amount of time? *The principal has lots of questions about this part of the lesson. She is trying to figure out the teacher's beliefs about mathematics learning in general and his students in particular. The principal's questions are rooted in her math content understanding, knowing for example that "the adding of four one-digit numbers is actually a second-grade mathematics standard." The principal's ability to notice a lack of alignment with grade-level–appropriate standards prompts her question about whether the teacher was trying to scaffold student learning based on his assessment of students' prior knowledge or if something else was at play.*

Subdimension: Teaching Point It is difficult to figure out Jacob's intended teaching point. The purpose statement reads, "using toothpicks to find the perimeter of rectangles, pages 15–18, lesson five." It seems to me that "using toothpicks" is a strategy that might help students to measure the perimeter of a shape and understand perimeter in terms of units around the outside. *Here, the principal is carefully analyzing the differences among the teaching point, standard, and the activity. This analysis is based on the principal's knowledge and understanding of standards and teaching points.* I wonder if he wants "using toothpicks to find perimeter" to be the teaching point. In the case of this class, however, "using toothpicks" became the *activity* for the students, not a tool or strategy for understanding measurement, shape, or perimeter. Although Jacob did ask "Who remembers how we learned to find perimeter?" and at the end of the lesson asked "OK, what is the perimeter of this rectangle?" for the most part, his comments during the lesson addressed the logistics of using toothpicks (or straws) to measure the lengths of the sides. For example, he asked, "what could Hillary do now to use the straws to find the perimeter of this rectangle?" The students have lots of advice for Hillary and each other about how to manipulate the toothpicks and straws against the white board ("she should just make a mark at the end of the straw") but less about other measurement strategies or methods for calculating perimeter, let alone the meaning of *perimeter* or its use in the world. The focus quickly became the usage of the supplies, not the mathematical thinking. I am further led to this conclusion by the inclusion of the textbook page in the purpose statement. Although this is not in and of itself a problem, it does reveal a possible conflation of the larger purpose (standard), teaching point, and task. *The principal is quite attuned to the differences among teaching point, activity, and standard. She is looking for evidence of thinking work.*

Furthermore, the students' advice for Hillary would not easily apply to their own manipulation of toothpicks on their horizontal desks. They would not be battling gravity to hold up the measuring tools (as Hillary did against the white board), and in fact they had plenty of toothpicks to use to measure the lengths of the sides of the rectangle. I have observed students using this strategy and counting individual toothpicks at the end, not using measured marks. It is possible, given the unclear teaching point, that the students might have tried to use one toothpick to measure each shape in their textbook, drawing little marks at the end of each one. This is not necessarily a bad strategy but also not the most appropriate or efficient. The modeling in front of the class did not match the task the students would themselves complete. During the lesson portion, the only skill that the students practiced on their own was adding four numbers. Was this the teaching point? *The principal is questioning the usability of the stated teaching point, which also became the focus activity. She is also attending to the appearance (or nonappearance) of the teaching point throughout the lesson. She understands that the teaching point is the immediate take away, that is, what the student will know and be able to do as a result of this specific lesson activity. She knows that the teaching point must be related to a larger standard that allows the students to transfer knowledge and skill. She noted several inconsistencies.*

I did not ask any students what the purpose of the lesson was, so I am wondering what they would say. Early in the lesson, one student asked her neighbor, "what's *perimeter* mean?" suggesting that she knew that word would be important. *The principal is careful to note that her wondering is based on what was or was not noticed and the fact that she might need more information.* The four most assertive and verbal students who spoke right away had lots of strategies for calculating perimeter, revealing that this was not a brand-new concept for them. These students, at least, had some concept of *perimeter,* even though they were conflating strategies for measuring with strategies for calculating perimeter ("use a ruler" and "add up the sides"). In fact, when Hillary went to the front of the class to model, they were able to start working on their own.

I would imagine that most students would say the purpose today had to do with using toothpicks to measure the lengths of the sides of a rectangle. At least one student (Hillary) knew this strategy at the start of the lesson. I am not sure students would know how and when to transfer this strategy to other shapes or could articulate why this particular strategy might be more helpful than another when figuring out perimeter. In the end, most students seemed able to calculate perimeter once they knew the lengths of the sides—at least they all raised their hands to volunteer an answer. I left before the students began independent work from their books. I would be curious to hear how they performed at that time. *Note that the principal can distinguish between what she knows for sure and what she observed. She is also trying to figure out for whom this strategy was new.*

The skill of finding the perimeter of a shape is certainly transferable and at least some students were transferring previous experiences with this kind of work to this task. The students were also practicing the mathematical skill of communicating understanding of mathematics. *The principal offers several examples of transfer in the lesson in addition to assessing the transferability of the stated purpose of the lesson. The principal understands that purposeful instruction requires a clear teaching point related to a larger standard that allows students to transfer their acquired knowledge and skills to other problems and tasks.* One particularly notable example of transfer came during the partner talk about how Hillary should proceed with the straws. One student said, "I think she should forget the straws and use the ruler." This student was transferring learning from another experience with measurement (a ruler) to this one. Ironically, the strategy of using a ruler was not the stated purpose of the lesson. It is unclear to me whether or not the students are likely to transfer the skill of counting straws or toothpicks to other perimeter experiences. Because it was not the focus, I am not sure whether or not the students will transfer the skill of "calculating perimeter" to other kinds of shapes. I would like to ask Jacob what he observed after this lesson and in subsequent opportunities to measure perimeter. I wonder what he hopes for the students as they develop a concept of perimeter. When and why does he think using concrete, nonstandard unit manipulatives would be helpful for finding a perimeter? *The principal assumes that the teacher has a long-term goal in mind for his students as mathematicians. She also is questioning the transferability of the skill as it was taught.*

I wonder how the students would have responded if Jacob had asked the group ahead of time, "What do we know about rectangles?" or "What do we know about finding perimeter?" Such questions would have elicited more student thinking in general rather than in relation to one strategy and one problem. I also wonder what would have happened if at the end of the lesson Jacob had asked the class, "What did we learn about calculating perimeter today? When might we use this strategy again? Why might we use it?" *Here the principal offers alternatives to the way the lesson proceeded. These alternatives would have reinforced the larger point of the lesson.*

I was struck that this lesson focused on finding the perimeter of a shape completely out of any context. Many of the teachers at our school have commented that their students need to practice the basic skills of math before they apply them to word problems. I have been pressing them on this idea, trying to understand why they hold it. *Here the principal is thinking about something she knows about teachers at the school in general. She is testing a theory she has about her teachers' math pedagogy. She understands that her ability to analyze the quality of teaching is necessary to inform how she orchestrates the professional learning of her teachers.* I noted in this decontextualized lesson that the students had limited opportunity to apply their number sense to figure out if their answers made sense. For instance, during the partner talk time, a student proposed two strategies that would not arrive at the same answer: "she could also use the straws to measure one side and add it by two" and "she should just measure one side and times it by two." If this student engaged in both of these strategies, what basis would he have for figuring out accuracy or logic in an answer? I had a similar question about the girl who counted tick marks to add the numbers. Although this strategy seemed to be guiding her to a correct answer, I wondered if she would have been able to assess its accuracy or if she had any more efficient strategies for addition. Measuring the sides of a rectangle in isolation did not appear to have particular meaning for the students. *The principal's critique of this pedagogical choice and understanding is anchored in student learning observations and knowledge of math pedagogy.*

What does Jacob believe about how students learn about number and distance? I started thinking about real-life uses for perimeter and wondered which uses would make sense to these students. In P.E. class the students have to run around the perimeter of the rectangular gym. I wondered if such an example would help them understand side congruence and what perimeter really means in context. Jacob could have asked students to imagine themselves getting ready to run a lap around the gym and consider how they would figure out how far they would run. I will ask Jacob his opinion about using examples such as this with his students. Furthermore, students were not invited to inquire about rectangles or about perimeter. Their conversation focused on procedures (like how to mark the ends of a straw) and Jacob *directly* told Hillary that the opposite sides of the rectangle were the same lengths—she had no space to try to figure that out. I want to ask Jacob about this moment. I wondered if he was surprised by her confusion about the lengths of the sides and that she was not sure how to respond. Did he choose to tell her this answer so that she could focus on her measurement and addition? What else explains this move? *Note how the principal knows the students' experiences in other classes and offers a suggestion anchored in the students' experiences. She also returns to a set of questions about Jacob's understandings and beliefs about math learning.*

Student Engagement

Student engagement has three subdimensions. *Intellectual work* refers to who is doing the work (teacher versus student) and what is the intellectual nature of that work. *Engagement strategies* refers to the specific strategies the teacher uses to engage students authentically in the lesson. *Talk* refers to how students make meaning of the lesson as evidenced by the intellectual substance of their conversations.

Subdimension: Intellectual Work   The responsibility for the work in this lesson moves back and forth among the teacher, a few students, one student, and, on a few occasions, all the students. Jacob selected the problem and controlled the questioning during the lesson. He had chosen the rectangle, its size, its context, and the conversation about measuring it. He asks the class what they know about calculating the perimeter, which invites all students to think. However, only four students raise their hands. Interestingly, these four students really wanted to share their thoughts and when they noted they were not the only ones with ideas to share, they each started shouting out. This makes me wonder about opportunities for students to be heard in the classroom. These students were quite excited to share but perhaps worried they would not get the chance if they had not shown some aggression. In fact, Jacob responded to the shouting out by asking for students to share one at a time. This might have been an opportunity for students to talk to their neighbors instead. He calls on one student (Hillary) to share at the board. I might ask Jacob about how he chooses students to come to the board and share and what he learned about his students' strategies during this part of the lesson. *First the principal describes in general how students are asked to do the work in this lesson. She describes "doing the work" as choosing what work is done, how it is discussed, and who gets to share. She understands that strong student engagement requires the teacher to be intentional and thoughtful about releasing responsibility for students to take on the work. She also suggests one alternative (partner talk).*

Hillary definitely had the opportunity to do the work while she was modeling at the board, although it was unclear what the other students thought their roles were at this time. Hillary had the pen and straws in her hands and was invited to produce mathematical writing for the class to examine. Jacob got a little frustrated with two boys who were whispering in the back. Yet, he did not comment on the four students who had stopped watching in order to solve the problem on their own. How does Jacob want the students to engage when another student is modeling? What does he want them to learn? When Hillary got stumped about what to do with the straws, rather than doing the work himself, Jacob asked the students to talk to a partner about what they thought. At this time, all the students were engaged in conversation with a partner and all were doing the work. I would like to ask Jacob about this decision—how does he decide the content of partner talk and how does he decide *when* to have students talk to partners? The students seemed really accustomed to this ritual and most had lots to say to their partners. *Here the principal continues to narrate who did the work during the lesson and starts to question teacher decision making about intervening to guide student behaviors. She is also examining how Jacob wants students to do the work.*

When Hillary chose a strategy and started measuring the rectangle, it was clear that at least John was watching and processing because he interjected with his information about the lengths of the sides of the rectangle. Rather than allowing others (including Hillary) to grapple with this, Jacob told her what to do, even taking the pen away, essentially doing the work for the class. This was a striking moment during the lesson that might reveal Jacob's discomfort with tension in the classroom. However, it might also reveal his careful decision making about what to emphasize during the lesson and what to just note and teach later. I would ask Jacob his long-term plan for student concept formation about shapes and perimeter. *Here the principal offers several interpretations of one striking moment in the lesson when Jacob decidedly did the work for the students. She is careful not to jump to a conclusion, instead recognizing she would need to have a discussion with the teacher to understand fully the nature of that moment.*

All students *seemed* actively involved in the work of computing the perimeter of the rectangle. Jacob prompted one student to start drawing the shape. It is unclear if the student had been uninvolved to this point or if he was simply calculating in his head. In the end, Jacob told the students "very good" when someone volunteered the perimeter, doing the work of evaluating the solution. *The principal notes that validating an answer is also doing the work.*

The majority of the student conversation during the lesson was devoted to procedures (how to find perimeter) or management of materials (how to use the straws to measure) rather than to the disciplinary thinking work of geometric sense making, measurement, and assessing measurements. For example, the students had a fair amount of independence to talk with each other during the partner talk portion of the lesson when they worked on giving Hillary advice. Although Jacob asked a fairly open-ended procedural question, "what should

Hillary do now?" the student conversation focused on logistics ("she should just hold the straw up there . . . ," "she should get Mr. White to hold the straw for her . . .") rather than mathematical reasoning or generalizations. I wonder how the students would have responded if Mr. White had asked, "How might a mathematician use tools to figure out perimeter of shapes like this one? Why might they do that?" Such a question might have prompted the students to think beyond the materials and problem at hand and start to generalize their measurement skills. The narrow teaching point led to a narrow conversation prompt and thus limited use of academic language and academic thinking. *Notice how the principal distinguishes among the prompt for student talk, the content of their talk, and the work of the discipline. The principal offers alternative questions with the understanding that purposeful teaching provides students with knowledge and skills that can be generalized and transferred to other subjects and settings. Notice also that the principal analyzes this particular partner-talk moment multiple times in this analysis. This moment can be considered for lesson purpose, transferable skills, intellectual work, and several other parts of the 5D framework. The dimensions are tightly related.*

The other moment in the class when students were all engaged in doing the work was the calculation of the perimeter (adding four one-digit numbers). It seemed students used different strategies from each other but did not have space to discuss them. In fact, when one student noted that his partner was performing an arduous calculation method he nudged her, "make tens," the girl ignored him, suggesting that this strategy sharing is not a norm in the classroom. *The principal notes additional potential for student interaction in the classroom based on a vision of an equitable, rigorous work environment that provides students an opportunity to engage in substantive, academic talk.*

The moment when John asserted his understanding of rectangles could have led to a mathematically rich conversation. *Note how the principal is sensitive to moments with potential for further exploration. Similar to the partner-talk moment, this one will also repeat in the analysis.* When John commented, "It's the same!!! You don't have to measure the top." Hillary was unsure what to do. The other students looked expectantly at Jacob, not at each other or at Hillary to reason out the geometric logic. This moment could have led to a conversation or inquiry about congruence and the definitions of quadrilaterals but instead Jacob chose to move on quickly to the computation of perimeter. I am not sure why he made this decision and would like to talk with him about it.

I wonder what would happen in the future in moments like this if Jacob invited students to reason through a tension on their own. He might say, "OK, some of us think . . . and others think. . . . As mathematicians we have to find proof for our ideas. What do we know that could help us? Talk to your partner." *The principal here poses another topic for discussion with Jacob and offers alternatives for what actually happened. Again the principal understands that student engagement is much more than students staying on task or students having the opportunity to talk. The principal understands that authentic engagement must provide opportunities for students to engage in academic discourse in order to deepen their own thinking and conceptual understanding.*

Jacob gave the whole class two opportunities for participation—the partner-talk part and the individual work computation of perimeter. In all other parts of the class, Jacob cut off whole-group discussion after hearing a few student responses (by calling Hillary up to the front) or made the decisions for them about correct answers ("very good, P = 20"). The partner-talk portion preceded a share out, and in that partner-talk experience, students had the opportunity to practice saying their ideas. I heard many more students sharing during that part of the class than in the other parts. After the partner talk, Jacob asked the students to share with the class and three students raised their hands right away. He called on John, one of these three students, then told him "good. Who else has an idea? Jody?" The two students gave basically the same answer and Jacob did not provide space for others to share. This might be because Hillary had already started working using the suggested strategy. Regardless, this was an opportunity for many more answers to be heard! I would like to talk with Jacob about figuring out ways to call on students who do not have their hands raised and to allow time for more students to raise their hands. Currently, he tends to arbitrate right and wrong in the classroom and let the most verbal and popular students dominate. This has become his role and the students seem to expect it by the way they look to him during disagreements. *Here the principal traces Jacob's responses to student talk throughout the lesson. She considers who spoke, when, and how Jacob's actions contributed to those patterns. She is attuned to equity of participation. She also suggests reasons why that might be happening, and offers suggestions that might change the patterns.*

I think Jacob could create more opportunities for less-verbal students or English language learners to *practice* saying their ideas and for students to say ideas that are still in development. For example, right at the beginning Jacob had the opportunity to get lots of information about his students' understanding of perimeter when he asked, "Who remembers how we learned to find perimeter?" Perhaps students could have turned to a partner or written a few notes before sharing out loud. Jacob could have wandered around and taken notes about what he heard or read. I wonder if he is uncomfortable asking questions to which he does not know the answer. He did wander around during the computation portion of the class when the answer was more black and white. *The principal notes a pattern in the kinds of answers that students shared and some hypotheses about why this is the case. She does not just note who spoke but the content of what was said and the patterns that explain this content. She also offers an alternative way to organize the talk.*

It is unclear to me what Jacob wanted to release to students to do on their own during this lesson. Students watched someone demonstrate finding perimeter using toothpicks and had time to practice adding numbers. The short practice period did not involve toothpicks or other ways to measure perimeter, just computation. Students were then asked to complete perimeter problems in their textbooks. I am not sure if Jacob allowed students to use other strategies (besides toothpicks) after I left the room or whether he expected students to decide if their answers made sense. In summary, because there was no alignment among the purpose statement, the modeling, the guided computation practice, and the independent work time, I could not determine what skills Jacob hoped the students would demonstrate on their own. *The principal here shows she understands the difference between doing practice problems and a transferable skill. She also shows her ability to trace a stated purpose through the different structures of the lesson. She understands that engagement (no matter how wonderful the opportunities for student talk) must be in service of the teaching point and related standard.*

Subdimension: Engagement Strategies   Jacob uses some strategies with the potential to engage all students in the content area learning. *The principal frequently notes potential in the lesson with the understanding that these strategies might be instinctual for the teacher but could occur with more intention. Areas of potential might also constitute areas for the teachers' professional growth.* Jacob gives all students the opportunity to talk to a partner to figure out how to help Hillary find perimeter. There was a lot of talk at this time, though limited academic conversation. At least one student said,

"I don't know" to her partner and her partner responded with two more strategies, though not an attempt to engage the student who did not know and figure out her problem. In fact, most of the partnerships just shared strategies, one by one, rather than having a conversation that would lead to increased understanding or extension of thinking. *Here the principal continues to discuss the content of the talk. She can distinguish between just hearing lots of student talk and the content and quality of the talk.*

Jacob uses two strategies to make sure that students talk to their partners. He says, "start with the partner who is oldest first!" and then jumps in to say, "OK, next partner should be talking now!" I imagine he uses these comments to make sure one student does not sit back and say nothing in the conversation; the comments created a structure for the talk. However, such conversation controls regulate the talk but do not push its quality. It seems that comments like these help the students get comfortable with partner talk initially but that now they might be ready to move on to more sophisticated partner-talk strategies. I wonder what Jacob's long-term plan for partner talk is? How does he want them to be running their conversations? How does he want them to be pushing each other's thinking by June? I wonder if Jacob knows what to teach his students next about answering each other's questions or asking each other "why do you think that?" to create richer dialogue. *Note how the principal can describe what Jacob did to create the level of talk that exists and poses questions about what might come next.*

Although students used basic math terms such as *add* and *ruler,* I also noted that students did not use academic language to talk about their thinking. Most of their conversation used colloquial language, "I think she should forget the straws . . ." or "you plus the length and width." Jacob's language (including the purpose statement on the board) is also fairly colloquial, though he uses some math terms like *perimeter* and *rectangle.* This might be an area to push for Jacob. Because he already uses partner talk, it might be an easy shift for him to say, "Talk to your partners about what Hillary might do to find perimeter. Use the terms *measure, height, length, rectangle,* and *congruent.*" Jacob could also create more visual support in the room to help students learn these words. He might try a word wall or poster with the terms and their corresponding pictures. Another alternative would be for Jacob to have posters of sentence prompts that will continue and enrich student dialogue such as "Why do you think that?" "What do you think?" and "How can you convince me?" *Here the principal continues to assess the academic quality of the conversation. She also proposes alternatives and support for greater amounts of talk.*

Jacob seems to be developing his ability to respond to and learn from student comments. Jacob only circulated to listen and watch students work on their own during the computation portion—that was also when he pushed in to support one student individually. Most of his responses to student comments were nonspecific and evaluative. He commented "good" or "John's right." After the partner talk portion he commented, "I heard lots of good ideas," but he did not circulate at this time, so perhaps he only heard the students in the front row. It is unclear on what he based this statement. Furthermore, he did not appear to hear the quiet student at the beginning of the lesson who asked her partner, "What's *perimeter* mean?" Later in the lesson, he specifically chose Hillary to come to the board to demonstrate her strategy. Because she had commented that she would use toothpicks, and this was the topic for the day's lesson according to the purpose statement, Jacob might be listening for answers that fit the direction of the lesson that he wanted. In the next year or so, I would like to work with Jacob on how he responds to student comments in ways that extend thinking and the way he listens to student talk to let him assess student understanding. *The principal noted an area of improvement for Jacob (changing his responses to student comments) and its connection to a larger area of improvement (changing the way he listens to student responses). The principal understands that her role requires seizing on her deep understanding of instruction to guide and support the improvement of teacher practice over time.*

I am curious about Jacob's decision to have Hillary demonstrate her thinking at the board. She seemed comfortable coming forward, so this is likely not the first time for such a strategy. I wonder if this strategy is intended to promote student interest. Most students watched Hillary and at least one student (John) gave her feedback. I wonder what other strategies Jacob has for promoting student interest in mathematics. For example, I wonder if creating a real-life scenario for solving perimeter might have engaged more students, such as the gym scenario I describe previously. I wonder if Jacob has asked students how they (or their families) use the concept of perimeter in their lives. Furthermore, it seems Jacob has some tolerance for students using different strategies to solve mathematical problems. He might capitalize on this strength by making student strategies public. For example, he might chart or record "John's strategy" for finding the perimeter of a rectangle (double the base and height) and "Hillary's strategy" for using toothpicks to measure the lengths of sides. This teaching strategy might also heighten the use of academic language in the classroom and promote algebraic thinking by generalizing strategies for finding perimeters of rectangles.

Here the principal is wondering about why Jacob chose to have a student come forward and demonstrate her thinking. She wonders if this was the teacher's attempt to increase student engagement and if so for what purpose. She offers alternatives based on other observations in the class. She will puzzle about Hillary coming forward in the classroom several more times. It is a rich moment for analysis.

Subdimension: Talk Jacob starts the class by attempting to access student background knowledge about perimeter. He asks, "Who remembers how we learned to find perimeter?" Three boys and a girl raise their hands and then start shouting out answers to this question. Jacob did not try to get information from more students; instead, he chose one student (Hillary) to model a strategy at the board. I am not sure how regularly Jacob starts class in this way—by asking students their prior knowledge—but it is a strategy with potential, particularly if he developed ways to access more learners. Jacob might develop other ways to hear more students and connect more student strategies to the new learning. For example, he might put the students in groups and ask them to discuss how they might find perimeter using an example problem. Then, he might circulate and share highlights with the whole class, asking students to respond to each strategy he presents. During such a share, he would be able to provide academic language. For example, if a student said, "You times it by two," he might say, "OK, you are saying you measure the length of the base and double it." Such language would bridge what the students say with the language and thinking of the discipline. *Here the principal shows knowledge of strategies that would help Jacob elevate the content of the talk and academic language in the classroom. She is synthesizing several observations to make this suggestion (Jacob's response tendencies, the level of academic talk, and the existing practice of preassessment).*

The majority of student talk in this lesson was accountable to the procedures of finding perimeter rather than to mathematical habits of thinking or to each other. For example, during the partner conversations, students were offering lots of strategies for Hillary but not responding to each other in ways that would push disciplinary thinking. After more practice and instruction, I would expect students to ask each other, "Why did you choose that strategy?" "Does that answer make sense? How do you know?" "Will that strategy always work? When might it not work?" "What about this shape makes that a good strategy?" I wonder how satisfied Jacob is with the level of conversation among his students. I would like to ask him what he thinks their strengths are as mathematical thinkers. I suspect he is satisfied with how much students talk in those partner conversations but I wonder if he is satisfied with the quality. It is possible that he does not know what they *could* be saying with some support. *Note how the principal can distinguish among types of accountability in students' talk (to the group, to the discipline, to the teacher, to the procedures). She also considers teacher satisfaction, a crucial factor in providing feedback and guiding teacher development.*

Jacob clearly values student talk and he wants students to feel comfortable participating. This shows in how he asks the class questions that invite multiple answers ("What should Hillary do now?") and offers some responses that would promote multiple responses ("Who else has an idea?"). He clearly does not want students to speak over each other; he emphasizes students raising their hands in the whole group discussion. Additionally, there is evidence that Jacob does not want students to feel uncomfortable. When Hillary struggled with the straws, he used language that encouraged the class to help her, "What should Hillary do now?" This comment allowed Hillary to save face and get some support. *The principal is skilled at noticing teacher strengths. She also provides evidence to back up assertions about teacher strength.*

However, Jacob also uses language that limits student self or group evaluation of answers and development of disciplinary thinking. Sometimes he replies to student comments with "good," or "you did a nice job," taking control of the flow of the discourse and general evaluation of performance. He might learn to say, as is accepted in the larger mathematical community, "What do the rest of us think about John's answer?" or "How did you find that answer?" *Teacher response patterns play a role in multiple aspects of the 5D framework (intellectual work, engagement strategies, talk, as well as curriculum and classroom culture).*

Interestingly, most students raised their hands after the computation portion of the class. Jacob had set them up with specific directions ("remember to add all the numbers you see"), gave them time to work, and then asked for students to raise their hands. I wonder what Jacob thinks about why this happened. Does he attribute it to the individual work time, the preceding modeling, the content, the directions, or something else? I also wonder why he called on Hillary to share out. I wonder what would have happened if Jacob had asked the students at this time, "turn to your partner and discuss Hillary's answer. Do you think it makes sense? Why or why not?" *The principal here is able to distinguish, again, between number of student hands raised and quality of the topic under discussion. She also wonders about Jacob's interpretation.*

At the end of my observation, I was not sure exactly how much and what the students learned about finding perimeter. I did not talk to students but I did notice that most turned to the textbook problems with some degree of confidence. Based on the hand raising at the end, it seems to me the students were relatively secure in their computational skills, but I am less certain about their ability to match strategies to the work of finding perimeter of rectangles. Based on the partner talk, I would guess many students could assign a procedure to finding perimeter (using either straws or rulers and some computation) but I am less sure if they would know why and what to do with other shapes. Except for John who seemed secure in his understanding of rectangles, I would guess most students would not be able to decide if their answers made sense. I don't know this for sure, however, and am curious what Jacob would say and what he noticed next. *The principal assesses the level of rigor based on what students seemed to come away understanding. Because this is a lesson in which the stated purpose was conflated with the activity, the principal also refers to her other content knowledge.*

There was limited opportunity for construction of new knowledge or metacognition in this lesson. Students were at the brink of constructing a rule for finding perimeter of rectangles (John's comment) but Jacob stepped in and stopped the conversation. Other than the initial question, "Who remembers how we learned to find perimeter?" students were not asked to explicitly connect their learning to previous experiences. Students were not asked to reflect on their current understandings of quadrilaterals, perimeter, or strategies for adding single-digit numbers. I am not sure if this is typical in this classroom. I would like to observe a few more times to study the role of meaning construction and metacognition in the classroom before proposing a professional development plan for Jacob. I wonder if he himself does not reflect on his own understandings of mathematical concepts on a regular basis. *The principal shows her understanding that rigor is not an isolated category (or dimension) in and of itself but that rigor must be present in the purpose of the lesson, in the quality and substance of student talk, and in other dimensions as we will see in the continued lesson analysis.*

Curriculum and Pedagogy

Curriculum and *pedagogy* have three subdimensions. *Curriculum* refers to the extent to which the actual curricular materials are age and grade appropriate and linked to the standards and teaching point of the lesson. *Teaching approaches and strategies* refer to the specific pedagogical choices the teacher employs in order to achieve his or her teaching point. *Scaffolds for learning* refers to how the teacher creates access to and supports student learning, understanding that students come to the lesson with different backgrounds, knowledge, and skills.

Subdimension: Curriculum   Jacob selected this lesson based on the district-adopted, math-pacing calendar and the district-adopted math textbook. The lesson (using toothpicks to measure perimeter) fits into a sequence of lessons that introduces different strategies for finding perimeter of various four-sided, three-sided, and five-sided shapes. The work of finding perimeter does appear in the third-grade standards and the associated arithmetic appears in the second-grade standards. Our students tend to struggle with mental addition, so the addition practice might have been a carefully designed review for the students. I intend to ask Jacob about that choice. I wonder if he wanted students to practice mental addition, but in reality, the majority of them used pencil-and-paper strategies. I wonder if he was assessing this. *The principal is knowledgeable about the district curriculum and understands enough about math subject content to assess whether or not the task and materials were appropriate for these students. The principal also understands that although she cannot be an expert in every subject content area, she needs to know enough about the core content areas (math and language arts) to guide and support her teachers' growth.*

The use of toothpicks to conduct measurement appears in the textbook. It is developmentally appropriate for third-graders to use concrete objects to develop their sense of number and distance. I wonder if Jacob's students tend to benefit from such concrete manipulatives and how he scaffolds for abstract representations of number concepts. It seemed like most students picked up the toothpicks and used them to aid their counting. A few seemed to skip the step altogether and prefer to use rulers or to simply estimate. I have observed in some classrooms that the objects themselves become the outcome of the activity rather than a tool to help them develop concepts. I would want to see how Jacob is thinking about this relationship—particularly for his more skilled math students—but also for all students. *The principal notes trends in teacher practice across classrooms, which helps her build her own pedagogical knowledge and ideas for professional development.*

Jacob used a large visual representation of a rectangle and actual straws to support Hillary's modeling of a strategy that students will try at their desks. Most students watched this visual demonstration carefully. This demonstration, complete with a few road blocks in the middle, likely supported visual learners in the classroom. I wonder how often he uses this style of demonstrating and whether or not he ever incorporates written words, symbols, or kinesthetic representations to access more learners. *The principal understands that the choice of curricular materials should not only be age and grade appropriate but also attend to specific student learning styles and needs.*

Subdimension: Teaching Approaches and Strategies The class period seemed to be divided into four parts: review question to activate prior knowledge, Hillary's modeling, the student addition practice period, then the extended time with the textbook problems after I left. The review portion ("Who remembers how we learned to find perimeter?") prompted responses from a few students but many waited quietly. It seems this "review" time, without a visual cue or other way to access background knowledge, elicited information from the most verbal students who could also quickly process the question. The others stayed silent. This silent majority included English language learners and the quiet girl who asked her partner what *perimeter* meant. I think Jacob would have accessed more learners if he allowed partners to talk at this time, too, and had he circulated to listen in and seize on students' conversation to access background knowledge. *The principal is keenly aware that every instructional decision—in this case the review portion of the lesson—must be linked to the overall purpose of the lesson, allowing students an opportunity to access and demonstrate learning.*

During the second portion of the class Jacob asked Hillary to explicitly model a strategy with support from the rest of the class. Hillary's modeling with physical materials (straws, pen, and the image on the board) actively engaged her. It is significant that Jacob did not model; he asked a student to do so and a student who may or may not have a lot of status as a strong math student. In fact, I would ask Jacob how he selected Hillary and what he knows about her as a math student. Jacob stepped in to help Hillary finish the modeling but there was little explanation beyond, "You don't have to measure the top, too, because it's a rectangle."

When she got stuck, Jacob chose to ask the rest of the class also to actively engage to help her get unstuck. Although the quality of the question he asked limited the students, they did all participate. This seems a useful structure for Jacob to develop in the future. I wonder if he ever also allows them to write or use objects at this time. I am not sure if students' conceptual understanding of perimeter or of rectangles is developed at this point, but I did see evidence that their procedural knowledge certainly is. Hillary carefully modeled using the straw to measure the shape. This demonstration likely helped visual learners, though I would have to talk with students to know whether or not it truly did. At the end of the modeling, it may have been more powerful if Jacob had asked students to turn and talk about "what they had just observed and how it might be helpful." *The principal understands that student talk provides a window into students' thinking that would then allow the teacher an opportunity to assess their conceptual understanding. Again, Hillary's modeling figures prominently into several parts of the framework analysis. Curriculum and pedagogy feeds and is fed by purpose.*

The third portion of the class, the arithmetic practice, engaged all students in computation. It is possible that some students missed the concept of perimeter but were able to engage in this task because they already knew how to add. Although it makes sense to ask students to practice a skill they already have, rather than to demonstrate it needlessly, the side effect of this choice was that students did not get perimeter practice. Jacob could not assess the students' levels of understanding of perimeter at this time; instead, he may have gotten information about their addition skills. He gave students immediate feedback on their answer after this brief practice. However, this feedback was about adding and not about perimeter. Students were then completely on their own during the independent practice of measuring perimeter. Because one of Jacob's strengths as a teacher is taking his time and making sure students are following a string of procedures, he could really grow if he used this practice-with-feedback portion of the lesson to assess student success with the new skill. This might be Jacob's most immediate next step as a teacher. I would like to pair him with another teacher who already does this well. I would also like to ask Jacob about what kinds of work he asks students to quickly try during the lesson portion of the class. *Here the principal knows her role is to help Jacob improve his teaching practice and is continuously looking for the best next step with the understanding that—just like with students—she needs to scaffold Jacob's learning one step at a time. She ponders the arithmetic portion here from an instructional-approach perspective.*

Jacob's choice of instructional strategies provided little space for student independent inquiry. The partner conversation mostly concerned logistics of manipulating straws. There was no inquiry concerning the nature of the shapes or the meaning of perimeter. Because of the mismatch among the review question, the modeling, and the short practice, there was not a clear gradual release of understanding or skills to students. Other than Hillary's demonstration, there was no other evidence of student ownership. Students had very few if any choices in the lesson. Everyone worked on the same sample problem, tried the same strategy, and ultimately worked on the same problems. Although students had choice about how to talk with their partner, this partner was assigned (seemingly by seating) and the content was predetermined. *Here the principal's analysis is grounded to her own subject matter and pedagogical content knowledge, knowing that students' conceptual understanding of mathematics is developed best through inquiry and that skill development is a process of the teacher gradually releasing responsibility until the student is capable of practicing independently.*

Subdimension: Scaffolds for Learning   Jacob employed several preplanned teacher moves to support student understanding. He made a large visual on the board and figured out to use straws to represent toothpicks (easier to see). Without talking with Jacob, I am not sure if he preselected Hillary to model or if he decided to call on her on the spot. It seems she named a strategy that Jacob wanted the students to practice (using straws). I imagine he planned to have a student model this particular strategy. I also imagine he planned for the students to practice their arithmetic silently. These choices definitely supported some learners (the more independent, visual ones). *The principal is aware that students are at different places in terms of their prior knowledge, learning styles, and needs and notes where and how Jacob's* *teaching decisions did or did not differentiate support so that all students can demonstrate understanding.*

I am guessing that when Hillary got stuck during the modeling, he chose on the spot to ask students to turn and talk to help her. This choice normalized her struggle, involved more students, and set up a norm of academic support. *The principal recognizes that the strategy of turn and talk can be a powerful way to scaffold students' learning if used with specific teacher intentionality.* I am also guessing that he did not plan for her to get stuck when figuring out which sides were of the same length. He made the choice on the spot to just tell her. This choice ended the conversation, moved the modeling along, and may have scaffolded Hillary's understanding because she had already grappled with a different mathematical concept (perimeter). It also might have made Hillary feel "dismissed" as she then headed back to her seat. I wonder how Jacob interpreted this moment.

The structure of the lesson and the space itself (rows of desks) did not allow Jacob to get more information about his students before this portion. It is possible that the student he approached during the arithmetic portion had been sitting confused the entire time. I would like to talk with Jacob about developing more strategies for assessment throughout the lesson and also for developing more places in the lesson to provide this support to students. *Here the principal shows her understanding that successful scaffolding for student learning is directly related to how and how often the teacher assesses student understanding.*

This lesson had limited gradual release of responsibility. The moment when Jacob asked the students to give Hillary advice represented the most significant moment of student-to-student support. *It is clear that the principal understands the importance of student conversations and routinely listens in on those conversations to aid in her lesson analysis.* Throughout the lesson, no ELL students spoke. The task itself seemed too complex for some students and not complex enough for others. Although Hillary was operating in her zone of proximal development (what she could do with support), the student who remarked "I don't know what she should do" was not able to access the task and John was able to finish quickly enough to read his book.

I want to talk with Jacob about his understanding of his students' mathematical development. I want to ask him how he learned math, how he learned to find perimeter, and what makes geometry useful in his life. It would be hard for Jacob to differentiate or deviate from the pacing guide and book without a sense of authentic mathematical development. *The principal is beginning to hypothesize a theory (based on her analysis) that Jacob may not have a deep enough mathematical subject matter foundation necessary for him to know how to support the different learning needs of his students. Through further conversation with Jacob, the principal can test this theory, which will inform her next steps to support Jacob's continued growth as a teacher.*

Assessment for Student Learning

Assessment for student learning has two subdimensions. *Assessment* refers to the systems, structures, and strategies the teacher has in place to gather real-time information related to student understanding and performance. *Adjustments* refer to how the teacher makes real-time, in-the-moment changes in her lesson to respond to her assessment of student understanding.

Subdimension: Assessment Jacob created multiple opportunities for assessment in this lesson (whole class talk, partner talk, and individual work time). I am unsure what he actually assessed about the learning of his students during these times, however. For example, initially, Jacob asked the students to share what they remembered about finding perimeter. Four students called out responses, including "you add up the sides," "you put your toothpicks there and count how many there are," and "you use a ruler," and "you plus the length and width." I am not sure what Jacob noticed about these comments. The third student who spoke ("you plus the length and width") revealed a misconception. I am curious if Jacob heard this comment and how he interpreted it. The other comments revealed that some students were conflating measurement with calculating perimeter. I would like to ask Jacob what he heard and if the comments surprised him at all. Jacob asked the student who had mentioned the toothpick strategy to share at the front of the class but did not probe the other comments.

Jacob also included a time for partner talk and individual work; both of these represent opportunities for assessment. During the partner talk, Jacob did not circulate and it is unclear how he selected students to share out. From my position in the classroom, I was able to hear several partnerships. Some of them seemed to understand the toothpick strategy but not its purpose. Others seemed unconvinced by the strategy and preferred to use the ruler. One student seemed to be confusing addition and doubling. "She could also use the straws to measure one side and add it by two . . . or she should just measure one side and times it by two." I am not sure if Jacob noted this. During the individual work time, Jacob did circulate and observe students working on their computation. I am not sure what he learned about the class's strategies at this time. He gave one student some feedback about copying the figure from the board. I do not think he heard the conversation between the two students near me (tick marks versus "making tens"). Interestingly, this individual work time was not directly connected to the objective. Had he gathered information at this time, it would have been about computation skills, not about the concept of perimeter or any other geometric reasoning. The partner talk was also not explicitly connected to the objective or transferable skills. *The principal knows that high-quality instruction should create opportunities for students to demonstrate their learning and she has identified multiple opportunities that were largely missed by the teacher during the course of this particular lesson. Notice how the partner-talk moment returns again here, this time in terms of assessment opportunities.*

These multiple assessment opportunities had the potential to provide lots of information to Jacob. Students who did not feel comfortable speaking in front of the whole class had the chance to speak with a partner or to work individually. I wonder how Jacob scaffolds students (particularly quieter students and ELLs) so they can share their thinking with the whole class. I also wonder if Jacob sees the potential to gather lots of data at all these different times. I would like to work with him on the habit of circulating and listening to student conversation throughout the lesson while keeping his objective in mind. Jacob might also benefit from collecting student notes at the end of his lessons because this is such a large class. I am not sure if he has this habit. It seems he has the structures in place that could support assessment but not the habit of listening. How does Jacob decide what to assess? Does he typically assess procedures and not thinking skills? In future visits I would like to study this. Furthermore, I am curious how Jacob tracks what he learns about student learning. *Here the principal considers how she will support Jacob's growth in this dimension. The principal knows that teachers (not just Jacob) routinely miss opportunities to assess student learning when they do not employ disciplined methods of just-in-the-moment assessment such as listening to student talk and jotting notes. In addition the principal is cognizant that Jacob (when he does assess in the moment) may only be assessing procedural understanding rather than the student thinking work necessary to develop conceptual understanding.*

During the portion of the lesson I observed, Jacob did not provide students with an opportunity to self-assess or reflect. All feedback on student answers came from Jacob. The preassessment question, "Who remembers how we learned to find perimeter?" provided some opportunity for students to recall previous learning but this moment was limited for several reasons. Jacob did not probe student answers or ask them to think about their own personal strategies, level of understanding of them, or their effectiveness. Additionally, only four students shared. Jacob could have asked students, "What do you think perimeter means? How well do you think you understand perimeter on a scale of 1 to 5?" or "Based on this lesson, what will you try in the future when you figure out perimeter? Why? What is the most important thing you learned about perimeter? What do you still need to work on?" I am wondering why reflection is not a routine part of Jacob's practice. I would like to ask him about his own habits of reflection. Does Jacob see value in reflection? How does he see it as connected to students transferring what they learn? *The principal understands the importance of student self-assessment and posits a theory that either Jacob does not use the habit of reflection in his own learning or perhaps if he does, he has not translated that habit to his own teaching practice.*

Subdimension: Adjustments   I have a lot of questions for Jacob regarding the connections between assessment and his teaching decisions. I noted that Jacob asked Hillary to model her strategy at the board and that her strategy happened to be most closely related to the lesson's stated objective (using toothpicks to measure perimeter). I am not sure if he preselected her or selected her in the moment based on her comment. It is also possible that Jacob had not intended to ask a student to model but that when he heard Hillary's comment he chose to invite her to the front. When Hillary came to the board and started her demonstration, she got stuck and Jacob asked the class to turn and talk to address the problem she had experienced. This seems like a decision based on his on-the-spot assessment of her needs. It is possible that he planned to have a turn and talk during the modeling ahead of time but chose when based on his observations. I would like to ask Jacob about when he made these various decisions.

However, I am also concerned about the amount of student confusion about finding perimeter that went unaddressed. Based on student comments during the preassessment and in the turn and talks, I wonder if students needed more time to discuss the concept of perimeter before moving into the procedures. After hearing the range of comments in the first whole-class sharing time, I would have asked students to turn and talk to elicit more student responses. I would have asked all partners to share and might have charted their responses, following up on each one with "why do you think that?" or "what would that allow us to see?" or "what do you mean by that strategy? Could you show us?" Also, based on the partner conversations about Hillary's modeling, I would have given students another perimeter problem to try with a partner and then discuss with the class. This added layer of support might have helped more students grasp the concept. *Here the principal is using her own in-the-moment assessment of student learning to make specific recommendations for the teacher's instructional decisions. Notice how these recommendations allow the teacher to have a window into student thinking, which could then further inform his own teaching moves.*

Jacob made two clear adjustments in the lesson. While Hillary was modeling, he chose to ask the class to turn and talk about how to help her solve the problem she encountered. He must have suspected that the students had ideas about how to help her. The content of this adjustment did not really address the concept of perimeter. Most of the conversations addressed the difficulty of holding a straw and using it to measure, a largely logistical concern. It seems Jacob is most comfortable making logistical or procedural adjustments in the lesson. He seems to value making sure students know what to do, perhaps more than he values their knowing why or how it might help them in the future. The other obvious adjustment occurred when Jacob chose to tell Hillary the definition of a rectangle (opposite sides are equal) and its implications for perimeter when John raised this issue. At this time there seemed to be some tension in the classroom. Rather than asking the class to puzzle this out—and recognizing a gap in Hillary's understanding—Jacob chose to tell the class the answer. It is unclear whether or not Hillary (or the class) left this experience with a clear understanding of rectangles.

There were other opportunities for Jacob to capitalize on or explore students' existing and emerging knowledge of geometry. For example, when John shouted, "It's the same!!! You don't have to measure the top." Jacob could have pressed him about why he thought this. I am not sure whether Jacob did not pursue these opportunities because he did not notice them, did not know to do so, or did not know how to do so. It is also possible that Jacob wanted to move the students on to calculating perimeter on their own. I am not sure whether or not he noticed some students' confusion about how to add the numbers up efficiently or whether or not he noticed an absence of larger conceptual knowledge about rectangles in general. I wonder if Jacob was more concerned about Hillary's feelings in this instance than the classes' learning. It is possible that Hillary does not typically share in the class and he wanted her to have a positive experience. *In this analysis the principal uses her keen eye not only to see when the teacher made adjustments in his teaching but also when the teacher missed opportunities to make further adjustments. Notice how the principal uses "wonder" statements when she has limited evidence to come to a firm conclusion. She will use what she notices and wonders about to focus the follow-up conversation with the teacher.*

Formative assessment of student learning, not just student procedures, is an important next step in Jacob's practice. Before suggesting some professional learning opportunities for Jacob, I would like to talk with him about how he understands formative assessment at this time. How does he gather information currently? What does he notice about student performance on formal assessments? Is he typically surprised by results? What did he learn about his students today? How does he track that information? Jacob helped one student one-on-one in this lesson. Was this a reaction to something he observed today? How does he design learning plans for students with certain patterns of behavior or understanding? How does he use formative assessment to plan small-group or individualized instruction? *The principal understands that formative assessment is critical for purposeful instruction. In the spirit of formative assessment, the principal plans on assessing Jacob's understanding so that she can guide and support his next steps to improve his teaching practice.*

Classroom Environment and Culture

Classroom environment and culture has three subdimensions. *Use of physical environment* refers to how the teacher sets up and uses the physical space of the classroom to support student learning. *Routines and rituals* refer to transitions before, after, and between lessons and how students are taught to be accountable to each other and the academic discipline during partner and group work. *Classroom culture* refers to how all students are included and acknowledged during the lesson.

Subdimension: Use of Physical Environment   Jacob has arranged his classroom in five rows of six students each. All student desks face the front of the room. This arrangement allows for students to all see the board from which Jacob directs the majority of his instruction. In this lesson, students were all focused on the giant rectangle on the board. Jacob (and Hillary) could easily use the front of the room to model mathematical procedures.

The row arrangement raises a few questions for me, however. I noticed that the students farthest in the back tended to start chatting during the lesson. Jacob directed several boys in the back to pay attention. The students in the far back have a long way to look in order to see the front. Most significantly, the rows make it very hard for partners to talk with each other. Students turn to face their neighbors but have to speak quite loudly to be heard. The rows also make partner work quite difficult; two students could not look at the same book or paper at the same time. I will ask Jacob if his students rearrange their seats for different activities. Furthermore, the rows also make it difficult for Jacob to navigate the room and listen to different partner conversations. He can move desk to desk to give individual feedback. I wonder why Jacob chose this room arrangement. It might be connected to his need for control of behavior. *The principal understands that the physical arrangement of the room is not for aesthetic purposes or the teacher's personal comfort but must facilitate student learning based on the purpose of the lesson and the instructional strategies employed during lesson delivery.*

The students seem to have the individual supplies that they needed at their desks. They had books, paper, pencils, and toothpicks. Jacob's room is highly organized. Students did not need to leave their seats to get materials during this lesson. The supplies for math lessons are typically stored in bins around the room. I did not observe the procedures for distributing and collecting materials today. In general, books, manipulatives, and office supplies all seem to have their place around the room and I will have to ask Jacob how students access these. My suspicion is that Jacob distributes them himself. Students remain seated for most of their time in his classroom.

Other than the writing on the board (the purpose statement and the rectangle), there are no visual cues in the room indicating the units of study or charts featuring student thinking. There are charts that list classroom procedures and rules. The remaining charts are generic and professionally published ("Reading Makes You Smarter!") and not connected to Jacob's students. There is student work posted on the back bulletin board. It appears to be a set of final tests for a previous unit in math. These papers are all corrected by the teacher and each one seems to have received an "A."

I imagine that Jacob's classroom reflects his values and his current understanding of student learning. It is clear that Jacob values order and predictability in his classroom environment as he does in his lessons. Jacob's students could benefit from seeing some of their own words and thinking posted in the room, including evidence of their personalized experience in this classroom. Students currently must rely on their textbooks as resources. The student early in the class who whispered "what's *perimeter?*" did not have any place to look in the classroom to find the answer to her straightforward question. Her neighbor was not close enough to her to be able to respond to her. ELL students would definitely benefit from more visual support in the room. Although Jacob's students know the routines and rituals of the classroom, they are ready to take on more ownership for their own learning. The physical environment provides many opportunities for increased access to resources (to materials, to each other, and to references) that could empower students. *Notice how the principal has done a very thorough job of scanning the entire room and looking at how the physical arrangement, including what is on the walls, may or may not support student learning. She also recognizes that the physical environment might reflect the teachers' values and understandings of student learning. Quick fixes to the structure of the room will not necessarily change the teacher's beliefs.*

Subdimension: Classroom Routines and Rituals   During this lesson, students participated in the classroom routines and rituals to varying degrees. Students all had the materials required of them (toothpicks, books, paper) and most students (except Tomas and Peter, initially, and one student who giggled) appeared to watch and listen to Jacob and to Hillary. Listening to each other is an expectation in the classroom. Few students shared answers in the whole-class structure but all students talked to their partners and attempted to solve the computational problems. It seemed that students were quite accustomed to turning and talking to their partners. Each student had a partner, knew who that partner was, and started talking right away. Jacob maintained the structure by directing each partner to talk at least once. Hillary seemed comfortable coming to the board and sharing her thinking. It seemed this was also a regular occurrence in the class because the students did not act surprised or question her.

I wonder what Jacob's long-term plan is for student participation in these structures. Does he hope students will volunteer to model strategies? Does he hope more students will participate in the whole-class conversation? What is his plan for increasing participation? I imagine the students are ready for small-group conversations about their learning and could easily chart their own thinking to share with the whole group. *The principal is aware of how classroom rituals and routines can be used to build student independence and ownership of their own learning and that the teacher likely has a plan for this over time.*

Students in the room mostly treated each other and Jacob with respect and compassion. Jacob models this respect with his affirming and polite comments to students ("Please . . . ," "What should Hillary do now?"). It is clear students are used to talking to each other in their partnerships because they did so quite easily. There was less evidence of academic respect among the students. There were a few moments when I sensed some competition among the students. During the first sharing of ideas, four students raised their hands and then immediately started calling out answers. Were these students afraid they would not get the chance to share if they did not shout out? John also started arguing with Jody about whether or not they had given the same answer and called out his observation of how to figure out a rectangle's perimeter. Was he concerned he would not get the chance to do so? Did he want to correct Hillary or help her? I could not read this moment. I would like to ask Jacob his interpretation.

There were also instances when students asked each other for help or expressed confusion to each other and all these moments went unaddressed by other students. A possible next step for Jacob's students might be to learn how to ask each other questions, express confusion, and offer advice to each other. Lessons addressing how to ask for help might facilitate a decrease in the competition among students and increase student metacognition. *The principal understands that in some cases students must be taught how to make the best use of the specific routine being employed by the teacher.*

Jacob's classroom appears to be extremely efficient. Jacob's students respond immediately to his verbal cues ("One-two-three eyes on me," "next partner should be talking now!" and "hands please"). Students engaged in the different structures right away (paying attention to student modeling, talking to their partners, working on the problem independently). Very little time was wasted getting students to do what was asked of them.

However, the pace of the structures might also limit the students. Very few students had the chance to share their thinking and there was little time for student questions throughout the lesson. Additionally, there were no alternative ways to work within the structures. For instance, if students needed to write their thinking before talking to a partner, they were not given this option. Furthermore, Jacob perhaps devoted more energy to moving students through the structures than he did assessing their ideas and thinking. I wonder if he ever selects students to share ideas that might be "wrong." I might suggest to Jacob that he try each day asking at least one question he does not know the answer to and calling on at least two students who did not volunteer information on their own. *Here the principal uses her understanding of how classroom structures can be used more effectively to engage students in mathematical thinking and how teachers start to learn to utilize these structures.*

Subdimension: Classroom Culture   I would say there is tremendous urgency in the classroom to get work done but not to explore divergent thinking. The students were engaged in mathematics work (talking about it, watching it modeled, or individually performing it) for the entire lesson. I am not sure if all students needed ten minutes to complete the computation of the perimeter but those who finished early started reading their books. Jacob did not hold all students accountable for their partner talk or written work. He only called on students who had raised hands. However, students all apparently felt capable of this work because they all seemed to engage in it. As Jacob's practice develops to allow more space for assessment, he might feel a slight decline in this rigorous pacing. However, the shift should also allow for more students to explore more ideas together. *The principal is aware of the tendency for teachers to move through content with a sense of urgency at the expense of deepening student thinking.*

Jacob's pacing indicates that he believes all students can produce the work required of them and follow procedures. He provides lots of time for students to practice computation on their own. Because less time was allocated to discussions of mathematical concepts or for individual practice of conceptual work, I wonder if he believes they are capable of more nuanced thinking work. I would like to ask him about this, in addition to what might be hard for him about asking students to engage in mathematical dialogue. Does he need strategies? Does he worry about students embarrassing themselves? Is he concerned about time? *Here the principal continues to wonder to herself based on the evidence she gathered, understanding however that without a deeper* conversation with the teacher, she will not know what Jacob believes about students' intellectual capabilities and how best to create a classroom culture that recognizes each student's unique gifts.

Based on his choice to call her to the front, it seems Jacob believed in Hillary's ability to model her thinking. By asking the class to help her, he seems to believe that Hillary was confident and open enough to receive suggestions. However, when he asked her to sit down after the interaction with John, I wondered if he started to doubt her ability to grapple with ideas.

All students participated in the turn-and-talk opportunity and in the individualized writing time. However, the same four students participated in the whole-class sharing opportunities each time. Although he seemed to call on both boys and girls, Jacob only called on students who raised their hands. All sharing out loud occurred from native speakers of English. I wonder how much Jacob notices these interaction patterns. I wonder if Jacob has other strategies for supporting more student participation. One simple strategy he might try is asking students to share ahead of time during the turn-and-talk period. He could even ask them to write down what they will share with the group so they are prepared. *The principal understands that an equitable classroom environment must allow all students to participate fully.*

In general, the students do not seem to know each other as mathematicians or thinkers. The most verbal students automatically raise their hands and do not respond to each other's comments, except to remark, "that's what I said." Turn and talk gives students the opportunity to share their ideas, but even in the turn and talks there was little evidence of students responding to each other's ideas. Jacob's choice to ask Hillary to model her thinking definitely contributed to a culture of risk taking. However, Jacob stopped the process and asked her to sit down when John challenged her. *The principal understands that the development of an intellectual community does not happen by accident. The teacher must be intentional about creating a classroom environment and culture in which students' status and authority are gained as a result of intellectual thinking versus popularity or assertiveness.*

Finally, I observed no evidence of work reflecting the lives, interests, and cultures of the students. There was limited choice in this lesson in general. *Here the principal simply notes what she observed without positing a theory. However, she understands that one strategy to create a culturally relevant classroom culture is by encouraging student choice.*

CONCLUSION

As we stated at the outset of this chapter, the preceding lesson analysis was written at the most granular, expert level to offer the reader a complete picture of the 5D framework. For those leaders interested in deepening their own instructional expertise we understand the analysis could be daunting. We acknowledge that some leaders may question whether they will ever be able to develop this level of expertise or whether they even need to in order to be an effective instructional leader. With respect to the second question we believe that the principal in this vignette is far more able (based on her expertise) to guide and support Jacob's growth and development than a principal with a less-refined instructional eye. Perhaps more important, the principal in this vignette (again based on her expertise) will be able to detect patterns and themes across classrooms that will allow her to orchestrate more effectively the professional learning of her entire staff.

With respect to the daunting question of whether you will be able to develop this level of expertise, the answer, of course, is yes. Malcom Gladwell in his book *Outliers* (2008) speaks at length about professional athletes, musicians, and others who are the best in their respective field. He found that it takes approximately ten thousand hours to develop the level of expertise necessary to perform at such high levels. Ten thousand hours is not an unreasonable expectation to develop the kind of expertise illustrated by the principal in this chapter. The important point, however, is that expertise is not innate; it is learnable and can be developed over time. In the ensuing chapters we will provide leaders with examples of how they can develop their own expertise as well as the expertise of their teachers in their daily leadership practice.

DISCUSSION QUESTIONS

- To what extent does your school or district use an instructional framework to define *quality instruction* and how does it inform your classroom observations, instructional leadership, and coaching?

- To what extent do you or your school leaders engage in the kind of fine-grained lesson analysis illustrated in this chapter?

- With respect to lesson analysis, what area(s) of expertise do you or your leaders need to develop in order to become more skilled at analyzing instruction and providing feedback to teachers?

PART THREE

Leading for Instructional Improvement

chapter FOUR

Observing Classroom Practice

Chapter Three took us inside a third-grade classroom where a principal with deep understanding of the 5D framework analyzed a math lesson. We saw how a sophisticated observer of teaching and learning thought and wondered about what she noticed as she carefully watched and listened to students and the teacher. We recognize that the robust nature of the 5D framework sets a high bar for the ongoing development of instructional leadership expertise and that most of us will have to learn, over time, to grow the depth of expertise this principal brought to her classroom observation. This chapter will introduce and provide tools for leaders to examine teaching practice in their schools and develop expertise along the way. A framework for classroom observations will illustrate the practical application of the 5D framework and classroom walkthroughs. This chapter also contains examples of memos, letters, and other documents created to support leaders to connect classroom visits with their school improvement goals.

LEADERSHIP BEGINS WITH PURPOSE

There is a striking parallel between good teaching and good leadership: *purpose.* As we have seen with the Five Dimensions of Teaching and Learning framework, *purpose* is the linchpin that holds everything together. *What will students know and be able to do as a result of the lesson?* is the first and foremost question asked by astute observers of instruction. The same concept can be applied to leadership strategies and actions, which should have a well-defined purpose with clear, intended outcomes.

For the case illustrated in Chapter Three, we can assume that Jacob White has a theory about how best to accomplish his purpose given the learning needs of the students, the complexity of the content being taught, the time and space available for learning, and his understanding of the trajectory of student learning for mathematical understanding. The principal observing wondered about what she saw and heard in the classroom and tried to better understand Jacob's intentions and his knowledge about content and pedagogy. Teachers have a theory of action for how they go about achieving the purpose of the lesson, in both the short term and long term, whether they are actually conscious of this or not. Expert teachers develop and refine their theories about using a particular approach or strategy that is anchored to and supported by appropriate materials; relevant, intellectually demanding tasks; and assessing the students' learning to reflect on whether or not the purpose of a lesson was achieved. The same is true for leaders as they embark on district or school improvement strategies and actions. First, leaders need to be clear about their purpose and intended outcomes. Second, they need to have a viable and articulated theory about why a certain strategy or action is likely to achieve the intended short-term and long-term outcomes. Finally, leaders need to understand the iterative nature of the development and refinement of their theories, their classroom observations, and their conversations and inquiry with teachers, all of which further clarify their purpose and outcomes. Indeed, the vision leaders have for the nature and quality of student learning will be continuously refined. It is not simply a moving target but the development of an increasingly robust picture for the end game of student achievement. Leadership begins with what we know, some awareness of what we do *not* know, and a strategy to develop our understanding while leading. It is with the idea of purpose and theory in mind that we examine more deeply the topic of classroom observations.

There are many reasons (purposes) to observe classroom practice. As we mentioned in Chapter One, we have observed as many local variations of the walkthrough as there are butterflies. The extent to which any of these walkthrough strategies actually result in improved teaching practice can be linked largely to the leaders' purpose and theory of action underlying the walkthrough. In cases in which there is a clearly defined purpose linked to a viable theory of action, the odds of improving teaching practice are measurably higher. Having a clear purpose, intended outcome, and a well-developed theory of action about how classroom observations will result in the improvement of teaching practice allows leaders to reflect on just how closely their own intentions and practices align. We have developed an observation framework (found in Appendix B) that can help leaders think about the purpose of their classroom observations, the supporting theory of action, the intended outcome(s) for that observation, and particular logistical questions and issues. We have identified three general categories of observations: *learning walkthrough, goal-setting and implementation walkthrough,* and *supervisory walkthrough.* Each one of these categories is distinct in terms of purpose and leaders must be mindful of their purpose and subsequent actions when they visit classrooms. We will devote the remainder of this chapter to a thorough examination of these different kinds of observations, with specific examples along the way to help leaders differentiate the purpose of their classroom visits.

THE LEARNING WALKTHROUGH

The primary purpose of the learning walkthrough is for individual and collective learning. Thinking back to our two-part leadership equation introduced in Chapter One, before leaders can lead the improvement of instructional practice, they must have a shared vision for, and understanding about, what constitutes quality teaching. The learning walkthrough is intended to accomplish just that through the following purposeful outcomes:

1. To develop a shared vision for high-quality teaching and learning based on an instructional framework (for example, the 5D framework)
2. To calibrate understanding of the dimensions of the instructional framework (for example, Student Engagement and Classroom Environment and Culture)
3. To calibrate understanding of best practices in a particular content area
4. To provide principals and teacher leaders a tool to assess their own classrooms against the emerging vision of instruction

5. To begin to use the language of the instructional framework to communicate learning to staff through which leaders identify, consider, and discuss issues of student learning and teaching practice

6. To develop a school and district culture of public practice

7. To gather data necessary to identify relevant problems of leadership practice

The learning walkthrough purpose is guided by the following theory of action and intended outcomes:

1. If we (as school and district leaders) spend regular and focused time in classrooms observing and describing student learning and teaching practice with the support of an instructional framework, then we will develop a common vision and shared understanding of high-quality instruction.

2. If we develop a common vision and shared understanding of high-quality instruction, then we will be able to identify the supports teachers need and lead with greater clarity the improvement of teaching practice.

3. If we are open and transparent about our own learning, then we will be able to engage in and model the kind of reflective learning necessary to support a learning community culture focused on continuous improvement.

An instructional framework can help accelerate the development of a shared vision for high-quality teaching and learning. Although we believe the Five Dimensions of Teaching and Learning is a particularly powerful tool, well suited to *developing a shared vision of quality instruction*, there are in fact other frameworks available for school leaders. In all cases, the process is the same. Ideally, prior to beginning learning walkthroughs, it is important to have an opportunity to become acquainted with the language and ideas in the framework. In our case we spend an entire day introducing the framework, allowing participants to interact with the five dimensions—*purpose, student engagement, curriculum and pedagogy, assessment for student learning,* and *classroom environment and culture*—through the use of classroom videos and teacher and student artifacts. It is not until we have spent time practicing outside of the classroom that we begin practicing inside the classroom. We have learned that this underscores the necessity of separating the observation from the person. In order to develop a shared understanding and vision of quality instruction, leaders must be open to examining their own practice in light of an emerging picture of quality. Psychologically, they must be able to separate themselves from their practice in order to create a culture in which they learn to be "hard on the work" while being "respectful with each other." This is not an easy process given that our very identify is often tied up with how we practice our craft. It is made even more problematic in a culture of privacy and isolation endemic to public education, which can make sharing our practice fraught with oversensitivity and defensiveness.

Several years ago we visited a high school in a small rural school district. We were preparing to provide some leadership development work with the district and school leaders and to that end we walked through a number of classrooms with the superintendent, principal, and assistant principal to get a picture of the quality of teaching. We observed a variety of subjects and after each short classroom visit we went out into the hall and debriefed what we observed. In one United States history class we observed the students sitting quietly, each at their own desk, working on an activity while the teacher sat quietly at his desk. We assumed that the students had just independently read a chapter in their history text because they were answering a series of multiple choice questions about the chapter on a worksheet provided by the teacher. The questions required the students to remember facts and figures and recall certain information from the text. Our hallway debrief conversation went something like this:

CEL consultant: What did you see happening in the class?

Superintendent: Students were just sitting there working quietly. I didn't see any evidence of student engagement.

Assistant principal: All kids do not learn in the same way. This type of classroom environment may be better suited for some kids' learning styles. The fact is that some kids learn better in this type of classroom environment.

CEL consultant: Can you tell me what student learning you observed?

Assistant principal [with great animation]: I don't like the accusatory tone you are taking. Our teachers work very hard and care about these kids, and I don't appreciate you coming in and being so critical!

This anecdote exemplifies what happens when the *personal* and the *practice* conflate. The assistant principal not only felt he had to defend this teacher but also the quality of the teaching practice at the high school in general. During the debrief in the hall we thought a question aimed at describing the actual learning they observed was rather innocuous but clearly the assistant principal heard something else entirely. Even when being careful with the tone and tenor of our questions so that the weight of each word is intentionally measured, often the very words can be offensive if the process of talking explicitly about teaching and learning is new. This example points to the importance of structuring a process that allows leaders to experience what it looks, sounds, and feels like to be hard on the work, respectful with one another. In our work we now always begin the process of developing a shared vision of instruction and having evidence-based conversations by watching classroom video from *other* school districts. We anchor the observations and conversations to the Five Dimensions of Teaching and Learning framework, guiding participants through a number of lesson videos and other artifacts. Even when leaders want to begin this work in their own district, our learning suggests practicing first by watching videos from other school districts. In this way, district leaders can begin to create the norms necessary to ensure a more successful transition to actual classroom visits.

Developing a shared vision for high-quality teaching happens over time as leaders have multiple opportunities to calibrate their understanding of the five dimensions of teaching and learning. Calibration is a recursive process that is informed not by the framework vision statements as much as the guiding questions. In fact when we lead learning walkthroughs we often use a template (Figure 4.1) without the 5D vision statements.

Calibrating understanding requires many hours of vigorous discussion with leaders using their descriptive notes to address the guiding questions in the framework. We cannot overemphasize the importance of teaching leaders how to stay in the descriptive mode as a critical component of the calibration process. The framework—whether it is CEL's Five Dimensions of Teaching and Learning or another framework—is not meant to supersede the descriptive voice. To the contrary, the ideas and questions in the framework are intended solely to support conversations using the language of the framework as a means of accelerating individual and group learning. In that context we still teach leaders how to see without judging. City, Elmore, and colleagues (2009) talk about the importance of "learning to see, unlearning to judge" (p. 83). We use the language of *noticing* and *wondering*. Specifically, we ask leaders,

Figure 4.1.

Guiding Questions for the 5 Dimensions of Teaching and Learning

SUBDIMENSION	GUIDING QUESTIONS	NOTES
Standards	• How do the standard and teaching point relate to content knowledge, habits of thinking in the discipline, transferable skills, and students' assessed needs as learners (in terms of language, culture, learning styles, etc.)? • How do the standard and teaching point relate to the ongoing work of this classroom? To the intellectual lives of students beyond this classroom? To broader ideals such as problem solving, citizenship, etc.?	
Teaching Point	• What is the teaching point of the lesson? How is it meaningful and relevant beyond the specific task or activity? • Is the task or activity aligned with the teaching point? How does what students are actually engaged in doing help them to achieve the desired outcome(s)? • How are the standard and teaching point communicated and made accessible to all students? • How do students communicate their understanding about what they are learning and why they are learning it? • What will students know and be able to do as a result of the lesson? What will be acceptable evidence of student learning?	

(continued)

Figure 4.1.
(*continued*)

SUBDIMENSION	GUIDING QUESTIONS	NOTES
Intellectual Work	• What is the frequency of teacher talk, teacher-initiated questions, student-initiated questions, student-to-student interaction, student presentation of work, etc.? • What does student talk reveal about the nature of students' thinking? • Where is the locus of control over learning in the classroom? • What evidence do you observe of student engagement in intellectual, academic work? What is the nature of that work? • What is the level and quality of the intellectual work in which students are engaged (e.g., factual recall, procedure, inference, analysis, metacognition)?	
Engagement Strategies	• What specific strategies and structures are in place to facilitate participation and meaning making by all students (e.g., small group work, partner talk, writing, etc.)? • Do all students have access to participation in the work of the group? Why or why not? How is participation distributed?	
Talk	• What questions, statements, and actions does the teacher use to encourage students to share their thinking with each other, to build on each other's ideas, and to assess their understanding of each other's ideas?	

Curriculum	• How does the learning in the classroom reflect authentic ways of reading, writing, thinking, and reasoning in the discipline being studied? For example, how does the work reflect what mathematicians do and how they think?
Teaching Approaches and Strategies	• How does the content of the lesson (for example, text or task) influence the intellectual demand (for example, the thinking and reasoning required)? • How do lesson content and instructional strategies provide all students with access to the intellectual work and to participation in sense making? • What does the instruction reveal about the teacher's understanding of how students learn, of disciplinary habits of thinking, and of content knowledge?
Scaffolds for Learning	• How is student learning of content and transferable skills supported through the teacher's intentional use of instructional strategies and materials? • How does the teacher differentiate instruction for students with different learning needs?
Assessment	• How does the instruction provide opportunities for all students to demonstrate learning? How does the teacher capitalize on those opportunities for the purposes of assessment? • How does the teacher gather information about student learning? How comprehensive are the sources of data from which he or she draws? • How does the teacher's understanding of each student as a learner inform how the teacher pushes for depth and stretches boundaries of student thinking? • How does assessment help students to become more metacognitive and to have ownership of their learning?

(continued)

Figure 4.1.
(continued)

SUBDIMENSION	GUIDING QUESTIONS	NOTES
Adjustments	• How does the teacher's instruction reflect planning for assessment? • How does assessment inform the teacher's instruction and decision making? • How does the teacher adjust instruction based on in-the-moment assessment of student understanding?	
Use of Physical Environment	• How does the physical arrangement of the classroom and the availability of resources and space to both the teacher and students purposefully support and scaffold student learning?	
Classroom Routines and Rituals	• How and to what extent do the systems and routines of the classroom facilitate student ownership and independence? • How and to what extent do the systems and routines of the classroom reflect values of community, inclusivity, equity, and accountability for learning?	
Classroom Culture	• What is the climate for learning in this classroom? How do relationships (teacher-student, student-student) support or hinder student learning? • What do discourse and interactions reveal about what is valued in this classroom? • What are sources of status and authority in this classroom (for example, reasoning and justification, intellectual risk taking, popularity, aggressiveness, etc.)?	

Source: Copyright © 2010 Center for Educational Leadership, University of Washington. www.k-12leadership.org.

"What do you notice going on in the classroom and what does that make you wonder about?" This is the first step in deepening understanding and developing a shared picture of quality instruction. Much like anthropologists taking field notes and relying on the notes to make sense of what they are seeing, leaders must learn how to script what is happening, paying particular attention to what the teacher is doing and saying and what the students are doing and saying. Scripting lessons is not something we learned in our formal preparation programs. The process of learning how to see without judging is a skill, similar to other skills, that requires practice in order to improve over time. Scripting lessons does not require fancy tools. One can simply use notebook paper or in cases when we work with our formal networks, we provide a template (see Exhibit 4.1) that is a simple tool designed to focus the observer's attention on the instructional core: what the teacher is doing and saying; what the students are doing and saying; and the text, task, or activity the students are working on. The purpose of scripting is to gather enough data to engage in an evidentiary-based discussion of the observation.

EXHIBIT 4.1. CLASSROOM OBSERVATION PROTOCOL

School: _____ Classroom: _____

Lesson Activity: _____

What Is the Teacher Doing and Saying?	What Are the Students Doing and Saying?

As a litmus test, we encourage our classroom observers to have enough descriptive detail so that someone who was not in the classroom would have a clear picture of what the teacher was doing and saying; what the students were doing and saying; the text, task or activity the students were working on; and anything in the interaction of teacher-student-task that prompts the observer to wonder. Exhibit 4.2 shows an illustration of one such example.

EXHIBIT 4.2. LESSON OBSERVATION SCRIPT

Ninth-Grade Language Arts
10:20

[T = teacher; S = student; T&T = turn and talk; IR = independent reading; . . . . = could not hear; observer's wonderings are in italics]

[Students up front in half-circle with notebooks and their IR books. On chart: Author's Stamp: point of view, narration, text structure, language]

T: . . . . and then she challenged me, made me support my point, and I had to turn to the text . . . . Look at your IR book and examine the first question. What is your author's stamp? Want you to do some brainstorming on your own. Stop and jot quickly and then we'll do some talking. Identify which piece you want to focus on for your author's stamp; use the tools learned in this unit . . . .

[T conferring with one student]: know what you're going to focus on for author's stamp? Know who the narrator is? Who wrote this book? Who told the story? Is it first person or third person? Let's take a look. Who is the main character? Warren? So someone is telling the story about Warren? . . . . So the fact that it's third person, is part of the author's style . . . . So for number one you can say, "third-person person point of view."

S: Do I just write that?

T: Yeah, and that someone else is telling the story about Warren, so it's a third-person point of view.

[T to whole class]: Some of you already into T&T, which I love, so T&T . . . . find a partner, what identified about your author's stamp . . . .

[*T conferring with a student*]: . . . . for identifying though, you can look for point of view, who's telling the story in *Snow Falling on Cedars*?

S: . . . . not really sure yet . . . .

T: turn to first page . . . . fact that says "he," . . . . third-person point of view, why, so focus on why author did that . . . .

S: . . . .

T: . . . . can at least focus on dialect . . . . even if you just read just first chapter . . . . when characters talk to each other . . . .

[*T to whole class*]: Just a reminder, so we can get a good assessment of where you are right now . . . . remember that the content is in the middle [refers to chart] and you are already masters of content. Want you to . . . . focus on author's stamp, the writing, and the choices the author made . . . .

[By content does she mean plot? Are students still primarily relying on retelling as their only way to make sense of their reading? Seems like she really is trying to figure out what her students currently understand about author's stamp.]

T: Lou, do you want to start for us?

[Lou reads what he wrote in his notebook]: In *Snow Falling on Cedars*, I think the author's stamp can be found in the text structure, excessively descriptive, detailed . . . .

T: Awesome, Lou, as always. Can you ask another classmate . . . .

Lou: ___'s reading the same book, *Snow Falling on Cedars*.

S: . . . . and text structure is formal and it's third person.

T: . . . . What reading?

S: *Boston Jane* . . . . the dialect is like formal pronunciation, uses a lot of big words, different pronunciation, like in Australia the word for *toilet* is *bucket* . . . . it's in first person and narrator is Jane . . . .

 . . . .

S: going to talk about my old book cause my new book I don't really like . . . . It was *Lovely Bones* . . . . talking in first person then third person . . . . kinda weird cause the narrator is dead . . . .

T: Who else in this room is reading *Lovely Bones*? Leanna, you know what that's called right? The narrator of *Lovely Bones* has passed away . . . . feels and knows how all the characters . . . .

(continued)

Leanna: . . . . can't say it . . . . omniscient narrator.

T: *so knows how all characters are thinking and feeling . . . . that book is really unique . . . .*

. . . .

S: . . . *Scorpions* . . . . so main person is a kid, so in third person, writes how a kid would talk, slang, whatever . . . .

T: so it's informal language . . . . any one else?

S: . . . . I think the author's stamp is like so many flashbacks, when he was the kid and then a few years later and realizes he can't take care of him . . . . gives up the kid for adoption, too hard to be a teenage parent, but then . . . .

. . . .

T: OK, you're moving into content, but you hit it at the beginning, the flashback structure, and your book's unique because—what genre is it? . . . . yeah, nonfiction . . . . makes it a bit different as well.

. . . .

S: I'm reading *Fellowship of the Ring* and it's a limited omniscient narrator and the author's stamp is that . . . . and every time one of the creatures talks they talk different and talk very formal.

T: . . . interesting, very good . . . .

S: *Volcano Disaster* . . . . sometimes first person and sometimes third . . . . and narrator switches off . . . . don't know . . . .

T: the piece that you've noticed so far, great . . . .

10:30

T: Let's move onto the second question, why did the author make the choices they did? . . . . Let's model it again for *Their Eyes Were Watching God* . . . . and I hypothesized about why she made choices . . . . about southern dialect . . . . I think that's why the author made the decision to put it into southern dialect . . . . [T shows what she wrote on the chart.] I also identified that it's in third-person point of view and that author might be the narrator and this allows me to see how all the characters are thinking and feeling and make Janey a dynamic character . . . . think that it's intentional decision by the author to allow all different perspectives of Janey . . . . I want you to do the same thinking with your book . . . . why did the author make the choices you identified? Authors make purposeful choices, why did he or she make the choices you identified in your book? Do some stop and jot just for a minute and then we'll turn and talk . . . .

[students stop and jot while T confers with a S . . . .]

S: . . . think it has something to do with how her mom . . . . thinks she's better, so talks very sophisticated, acts like she knows more than she really does . . . .

T: So why does the author want you to have the experience of having the character talk that way? Why make that decision? . . . . So not looking at content, just why the author made that choice?

S: To show what she's been through, I guess.

T: Yes . . . .

T [T&T]: Why did the author make the choices that he/she did?

[Students T&T.]

[She seems to value student-to-student interaction and uses several strategies to prepare them for it. I wonder how satisfied she is with the students' current interactions? I wonder how she'd like the student interactions to function by June?]

Without ever stepping into this classroom we can tell from this detailed script how students were engaging with text, what they were asked to do, strategies the teacher used, and how students interacted with each other. From this script, we see that the teacher had her ninth-grade language arts students sitting up front, versus at their desks, and that they were working on figuring out the author's stamp of their independent reading books. The teacher modeled her own thinking and as the students wrote in their notebooks, the teacher conferred with individual students. After the students had time to write in their notebooks, the teacher asked them to turn and talk. The teacher also asked her students to engage in whole-group discussion about what they noticed about the author's stamp in their books. The times noted on the script allow us to see how much time (roughly) the students had to talk and how long (roughly) the teacher modeled before turning the work over to the students. This level of detail allows us to have a conversation about what we *actually* saw and heard, versus basing the conversation on our judgment about what we saw and heard. Notice that what the observer wondered about is separated from the script with brackets, indicating potential questions that could later be posed to the teacher.

Calibrating understanding is actually a two-part process in which leaders first discuss what they observed in the classroom relying solely on their notes (scripts.) After there is general agreement about what was observed, we can then use the framework's guiding questions to calibrate understanding within a particular dimension, for example, student engagement. This process becomes even more important as leaders begin to wrestle with the question of best practices within specific content areas. Invariably an emerging vision of instruction must be anchored to a deepened understanding of content. For example, what does it mean for students to think and talk like mathematicians or scientists or writers? From a leadership perspective, more important, how much content understanding do leaders need to have in order to lead the improvement of teaching in a given content area? Learning how to script lessons with depth and clarity to answer the framework's guiding questions is the first important step in the calibration process, whether leaders are calibrating for general understanding or content specific understanding.

The learning walkthrough also provides principals and teacher leaders a tool to assess their own classrooms against an emerging school or district vision of quality instruction as they begin to use the language of the instructional framework to communicate learning to staff. Of course this does not happen by accident. It can and should be an outgrowth of the district learning walkthrough process but relies largely on how intentional school leaders are about connecting their learning to stimulate learning among their colleagues and staff. In fact the district learning walkthrough process provides the thoughtful school leader with a platform from which to build a culture of public practice, create a shared understanding of quality instruction, and guide the professional learning at the building level. How principals frame this process for their teachers is a critical first step in connecting their learning to stimulate learning among staff. Principals (and all leaders) should use multiple means to put voice to their leadership actions. This leads to perhaps the most important piece of our observational framework: the specific actions leaders choose to take prior to and following a walkthrough. Although not meant to be an exhaustive list by any means, we do believe leaders at a minimum should consider how they will do the following:

- Communicate with staff about the walkthrough
- Model what it means to be a learner
- Highlight and celebrate what they want to reinforce
- Strategically plant seeds for future dialogue and reflection
- Articulate their vision for teaching and learning

It is through these and other actions that leaders achieve the purpose(s) of the learning walkthrough. It is through these and other actions that leaders consciously and purposely go about developing a culture of public practice. As we discussed in Chapter One, practice does not improve in isolation. It can only improve in a culture in which public scrutiny, feedback, and critique define the cultural norms and ethos of a school and district. Thus, how and what leaders choose to communicate before and after learning walkthroughs to model their own learning, articulate their vision for teaching and learning, and plant seeds for future dialogue will either promote or inhibit a culture of public practice. Creating a culture of public practice is the lynchpin from which the learning walkthrough can achieve the other important purposes.

Exhibit 4.3 is an example of a letter written by a district assistant superintendent to principals, preparing them for a series of learning walkthroughs

EXHIBIT 4.3. LETTER WRITTEN BY AN ASSISTANT SUPERINTENDENT TO PRINCIPALS

Dear Principals,

As I reflect on our work together and our theory of action, I keep coming back to these essential questions:

- Even though we have state standards, what are the critical skills, knowledge, and dispositions students need in order to be successful in our changing world?
- How can we focus our efforts to ensure that each of our students have these critical skills, knowledge, and dispositions? What does this look like in all classrooms, regardless of context or content?

(continued)

- How do our instructional and leadership practices need to change in order to meet these shifting demands and to support the ongoing improvement of instruction in all classrooms?

The 5D framework will support us as we look for guidance and answers to these questions. If all of our classrooms were organized around these dimensions our students would have experiences to gain the critical skills, knowledge, and dispositions needed to be successful. As we learned in August, the Five Dimensions of Teaching and Learning look deceptively simple on the one-page handout. When we used the dimensions to notice and wonder, analyze our observations, develop theories, and consider implications, the true complexity of classroom instruction felt overwhelming. Our ongoing work with the five dimensions, the University of Washington Center for Educational Leadership, and the Leadership Academy should help us feel more and more confident about a vision and understanding of effective and powerful instruction.

As we experience learning walkthroughs and videos together with our teacher colleagues, we will continue to develop a shared vision of instruction. We will notice and wonder, analyze, and develop theories together. We will also use the data collected during the observations (what we noticed and wondered about) to practice the habits of thinking while considering implications for further study and leadership. I'm convinced it will be challenging and rewarding work.

Although we do not have a formal presentation plan for all staff, we are not keeping our purpose a secret. Before we visit the classes in your building I encourage you to talk to teachers about the importance of a shared vision of effective instructional practices that align to what students need to know and do to be successful in our changing world. Talk to them about how all of us, regardless of position or years of teaching, will work together to continue to learn and make improvement in practice. Remember, this work is important, we can do it, and we won't give up!

See you on Friday,
Cindy

after an initial instructional framework overview training session. In this letter the assistant superintendent provides important framing questions that serve to provide a foreground for the upcoming walkthroughs. Notice how the assistant superintendent conveys in multiple ways the importance of her own learning in this process.

The letter to staff in Exhibit 4.4 provides an illustration of a principal's leadership voice in action. Notice how the principal first talks about her own learning as a prerequisite for supporting teachers. She goes on to discuss the issue of agreed terminology as a precursor for involving her staff in future conversations aimed at developing a shared vision for quality instruction. Then she frames the purpose of the walkthrough process and sets the stage for how this district-level process will serve to stimulate similar conversations within their school for the upcoming year.

EXHIBIT 4.4. LETTER FROM A PRINCIPAL TO HER STAFF

Dear Staff,

Before school started, while you were setting up your classrooms and relishing your last few days of vacation, I participated in a professional development workshop with the rest of our district administrative team to launch a study group focused on student learning. The basic premise is that the more I understand the complexities of teaching and learning within and across content areas, the better I am able to support each of you in the challenging task of ensuring that all students are successful in our school.

During the workshop, facilitated by the Center for Educational Leadership at the University of Washington, we watched lots of video clips and examined student work samples. Most important, we spent a lot of time talking with each other about our own beliefs about powerful instruction and student learning. One thing that struck me is that though we may use some of same terminology when talking about *best practices*, we don't often spend the time to talk about what we mean by the words we use. We all believe, for example, that *student engagement* is critical to learning, but what does that actually mean? Is it about

(continued)

classroom management? accountability? time on task? hands-on learning activities? Or does it have more to do with the nature of the intellectual work with which students are engaged?

The workshop was just the start. We will continue our learning together throughout the year by visiting each other's schools and participating in learning walkthroughs as a group. During these learning walkthroughs, we will be popping into classrooms for less than fifteen minutes at a time. The purpose of these visits is not to evaluate your teaching; we all realize that a ten- to fifteen-minute chunk of time is just a snapshot of what's going on in the classroom. We are not looking for anything in particular and only want to see what would usually be happening in the classrooms we visit. These learning walkthroughs are simply food for thought, fodder for our own learning about student learning. Thank you, in advance, for opening up your classrooms for the sake of our learning.

Just as I will be participating in ongoing conversations about teaching and learning with my administrative colleagues, we will be engaging in similar conversations as a staff. I'll continue to share with you what's on my mind as a result of time spent in classrooms and we'll use those musings as food for thought, as fodder for *our* learning about student learning. After all, it is what you do in the classroom—day in and day out—that has the greatest effect on students' success.

Cheers,
Diane

THE GOAL-SETTING AND IMPLEMENTATION WALKTHROUGH

As with learning walkthroughs, a leader's purpose and well-defined outcomes guide the goal-setting and implementation walkthrough. Although there is much overlap between the learning walkthrough and the goal-setting and implementation walkthrough, there are also distinctions. The specific purposes for the goal-setting and implementation walkthrough are as follows:

1. To determine the level of implementation of curriculum materials and guidelines along with further support and professional development needed to implement the curriculum with fidelity

2. To determine the extent to which new learning(s) resulting from specific professional development offerings are being applied in actual practice

3. To determine additional supports and professional development needed to implement learning(s)

4. To establish the school instructional improvement goals

5. To determine schoolwide patterns across grade levels and subject areas to inform professional development

6. To determine individual goals and supports for teachers

7. To monitor student progress

8. To help identify a problem of leadership practice

Similar to the learning walkthrough, the goal-setting and implementation walkthrough can be used to develop a school and district culture of public practice, gathering data necessary to identify relevant problems of practice and observing and analyzing the effect of teacher practice on student learning. Similar to the learning walkthrough, the goal-setting and implementation walkthrough can include central office leaders, principals, teachers, and instructional coaches. The logistical and possible leadership actions to consider are also similar. What distinguishes the goal-setting and implementation walkthrough is the intentional connection to teachers' professional learning. The theory of action that guides this type of walkthrough is as follows:

1. If we carefully monitor an expected level of implementation of new curriculum and professional development learning(s), then we will be able to measure the level of implementation across the district and school.

2. If we are able to identify the level of implementation of new curriculum and professional development learning(s), then we will be in a position to bring focused and differentiated support when necessary to improve the implementation and application of new practices.

3. If we, as leaders, examine our teaching practices in light of our deepened understanding of powerful instruction, then we will be able to establish specific improvement goals (district, school, or individual) along with the professional development necessary to improve practice.

The goal-setting and implementation walkthrough is a *support* for teachers' practice. As leaders, we need to understand teachers' strengths and needs—what makes particular curriculum or instructional strategies challenging to implement—and then align our support with the teacher's own assessment of her needs. We need to create ongoing learning opportunities that anticipate the kind of learning required for the changes in practice we seek. For instance, teachers need time for collective reflection and discussion and job-embedded coaching in order to anticipate students' thinking and needs, plan lessons with this in mind, and teach in a way that allows opportunities for ongoing assessment of student learning.

The goal-setting and implementation walkthrough helps leaders assess the level of implementation of curriculum materials and instructional strategies and supports more intentional decision making about subsequent professional development. Teachers are too often targets of drive-by professional development, attending workshops and receiving training of various stripes that, at best, promote a layering effect: the addition of an activity or strategy layered onto current established practices without the deep learning that could actually change teaching beliefs and practices. District and school leaders too often bring back the latest thing without considering how or if this thing could support the short-term and long-term goals for the school and district. Again, leaders' clarity of purpose and their subsequent theory of action to achieve the goals allow leaders to intentionally sort and sift through what is most important and what the reasonable expectations for implementation are. Even if research-based, high-leverage practices are identified, they require consistent use over time and a 90 percent implementation level across a school or department in order to see improvement in student learning (Reeves, 2002). Leaders need to understand what will actually make a difference for student learning and understand what it takes for teachers to move new practices from novel to routine.

Exhibit 4.5 shows an example of a letter from a CEL leadership coach to the superintendent and assistant superintendent that provides a picture of what a goal-setting and implementation walkthrough could look and sound like. In this example, you will note that the CEL coach supports the superintendent and assistant superintendent to consider their roles and positions as district leaders on this type of walkthrough. Following a summer workshop on reading for upper elementary teachers, this district wanted the teachers to incorporate specific teaching strategies that would support their students, especially their English language learner students. The district wanted their

EXHIBIT 4.5. LETTER FROM CEL COACH TO DISTRICT LEADERS

Dear Minerva and Kevin,

It was such a pleasure to spend time with you over the last couple of weeks and I'm really looking forward to working with you this year! The CEL team will work hard to align all of our coaching work with your district goals. So, these coaching notes are in the spirit of alignment and coherence while addressing Minerva's specific requests for support:

1. More focus for her role in the delivery of expectations: how to have a clear message that is heard as *support*, not as a *mandate.*

2. How Minerva and Kevin can support principals toward their district expectations:

   a. How to further leverage walkthroughs with principals

   b. How to help principals move beyond whole-group professional development activities to more strategic capacity building

   c. How to help principals better use their instructional support teams as a key capacity-building structure

In general, it seems to me that you will continue to need to (1) develop principals' pedagogical content knowledge, that is, they (principals) need to know what good instruction does and does not look like, including the relationship between the reading work and EL strategies. This knowledge has to become fine-grained enough so that principals can (2) act more strategically and assertively in terms of pushing the improvement of teaching practice. More specifically, we'll work on the improvement of principals' overall leadership strategies and actions, including but not limited to their leadership voice, how they conduct themselves as lead learners, recognizing patterns of needed improvement in teaching, orchestrating the professional development supports necessary to address those patterns, and learning how to provide both just-in-time and developmental feedback to teachers (for example, how to have tough conversations and how to be more precise in your language and expectations).

(Page 1)

I believe our work together to address your own specific requests for support will mirror what you want your principals to know and be able to do. We will work on how you can model and demonstrate (teach) what you want principals to learn.

So, given our goals, I provide (following) some specific language and actions you might use as you follow up with principals from the August 24 session with Shannon. Please note that because I spent my time with the elementary group, these follow-up suggestions do not necessarily apply to the middle and high school work, though some might. One caveat before you proceed: I am candid and straightforward with what I say—I get right to the point! As always, if this style does not work for you, tell me!

From Shannon's notes:

Each group of fourth- and fifth-grade teachers from the elementary schools agreed to implement three elements in their classrooms during the first week of school:

- Setting up a classroom environment that includes a meeting area, student seats arranged for group work, and a classroom library
- Reading aloud to students and facilitating student talk about the text
- Administering student surveys to get to know students' reading histories and interests

Here's how I think you might follow up with principals in a way that conveys your expectations in a supportive way.

Regarding Student Surveys

Ask principals what they found out about their students as the result of the surveys.

- What surveys did the school decide to use? Why?
- Are there patterns across grade levels? If so, what are they? Anything surprising?
- Have they mined the surveys to uncover (with their staff) what strengths or interests their students have? What needs were uncovered? How do

(Page 2)

both the needs *and* strengths of the students inform what they might need to do with their teaching practice and school environment? What are the implications for classroom libraries?

How are *principals* using the information the teachers gathered?

- Did principals use the surveys in a staff or grade-level meeting where the teachers were gathered together so that they could collectively engage in the analysis of what they learned about their students? Based on their collective learning, what are their next steps?

[Just by making it a point to ask these questions, you are modeling the kind of thinking you want the principals to engage in with their staff. You also don't want to ask the principals to do anything you wouldn't do yourself, so you need to model a genuine curiosity about who the students are, the strengths and challenges they bring to your schools, and how you'll all work together to support your students.]

Regarding Classroom Environments

Do a focused walkthrough with the principal and coaches at each school to look for meeting areas, student seats arranged for group work, and a classroom library across the fourth- and fifth-grade classrooms.

- Do the meeting areas and student seating arrangements allow for students to engage with one another (not just the teacher)? Do students know what is expected of them in the meeting area and during group work? How do students talk about these expectations (are they describing expectations about *behavior* or their *learning*)? Are there established routines for how students come to the meeting area and interact with one another?

- How is the classroom library arranged (for example, levels, genre, topic) and is the library accessible for children? What does the library consist of (think of *quantity* and *quality* here), for example, historical fiction, realistic fiction, picture books, magazines, and so on? How many books, magazines, and so on are in the classroom? Are there routines for how children select books, talk about their books, and keep track of their thinking while they read?

(Page 3)

After the walkthrough, ask yourselves if you detect any patterns across the classrooms, where strengths lie, and which teachers might need help in setting up their rooms or establishing routines.

- How will you communicate what you learned to the teachers? What kind of support (if needed) can teachers expect? If you find that teachers do not have enough books in their libraries or they are in need of more nonfiction, for example, how will you get these materials for them (they can't do the reading work without reading material!)?

[Again, the main point here is to actually go to the schools and ask the sort of questions that you want the principals to be asking when they are in their classrooms following up on the specific professional development. Equally important is the modeling of note taking so that you can look for patterns from which to plan next steps.]

Regarding Read-Alouds

Do a focused walkthrough (could even be simultaneous with the previously described walkthrough) in order to gather more specific information about teachers' understanding and use of read-alouds. Ask yourself these questions:

- What are teachers choosing to read aloud? Are teachers' choices based on student interests, genre, as a comparison to other books by same author, or other intentional reasons?

- What reading strategies or teaching points are addressed with the read-aloud?

- Is the read-aloud connected to prior read-alouds or literacy experiences?

- Are children gathered in the meeting area?

- How is the book introduced (for example, are story elements or key vocabulary introduced in a natural way, as part of a conversation about the book? How does the teacher introduce the writing style, characters, setting, and language that a series author uses)?

- Does the teacher model her or his own understandings and meaning making in a way that engages students in *accountable talk* about the text?

(Page 4)

- How does the teacher respond to student thinking to extend conversation and collective learning?
- What is the academic language being used by the teacher and students as they discuss their thinking and responses to text?
- Does the read-aloud foster an excitement for shared literature?

I am excited to visit again on September 20 to hear about how your follow-up school visits went, what you learned from the visits, and how the visits will inform your own next steps. In the meantime, please do not hesitate to call or e-mail.

Best regards,
Anneke

---

students to have access to higher-level thinking and communication about their reading and provided a week-long reading workshop focused on creating print- and language-rich learning environments, supporting the role of student talk in learning, and identifying how teachers could support their students' access to increasingly rigorous thinking. The school principals also participated in the workshop, learning the content alongside the teachers and learning how to follow up back at their buildings. The district expected the principals to support teachers in their implementation of particular strategies while they cultivated a learning community among their staff.

The goal-setting and implementation walkthrough allows district and school leaders to determine the extent to which new learning(s) resulting from specific professional development are being applied in actual practice and to determine the additional supports and professional development needed to implement learning(s). It supports leaders in establishing school instructional improvement goals based on the strengths and needs of the students and teachers, to help teachers determine individual goals aligned with the school focus, and to determine schoolwide patterns across grade levels and subject areas to inform professional development. The goal-setting and implementation walkthrough is part of an ongoing process to help identify a problem of leadership practice grounded in the actual teaching and learning of the school. This focus depends on having and communicating a vision for student learning and the rationale for improvement in specific enough ways so that planned actions and assessment of those actions is clear, aligned, and measurable. It provides a leader with a rationale for the decisions he or she will make—where to target resources, how to spend limited time with staff, and where to focus attention so that capacity is continually developed. Possible leadership actions might include the following:

- Communicating with staff about the walkthrough, highlighting and celebrating what you want to reinforce
- Creating and communicating new expectations if necessary
- Using teacher and principal expertise to build collective learning
- Modifying professional development as needed
- Considering strategic provision of new and additional supports, for example, professional development, coaching, study groups, readings, and so on, if necessary
- Articulating your vision for teaching and learning
- Providing an avenue for feedback and conversation on both the process and subsequent learning

THE SUPERVISORY WALKTHROUGH

The third distinction we make for observing in classrooms is the supervisory walkthrough. Intended for district and school leaders, the supervisory walkthrough will both support principals and allow their district supervisors to establish meaningful goals for which school leaders can be held accountable. The following demonstrate the various purposes that guide the supervisory walkthrough:

1. To examine the teaching and learning process as it relates to the school's and district's instructional goals
2. To examine relevant student performance data and monitor student progress
3. To focus on progress made since the last walkthrough visit and the best type(s) of professional development to meet teachers' needs
4. To identify specific leadership actions necessary to support the improvement of teaching practice

5. To assess leader's understanding of new learning

6. To hold leaders accountable for agreed-on leadership actions

When district and school leaders collaboratively examine relevant student performance data and monitor student progress in the context of the school and district's instructional goals, together they can identify specific leadership actions necessary to support the improvement of teaching practice. When district leaders accompany principals in classrooms and focus on progress made since the prior walkthrough, they assist the building leaders to address their problems of practice. The theory of action that guides the supervisory walkthrough is as follows:

1. If we carefully examine and monitor student performance data and the quality of teaching and learning in light of our deepened understanding of powerful instruction, then we will be able to identify specific leadership actions necessary to improve practice.

2. If we carefully examine and monitor the extent to which agreed-on leadership actions are enacted, then we can hold leaders accountable for the improvement of teaching and learning.

In the Exhibit 4.6, the supervisor of high school principals, Max, communicates the purpose for the supervisory walkthroughs he will take with principals as well as the logistical considerations for these visits. Max uses the supervisory walkthroughs to support individual principals with their problems of practice as well as to establish community among the principals.

EXHIBIT 4.6. MEMO FROM HIGH SCHOOL SUPERVISOR TO PRINCIPALS

To: High School Principals
From: Max
Re: High School Principal Quads
Date: March 5

This memo will lay out in detail the initial process, protocols, and expectations for our quad visits starting this week. Thanks to Rick, Stace, and Joan for being willing pioneers and hosting the initial visits. No doubt we will be revising this process as we move forward.

(Page 1)

Step One: Formulation of Problem of Practice

Prior to your visit day, I will meet with you for one hour to help you formulate a problem of practice. Lora will be in touch to schedule this time. This step is critical to ensuring a visit that is focused on the work of your school as well as on the skills we are trying to emphasize in our focus on instructional leadership. When we meet, we will craft a problem of practice based on these three principles:

- *That it is rooted in your school improvement plan (SIP) action plan or your instructional strategic plan*—I want to make sure that we use each visit as a chance to check in how your school is progressing with its plan as well as have a chance to consider revisions for this spring (depending on your visit date) or for next year. Continually monitoring our strategic plans is a critical component of strong instructional leadership.

- *That it is based on a current data set that concerns you or your staff*—This is your chance to get a new set of eyes on data that you are monitoring and are concerned about. Possible data sets include individually or a combination of measurement of academic progress (MAP), student grades, student work, conferring notes, student survey or focus groups, compilation of classroom visit observations, student discipline, and other data you might be tracking. Again, we will work together to pick a data set that will help us form a focused problem of practice. Continually using data to make decisions is a critical component of strong instructional leadership.

- *That it is directly connected to school-based theory of action focused on all students accessing and engaging with content and tasks that demand critical thinking*—I think this one says it all. As leaders we all need to be vigilant about ensuring that all students have the supports and scaffolds they need to do the critical thinking and communicating necessary for success after high school. In this component we will make sure that we are addressing issues of inclusion and student relationship to the work (engagement, intent, independence, and authenticity). Our work in this area is a critical domain for instructional leadership in our district.

(Page 2)

Step Two: The Visit

If we do a good job of crafting the problem of practice, then the visits should go smoothly. Keeping in mind that one of our goals is to create more permeable and public practice, we need to realize that this won't happen on one visit. It is critical that these visits allow us to give feedback that honors the work of the host school while giving them input that assists them in determining next steps. Feedback that is too critical or not rooted in the problem of practice can ruin a well-planned visit as can feedback that is too warm or "nice" and not focused on next steps. The protocol we use will create a collegial environment for this balance. The basics of the protocol are as follows:

- *Presentation of problem of practice*—The host principal will share the problem of practice with a rationale for the choice and the work that has been done to get to this point. This presentation can last up to thirty minutes with clarifying questions.

- *Brainstorming of evidence and indicators*—Together we will discuss and chart what evidence we will look for to support observations about the problem of practice.

- *Observations*—This is the bulk of our time together and will be focused on appropriate observations based on the problem of practice. Appropriate observations can include classroom visits, looking at student work, interviewing students, and looking deeper at data. We will decide the most appropriate observation during our formulation of the problem of practice.

- *Debrief*—This is when we discuss what we observed and the next steps for the host principal based on the following questions:

  - What did we see and what is resonating with us?

  - What are the implications of these observations?

  - What are potential next steps for the host principal including conversations around the use of professional development, coaching, resources, and further data analysis?

(Page 3)

- *Reflection*—We will end each visit with personal reflection and sharing on these two questions:
  - As a result of our learning today what am I going to do next?
  - What evidence would I like to evaluate during my next step?

Step Three: The Summary

After each visit I will write a summary of the visit including problem of practice, next steps, and each participants' reflective next steps.

Step Four: Visit Calibration

I have not fully figured this step out, but we will use time in our principal meetings to discuss what we are learning across quads.

Responsibilities

Host Principal	Visitors	Max

• Make sure that the following is ready for your visit:
  • Space for meeting
  • Chart paper and markers
  • A schedule of observations or copies of what we will observe
• Copies of all pertinent documents
	• Arrive on time
	• Be fully present and focus on problem of practice
	• Reflect on visit and own work in the school
		• Meet with host to determine problem of practice
		• Facilitate initial round of visits
		• Prepare summary

In the supervisory walkthrough, the possible leadership actions that both district and school leaders might consider are parallel and intended to support reciprocal accountability between the school and district. Possible leadership actions include the following:

- Communicating with staff about the walkthrough
- Highlighting and celebrating what you want to reinforce
- Creating and communicating new expectations if necessary
- Providing new and additional supports, for example, professional development, coaching, and so on, if necessary
- Articulating your vision for teaching and learning
- Holding leader(s) accountable for agreed-on actions
- Assessing the implementation of agreed-on actions using student learning as a measure

A deeper elaboration of reciprocal accountability will be provided in Chapter Eight, but as we can see from the previous example, Max, the high school supervisor, communicates purposes, expectations, and articulates his vision for teaching and learning. Max will also use his supervisory walkthroughs and subsequent written memos to highlight and celebrate what he wants to reinforce and stir new thinking about the professional development he wants the principals to consider. Exhibit 4.7, a letter written by Max after several of his supervisory walkthroughs, is an example of a district leader explicitly connecting the visits to schools with the district's ongoing professional development—communicating a vision of the collective work in the district.

Perhaps the most important aspect of the supervisory walkthrough is the idea that instructional supervisors actually have a formal role in leading for instructional improvement. At one level this is an obvious assumption; however, there are many school districts in which district leaders do not play an active role in leading for instructional improvement. Some district leaders subscribe to a loosely coupled leadership theory that places the sole responsibility for instructional improvement in the hands of the school principal. The district's role in this case is simply to provide material and other support to schools as well as ensuring districtwide expectations and accountability systems are in place. In other school systems, district leaders believe they should play some role in leading for instructional improvement but they have little idea how to engage in the practice of district-level instructional leadership. We will treat this in much greater depth in Chapter Eight but for now suffice to say that district leaders do in fact play an instrumental role in improving instruction and the supervisory walkthrough is an important tool in that regard.

EXHIBIT 4.7. A TALE OF TWO VISITS— STUDENT INDEPENDENCE, CRITICAL THINKING, AND CROSS-SCHOOL VISITS

Dear Colleagues,

I took some time over the weekend to review my weekly messages to you all. I was bothered but not surprised by the lack of coherence in my writing. In my mind, I know that we are focusing on getting all students ready for college and I know that we can only do this by improving their ability to learn, think, and express their thinking in various forms. So, I was concerned at how rarely I focused on these topics in writing. I know I need to get better at communicating important administrative and NCLB information while always keeping my eye on what we are doing to prepare our students for citizenship, college, and career.

The beautiful thing is that each of you and your teachers are working hard to keep student thinking and independence in the center of your work. The better we get at teaching our students how to learn (I think this is the sum of critical thinking + independence) and communicate, the closer we will be to playing a role in improving life outcomes for them.

My confidence in what you all are doing was reaffirmed in my visits to two schools last week. At one school, I joined the principal while she was working with four teachers and two coaches. Specifically, they were spending half a day on what they can do to put student thinking at the center of their work. Although the teachers struggled to name the specific types of thinking they wanted students to engage in, all participants worked hard to home in on the critical thinking necessary to be successful in their particular discipline. It was powerful to hear a social studies teacher move from saying he was teaching the Treaty of Versailles to his desire to see students read documents for bias and main ideas. This session ended with the principal asking her teachers to reconsider their lesson for that same afternoon to explicitly focus on the specific thinking they want students to do. In addition to being excited about the focus on student thinking, I was equally pleased to see a principal working so closely with coaches and teachers. This was a strong example of how a principal can assess what students need and what teachers need to improve on to better serve students. Additionally, it was great to see a principal leveraging coaching resources to support teachers within the mission, vision, and direction of the school.

On a second visit I visited a school in which the staff has agreed on the common practices of meeting space, conferring, and reflection. These common practices are all in support of students working and thinking with independence. The highlight of this visit was going into a geometry class in which a teacher and literacy coach were both conferring with students. In this class the coach and teacher had scripted a series of conferring questions to help uncover student thinking on a particular concept. As I was leaving the class, the coach and teacher were beginning to discuss what they had discovered about student thinking during the class period. Again, I was very excited to see a focus on student thinking, a clear instructional direction for the school, and the use of coaching resource to support teacher practice.

While I wrote about my two visits last week, this could have easily been about other schools I visited in the past month. As we move into our conversation on Thursday about visiting each other's schools I am more confident than ever these visits will support both the host principal and visiting principals. By critically observing classroom practice for evidence of student thinking, being discerning in our analysis of what students are doing, and then brainstorming next steps (professional development, use of coaches, messaging to staff, and so on) I know that we will each improve in our leadership practice.

Max

CONCLUSION

The three types of observations discussed in this chapter—the learning walkthrough, the goal-setting and implementation walkthrough, and the supervisory walkthrough—are distinct because of the leader's intentionality and a clear theory of action to guide the observations. These types of walkthroughs also overlap in that they inform, and are informed by, school improvement efforts and the district's professional development strategy. When leaders can trace the through-line from classroom observations to professional learning needs to the school's improvement agenda to a vision for student learning, then they have honed a tool for their own learning as well as for their strategic decision making.

When teachers' classrooms are visited during walkthroughs, they tend to ask, "What did you see?" or "What did you think?" Leaders need to respond to teachers' questions honestly, honoring teachers' work, being mindful of the culture they are attempting to nurture *and* their potential to effect teachers' practice. Navigating the terrain of culture building, honoring the extant expertise of teachers, and relying on teachers' shared leadership while pushing their practice is wrought with land mines. In the next chapter, we will explore how leaders can respond to what they see in classrooms.

DISCUSSION QUESTION

- What is the purpose for your classroom observations? To what extent do your own classroom observations align with the three purposes discussed in this chapter?

Responding to Observations

A s we have noted, there is a vast difference between experts and novices in terms of what they notice and wonder about during classroom observations. Learning how to "see" and to describe student learning and instructional practices in rich, nuanced ways has everything to do with posing relevant problems of leadership practice and with improvement efforts. Novices tend to make evaluative judgments or jump quickly to interpretations. Experts tend to withhold judgment until they can describe in evidentiary terms what they are seeing. We have argued that the Five Dimensions of Teaching and Learning can provide guidance and support the development of observational expertise, offering a tool for honing our observational lens on particular aspects of teaching and learning. We have argued that the 5D framework can help observers see more in classrooms and provide language that helps analyze what they are seeing.

In Chapter Three, we saw what a principal with deep subject matter and pedagogical content knowledge, an established relationship with the teacher she observed, and with three years as the school's principal, noticed and wondered about as she observed a portion of a third-grade math lesson. We saw how the 5D framework informed her thinking. In Chapter Four, we described three types of walkthroughs in which student learning and teaching practice are the focal points. We described how these types of walkthroughs are tools for leaders' own learning, for strategic decision making, and for reciprocal accountability. We asserted that these types of walkthroughs help leaders to connect a through-line (see Figure 5.1) from classroom observations, to professional learning needs, to the school's improvement agenda, and finally to a vision for student learning.

In this chapter, we will explore two cases that illustrate how leaders connect this through-line and consider the kind of feedback they might provide to teachers in light of the school and district context. Readers will be taught how to shape responses to their classroom observations and connect those responses with the broader educational improvement goals of their schools and districts. We will provide an example of a district leadership team that is just beginning to consider how to establish a through-line in their schools and as a district. The district case is one example of how a district might *begin* the work of intentionally connecting the through-line from observations of teaching and learning, to professional learning needs, and to their vision of powerful student learning. We illustrate how responding to classroom observations is grounded in the development of a collective vision and shared understanding of teaching and learning and how the creation of shared processes nurture this development. We will also examine how one middle school principal thinks through how he responds to classroom observations, paying attention

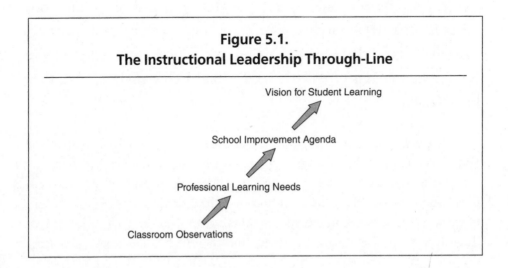

Figure 5.1.
The Instructional Leadership Through-Line

Vision for Student Learning

School Improvement Agenda

Professional Learning Needs

Classroom Observations

to the through-line from the observation to a vision for student learning and the cultivation of the kind of school community that creates and sustains collective inquiry into practice.

OBSERVATIONS, INTERPRETATIONS, AND FEEDBACK

When we think about responding to what we see in classrooms we often think about the kind of feedback we would give. In our experience working with many leaders across the country, we know that a certain kind of feedback does little to effect teaching practice. That is, an occasional visit into a teacher's classroom, sharing what the observer noticed, and making suggestions about what the teacher might do to improve the lesson carries the burden of a too-tall order: by virtue of the observer simply making a suggestion, the teacher (1) finds it relevant and useful and (2) can simply do what was suggested. At best, this sort of feedback provides possible helpful hints; at worst, it breeds cynicism and corrupts more authentic attempts for critique and dialogue. Often, the classroom teacher is left thinking, "Well, if I knew how to get the students to X (the suggestion that was made), then I'd have done it!" or "This person has no idea why I do what I do and couldn't begin to understand the dynamics of my classroom and my instructional decision making in that visit." Or, "I really do not understand or agree with those observations." At the same time, if the observer is "supposed to be" an instructional leader, she knows that her classroom visits should provide some kind of data about the state of teaching and learning in her building or district and that she will connect this data with ongoing opportunities to support teachers' growth. Especially if there is a formally designated role for the principal, coach, learning facilitator, and so on, and if that role is intended to support the improvement of instructional practice, then one might assume some self-imposed pressure to say something smart or helpful after being in a classroom. After all, as a designated instructional leader, one might ask, "Shouldn't I know something and shouldn't I help classroom teachers to improve their practice? I have to say *something*! How will we learn to have honest conversations about the quality of instructional practice if I don't speak up?" All true. The challenge and potential barrier lie in the unexamined conflation of what we see, how we interpret what we see, and when we do not evaluate our feedback alongside our short-term and long-term improvement strategy.

Let us be clear: we view the role of instructional leaders as one that is constantly holding the tension between communicating and acting on the urgent while tilling the soil for the kind of relationships with and among school staff that allow the ongoing scrutiny and public critique of practice to become part of the culture of the school. We do not want leaders to ignore, diminish, or condone practices that are harmful to students. In fact, removing incompetent teachers is also part of the school and district leadership role. For our purposes, let us imagine that as we discuss classroom observations we are not referring to a dysfunctional classroom or a brand-new teacher caught in the headlights of basic classroom management issues. Let us imagine that we are referring to observing a competent or above-average teacher who is still struggling to get *all* of her students to achieve at high levels. How might instructional leaders have conversations with teachers that are satisfying for teachers and leaders, that develop and deepen collaborative relationships, that allow for honest communication about the state of teaching and learning in that classroom, and that stimulate and support instructional improvement?

The 5D framework is not intended to be a script or checklist but a tool to guide observations and to support analysis and conversation. As such, we need to consider the relationship among observing, interpreting, and how we craft a response to our classroom observations. We have found that educators—no matter if they are teachers, principals, or district level staff—are challenged to describe what they see in classrooms. Educators seem more inclined to judge what they observe. For example, after being in classrooms we might hear, "I really like how the teacher (fill in the blank)." "The teacher could have (fill in the blank)." "The teacher should have (fill in the blank)." "When I was teaching, here is how I would have done (fill in the blank)." These sort of responses are understandable. As human beings, we are constantly interpreting what goes on around us and we are constantly making sense of things based on our own knowledge, experience, and understanding. But there are two inherent problems with only bringing our *personal* inclinations to classroom observations: (1) because we likely do not share collective agreement or have agreed-on definitions of teaching practices, the conversation about what was seen quickly becomes a matter of opinion; (2) because the conversation is likely to focus on trying to get the teacher to do what you would have or should have or could have done, there is no entry for authentic inquiry with the teacher. The conversation becomes a vehicle for convincing the teacher to do things differently, even if we do not completely understand the teacher's decision making or have a complete grasp of the content or the students as learners. If our conversations are simply an occasion to inform the teacher about what she should be doing or might do in the future, we lose a valuable learning opportunity.

Table 5.1 helps to illustrate the distinction between description of an observation and assigning an interpretation to the observation. You will note that there could be multiple interpretations of this snippet of teaching and learning in this classroom. You will note that when the observation and interpretation are conflated, it leads to judgment; when the observation is separated from the

---

Table 5.1.
Observation and Interpretation

OBSERVATION AND INTERPRETATION CONFLATED	OBSERVATION AND INTERPRETATION SEPARATED
Observation and Interpretation: I wonder why she's asking the students to line up when they are clearly ready to go back to work. She seems like she's holding them back. She has alluded to the students being out of control but they seem fine and ready to work. She's micromanaging the students' learning. There is so much time being wasted. The students just need to get back to their tables and get to work. She's not paying attention to the students who are already back at their tables. She's missing a lot of assessment opportunities.	*Observation:* The teacher is asking the students to show their exit tickets from the meeting area before they go back to work. Several students are asking if they can go back to work. The teacher has asked them to wait until she checks their tickets. She's reading them over and stamping them. *Interpretations:* I wonder what information she is getting from the exit tickets. Is she checking for a certain level of understanding? Every ticket is getting stamped, so I wonder if this is just a way for her to check in with her students. I wonder in what other ways she is getting information from the students. Her classroom and routines are very clear and organized. Everything is very orderly. I wonder if this is a ritual that has helped the students manage themselves.

interpretation, it leads to authentic questions about the teacher's decision making. You might also note that learning how *not* to base our response on our own personal inclinations will most likely require a more disciplined approach to classroom observations than we're accustomed to, especially if we are interested in creating and sustaining a co-inquiry stance with teachers. We will need to develop clarity between our own *assumptions* about what we see versus a *description* of what we see.

When we conflate our observations with interpretation, we leave ourselves little opportunity to engage in an authentic conversation with teachers. When we are careful to separate what we see from our interpretation of what we see, we can pose questions that we do not have the answers to and set ourselves up for co-inquiry with teachers. Such an orientation allows leaders to discover how teaching practices are products of what teachers believe about how students learn in a given content area and what they believe about their students as learners. This way, leaders will be better equipped to make decisions about how best to support teachers and what might get in teachers' way of making significant shifts in their practice.

As leaders, we need to understand teachers' rationale for their decision making. Teachers not only do what they know how to do, they also develop practices that may not align with their intentions. For instance, a teacher might say that she wants her students to own the conversations about the books they are reading but what you observe is the teacher in front of the classroom directing students' responses and most students do not talk at all. This teacher's stated desire does not match what she is actually doing in practice. Initially, you do not know why. You do not know if the practice and intention mismatch is that the teacher needs to learn some strategies or if she is afraid of losing control of her students or if she has not fully considered the role of talk in developing and articulating ideas and how that influences students' learning. Perhaps all of these things are in play. You cannot know by observing and if you approach a conversation with this teacher from a "here's what you should or could do" perspective, you set yourself up for a conversation bent on convincing the teacher versus a conversation with the potential to learn something—for the teacher and for you.

Learning how to observe versus interpreting what we see does not come naturally. We need to be aware of our tendency toward judgment versus description and then learn to discipline ourselves in order to develop a learning stance that will support our desire for authentic inquiry. As leaders, we are also prone to having our own intention and practice mismatch. There are some warning signs when we conflate observing and interpreting that prevent our response to classroom observations from becoming authentic inquiry. Such warning signs include the following:

1. A sense of anxiety about finding something positive to say
2. Relying on sentence stems or conversation prompts; reliance on the "compliment sandwich" (say something positive, then something negative, then something positive)
3. Thinking something different than what we actually say
4. Using instructional frameworks to guide our observations but not knowing how to use the information from the observations in conversations

CLASSROOM OBSERVATIONS AND HONEST CONVERSATIONS

Before we move to a more thorough discussion of responding to classroom observations, let's consider the broader context for our responses and what we are hoping to accomplish in the moment and as part of our long-term plan for collaborative problem solving and honest conversations about student learning and instructional practice. Although CEL considers leadership the nexus for instructional improvement efforts, we do not believe that teachers are *objects* of change; rather, we believe that teachers need to be part of the *creation* of our instructional improvements efforts or our efforts will ultimately fail. Ultimately, it is the collective wherewithal of teachers to improve their practice on behalf of their students, and teachers, similar to all learners, need to be active agents in their own learning.

The role of teachers' learning in their school community has been described as "opportunities to collaboratively examine, question, profoundly study, experiment, implement, evaluate, and change" (Calderon, 1996, p. 2) and when "shared values and visions lead to binding norms of behavior that the staff shares" (Hord, 1997, p. 12). With leadership as the nexus for instructional improvement, the onus is on leaders to cultivate a culture in which authentic conversations about student learning and instructional practices can thrive, when relentless scrutiny of teaching practice and the development of respectful critique can thrive, when an examination of teachers' particular work with their students are shared values and practices. Teaching norms of privacy, isolation, and an orientation toward egalitarianism that can trump expertise are bedrocks of current school culture (Johnson & Donaldson, 2007; Little, 1982; Lortie, 1975). The creation of a school culture in which teaching practice is truly public, in which dialogue among teachers is not only reflective but also situated in the actual terrain of teachers' work in the instructional core, and in which the strength of mutual trust allows the collective scrutiny of instructional practice is a long-term process. In the short term, each and every conversation a leader has with individual teachers, grade levels, departments, or the whole staff has to model the qualities of the conversations she intends to inspire and nurture. Our conversations, the letters we write, the way we open or close a meeting, or any other way to communicate is also an opportunity to cultivate and nurture co-inquiry into teaching practices where teachers are authentically part of the conversation.

With an eye toward both an immediate response to our classroom observations as well as toward the development of a long-range vision for collective inquiry, let us now closely examine how our response to classroom observations can be an authentic conversation: honest, connected directly to classroom observations, and ones that will develop and sustain a school culture to support collective critique and inquiry into teaching practices. In our response to classroom observations we want to connect the through-line from the vision for student learning and quality instruction to an emerging theory of action to actual practice. This requires a leader to hold several lines of thinking simultaneously: an advocacy stance on behalf of the assurances the district and school has made to its students; a learning stance that allows theory, research, and inquiry to drive an ongoing examination of our practices; and attention to the cultivation of an adult learning community that allows us to be hard on the work, respectful with each other. Holding onto these lines of thinking, making explicit connections among them, and constantly scrutinizing our actual practices against our best intentions is a never-ending cycle of improvement. A leader's work is never done—it is an ongoing process that requires heart, mind, and vigilance. Indeed, there is no short cut: we learn to do the work by doing it, creating and re-creating the opportunities that compel us to develop shared meaning through collective experience and evidence-rich conversations. We learn to respectfully press one another's thinking, ask for evidence, and collectively problem solve by doing it. We learn how to navigate the terrain of authentic conversations by trying them on and reflecting on them. The poet Antonio Machado (1982) was correct: "se hace camino al andar" ("we make the road by walking") (p. 142).

We cannot stop at a conversation—it is an essential vehicle of leadership that takes time to cultivate and sustain but we should always keep our eyes on the prize: equity of outcomes for each and every student. We need to learn enough about teaching and learning to analyze what we see in classrooms *and* we need to be courageous enough to make explicit connections between what we see and the race, class, or language fault lines that permeate relationships between teachers and students. Ultimately, if our effort to develop authentic conversations and a culture of collective inquiry does not affect teaching practice and learning outcomes for our students, then learning how to have a different kind of conversation is only a nice exercise. The conversation is not the ultimate outcome: it is a vehicle and a vital one for the depth of changes in teaching practices that are called for in current educational reform. As humans, we are hardwired to make sense of things. Opportunities to wrestle with, develop, and communicate our thinking and understanding is *the* venue for learning. As leaders, we need to engage in this practice ourselves and create ongoing venues for teachers to engage in this practice as well.

In the instructional memo shown in Exhibit 5.1, you will see how this director of K–12 schools thinks about the purpose of walkthroughs and the role of inquiry and learning during the course of walkthroughs and feedback to

EXHIBIT 5.1. INSTRUCTIONAL MEMO FROM THE DIRECTOR OF SCHOOLS TO THE DISTRICT PRINCIPALS

Dear Colleagues,

Instructional leadership, including classroom walkthroughs, have been a focus in our district for many years. Many of you have continued spending significant time in classrooms as is evident by your deep knowledge of classroom work during instructional visits. Recently I had the chance to spend the day with our consultant from CEL in high school literacy. Although we spent the day visiting high school literacy classrooms, my deepest learning was on the practice of classroom walkthroughs and how our

(continued)

work as administrators can either support and enhance what is happening in the classroom or at times create unintended results, frustrate teachers, and cause distractions for instructional improvement.

In both our math and literacy work over the years, we have asked teachers to know their students as learners—deeply understand what students can do and use that knowledge to build further skills and ability. My question to each of you is, "How well do you know your staff as instructors?" Although I know that it is extremely time consuming, two thirty- to sixty-minute observations a year in addition to a couple of informal classroom visits does not provide you with the quality time you need to truly know your teachers' instructional skill and provide meaningful and supportive feedback. Daily visits into classrooms where you have the ability to understand the story line of the instruction (the trajectory of the objectives as well as the various instructional routines and strategies used) are needed to provide effective feedback. It reminds me of Doug Reeves's 90 percent implementation theory (you need to get to 90 percent implementation before you will see your desired results). If we implement classroom visits at only a 30 percent level and give teachers next steps, we can actually do more harm to staff morale and instructional skill; if we implement 50 to 70 percent we may not see much improvement. It is only when we implement the practice well at a 90-percent level that we will see trust with staff and instructional practice improve.

Here are my current thoughts about walkthrough practice:

- We began our work in this area asking all principals to schedule two hours a day in classrooms (or with instructional teams). I still believe and stand behind this expectation. When we decrease to one or two hours a week it is impossible to understand the story line of instructional practice in our classrooms. Not only does our presence make a difference in improving instruction, we must also have a good idea of what is happening in classrooms on a daily basis before giving feedback that is meaningful and useful.

- Periodic walkthroughs can be very effective if they are used for collecting evidence for implementation trends (for example, school improvement plan agreements). However, if it is only periodic, it must be used only for trends that can be shared in aggregate comments and percentages (example: In 75 percent of our classrooms, we observed evidence of students asking higher-level questions of each other and the teacher).

- When we are involved in grade- and department-level planning and understand the collaborative agreements, or when we are in classrooms on a consistent basis, then meaningful feedback can be provided to teachers to push their practice forward. One way to do this is to provide evidence of what is occurring in the classroom to the teacher as well as provide inquiry-based questions that will encourage reflection on teaching (reflective practice should be one of our top goals in working with staff!). The structure of walkthroughs that are not consistent do not lend themselves to giving feedback and should only be used for trends.

- For large schools: dedicating even two hours a day to classrooms leaves you far from being in any given classroom on a regular basis. Consider focusing on a grade level and department for three-week cycles to get to know the work deeply.

- Classroom visits do not occur when they are not scheduled. They must be a priority driver in your schedule including both core classroom instruction as well as interventions. Take time this week to look at the your classroom visit schedules. How often are you getting into classrooms outside of your formal observations? Do you have a deep knowledge of the story line happening in your classrooms and interventions? Do you know what grade- and department-conversations are happening? It is some of the most important work we do!

Best,
Susanne

---

teachers. Notice how this district leader communicates with the principals she supervises about the nature of their classroom visits and conversations with teachers. This district leader frames the idea of classroom observations and feedback with a teacher in the context of the story line of the teaching and learning in that classroom. This district leader situates the walkthrough and feedback to teachers as part of an ongoing narrative about student learning, the improvement of teaching, and the creation of a school culture that is hard on the work, respectful of each other. In doing so, she underscores the *habit* of classroom observations in order to truly understand what the teacher is doing in order to provide meaningful feedback and to have honest conversations with the most potential to move a teacher's practice.

Susanne's letter to her principals reiterates the importance of consistent classroom observations as she makes the case for understanding the story line of the classroom as the basis for meaningful feedback to teachers. In this case, the district had practiced walkthroughs for several years and Susanne's letter spoke to the ongoing challenge of responding to observations in substantive ways. Next, we share a case of a district just embarking on the practice of learning walkthroughs and that is in the first stages of learning how to respond to what they observe.

THE DEVELOPMENT OF SHARED VISION: A DISTRICT CASE

In one of our partnerships, the district recently created a set of teaching standards and wanted to eventually use it as a tool for their teacher evaluation system. In the short term, the district leaders—including principals, teacher leaders, directors, and other district level leaders—wanted to calibrate their own understanding of the terms used in the document and begin to develop shared instructional leadership practices. The role of coaching as part of the teacher leaders' job description was a new one and the use of classroom walkthroughs as a data source for instructional leadership was also new. As a system, the district, its leaders, and its teachers were not accustomed to having collective, concrete conversations about student learning and teaching practices. Besides supervisory classroom visits, there were few other opportunities for the district's leaders and teachers to have conversations focused squarely on the instructional core. They did not want their teaching standards document to simply became a notebook that would sit on a shelf; they wanted to develop shared understanding so that their standards document could actually become a helpful tool. One of the main concepts in their teaching standards document was that of student engagement. We agreed that unpacking the notion of engagement would help better frame how to go about collectively working on it. By painting a common picture, we would have a more fine-grained understanding of the relationship among what teachers actually taught across grade levels, how teachers engaged their students, and the role students played in their own learning. Having a better defined—and shared— understanding about the relationship among teaching, content, and the students' role is the foundation of our instructional leadership decision making. Educators generally share jargon and words but do not share understanding and agreement. This district wanted to build a leadership team that would go first and become the leaders in making their teaching standards a living document. These leaders knew that in order to support teachers to analyze their own practice against the vision in the new standards document and use it as a districtwide tool, they needed to hone their own skill at developing shared understanding and having concrete discussions about the instructional core. They wanted to learn what to *do* with the observational data they would collect in classrooms and how to have conversations with teachers that would leverage improvement efforts.

Prior to getting into classrooms and in order to begin to calibrate collective understanding, we briefly looked at some definitions of *engagement* in the research literature:

- Relationships between students and adults in schools and among students themselves (Williams, 2003)
- Time-on-task behaviors (Brophy & And, 1983)
- Students' willingness to participate in routine school activities, such as attending classes, submitting required work, and following teachers' directions (Natriello, 1984)
- Students' use of cognitive and metacognitive strategies to monitor and guide their learning processes (Pintrich & De Groot, 1990)

We also asked the leadership team to consider what Schlechty (2002) had to say about how students might respond to school tasks:

- *Authentic engagement.* The task, activity, or work the student is assigned or encouraged to undertake is associated with a result or outcome that has clear meaning and relatively immediate value to the student—for example, reading a book on a topic of personal interest to the student or to get access to information that the student needs to solve a problem of real interest to him or her.

- *Ritual engagement.* The immediate end of the assigned work has little or no inherent meaning or direct value to the student but the student associates it with extrinsic outcomes and results that are of value—for example, reading a book in order to pass a test or to earn grades needed to be accepted at college.

- *Passive compliance.* The student is willing to expend whatever effort is needed to avoid negative consequences although he or she sees little meaning in the tasks assigned or the consequences of doing those tasks.

- *Retreatism.* The student is disengaged from the tasks, expends no energy in attempting to comply with the demands of the task, but does not act in ways that disrupt others and does not try to substitute other activities for the assigned task.

- *Rebellion.* The student summarily refuses to do the task assigned, acts in ways that disrupt others, or attempts to substitute tasks and activities to which he or she is committed in lieu of those assigned or supported by the school and by the teacher.

Leaders had an opportunity to discuss these research findings and ideas in light of their own standards for engagement and in light of what they actually see in classrooms. As in many districts we work with, this leadership team believed that most of their students were either passive, compliant, or ritually engaged. As is the case in virtually all of the districts we work with, these educators want their students to be motivated, self-aware learners who take an active part in their own learning.

Leaders also participated as learners in a shared experience and debriefed the process in light of the quality of their own engagement. The following list synthesizes the participants' descriptions of the qualities of their own engagement with the shared experience:

- We were expected to function in the large group and had the responsibility to share our ideas.

- Throughout the activity, we were synthesizing, analyzing, developing, and defending our ideas.

- We had ownership for our learning and learned from and valued one another (navigating conversations, listening, agreeing, and disagreeing).

- Our thinking and experiences were affirmed, valued, and were central to the learning experience.

- The CEL teacher made decisions and used instructional approaches in ways that intentionally supported her instructional purposes.

With some emerging ability to talk about specific aspects of engagement among the district, school, and teacher leaders, we wanted to help this leadership team extrapolate from their collective experience and discussion about engagement to create concrete guidance for our upcoming learning walkthroughs as a leadership team. Table 5.2 shows how to build a bridge to application from their shared learning experience. Because these educators had little experience working

Table 5.2.
Application of Leaders' Shared Learning to Classroom Observations

OBSERVING STUDENT LEARNING	5D GUIDING QUESTIONS
Students are *expected* to function in the large group and have the *responsibility* to share their ideas.	What specific strategies and structures are in place to facilitate participation and meaning making by all students (for example, small-group work, partner talk, writing, and so on)? Do all students have access to participation in the work of the group? Why or why not? How is the participation distributed?
Students are *engaged* throughout the lesson or activity, synthesizing, analyzing, developing, and defending ideas.	What is the level and quality of the intellectual work in which students are engaged (for example, factual recall, procedure, inference, analysis, and metacognition)?
Students have *ownership* for their learning and learn from and value one another (navigating conversations, listening, agreeing, and disagreeing).	How and to what extent do the systems and routines of the classroom facilitate student ownership and independence? How and to what extent do the systems and routines reflect values of community, inclusivity, equity, and accountability for learning? *(continued)*

Table 5.2.

(continued)

OBSERVING STUDENT LEARNING	5D GUIDING QUESTIONS
Students' thinking and experiences are affirmed, valued, and are central to the learning experiences.	How does the teacher's understanding of each student as a learner inform how the teacher pushes for depth and stretches the boundaries of student thinking?
The teacher makes decisions and uses instructional approaches in ways that intentionally support his or her instructional purposes.	If students were to accomplish the purpose set by the teacher, what would students know and be able to do? What evidence do you observe of students' learning in relation to the lesson purpose? How is the purpose connected to external standards for what students should know and be able to do at this age or grade level?

together as a collective team, the CEL team wanted to model classroom observations as an inquiry rather than a checklist of things to look for. Taking the language that was used to describe the shared experience the leaders had, we aligned questions from the Five Dimensions of Teaching and Learning with what they hoped to observe in their learning walkthroughs. The guiding questions were intended to foster a focused conversation about what was observed during the classroom visits and provide a scaffold for the leaders to bridge from describing what they saw and heard to an emerging analysis of their observations.

Although this leadership team knew that conversations with teachers would be an extension of their classroom observations, they also knew that they had to learn to have a different kind of conversation with classroom teachers and among themselves than they were accustomed to having. The newly appointed coaches needed to learn how to talk with classroom teachers in a way that could influence teachers' practice and they needed to learn how to have conversations with building and district administrators to develop a coaching plan. Administrators needed to learn how to have conversations that were not like the evaluation conferences they were used to having and they needed to learn how to talk with their newly appointed coaches about supporting instructional practices. This team of central office supervisors, principals, and coaches understood that they had to adapt, develop, and hone their knowledge and skills among themselves first.

In order to develop their own capacity to observe, analyze, and discuss classroom observations, we guided this leadership team on learning how to conduct walkthroughs. This experience was an opportunity to try on description (versus interpretation) of what was observed, to use descriptive classroom observations as data for analysis, to reflect on what was observed in relation to the qualities of engagement they had agreed on, and an opportunity to have conversations and pose questions as inquiry. During the learning walkthroughs the leadership team could focus on the development of these skills as well as develop shared language and understanding. Remembering experiences such as engaging as learners themselves and observing teaching and learning in order to come to some shared understanding of engagement was new to the members of this team. They were more accustomed to wordsmithing documents and talking *about* the language in the document versus *using* the language in the context of teaching and learning to arrive at a collective understanding. With the following essential questions that guided this CEL-district partnership for an entire year, we could have spent our time exclusively in a large room hammering out detailed plans and agreements:

- What is our vision for quality teaching and learning?
- How will we develop and hone our own habits of leadership practice in order to lead our district's instructional improvement agenda?
- How will we develop and align our practices and routines in order to create a system to support our work?

Instead, we intentionally used the experience of the learning walkthroughs to cultivate a common vision and shared understanding, to provide leaders with actual data from classrooms in order to ground subsequent conversations, and to develop the practices that could influence the system as a whole. These practices included getting into classrooms on a regular basis in order to study teaching and learning, using classroom data to drive the analysis of teaching and learning, cultivating the kind of conversations that have the potential to lead to inquiry with classroom teachers, and creating the expectation that teaching and leadership practice is public and open for observation and critique.

We asked this team of leaders to consider what they wanted to accomplish with their responses to classroom observations, whether verbally or in writing, and with individual teachers and the entire staff at their schools. They needed to think about what needs to be communicated *now,* for whom, and in what ways. We also asked them to consider teachers' current understanding and expectations of classroom visits. The letter shown in Exhibit 5.2 was sent by the assistant superintendent, Brenda, to all the teachers in the district. You will note that she reiterates the district vision, explains what the administrative team is learning, and why they are not necessarily providing feedback to individual teachers

EXHIBIT 5.2. ASSISTANT SUPERINTENDENT LETTER TO DISTRICT TEACHERS

Dear Teachers and Administrative Colleagues,

As most of you are aware, this year we have engaged in a project working with the Center for Educational Leadership (CEL) through the University of Washington. CEL's mission, much like our own, is to overcome and close the achievement gaps that divide students along racial and economic lines. We view this collaboration as a long-term commitment. We also believe strongly that one of the most powerful ways a district can improve student learning is to ensure our teachers receive the instructional support they want and need.

During this first phase of our work, I'm sure that you have noticed that the administrative team and teaching and learning facilitators (TLFs) have been practicing *walkthroughs* or *learning walks,* as they are sometimes called. The purposes of this activity are as follows:

- To build effective instructional leaders across the district
- For administrators and TLFs to practice and hone our skills of observation
- To learn to collect data without interpreting or judging the information

(continued)

This process, much like working on reliability and scoring student work, takes practice to gain agreement on what we are seeing. We are not yet ready to provide individual feedback to teachers. Instead, the focus is to provide more general feedback to staff that purposely does not single out anyone.

As a leadership team and after visiting many classrooms we know that our students learn in a very respectful environment and that our teachers work hard to adapt their instruction to best meet students' needs. Our visits to your classrooms also prompted us to wonder about a couple of things:

1. How can students be nurtured toward *independence* in their learning?

2. How do students show what they are thinking and understanding? How do we know?

As a leadership team, we will be thinking about these questions.

The next phase is to provide teachers with relevant and meaningful feedback as you all work to achieve your own personal instructional goals. As your leadership team gets better and more aligned with how we observe teaching and learning, we can better support you and your work with students as we all continue moving together toward our collective mission.

It is an honor to work alongside all of you.
Brenda

---

at this point. She does pose a couple of questions that the administrative team wondered about—questions that plant the seed for collective inquiry into problems of practice germane to the complex work of teaching.

In the last part of Brenda's letter, she poses a couple of questions that the administrative team wondered about as they began their initial learning walks as a team. These questions were the result of many classroom observations and subsequent analysis of classroom evidence as the administrative team calibrated their collective understanding of *student engagement*. Although not intended to provide feedback to individual teachers, questions such as the ones posed in Brenda's letter are examples of an honest response to classroom observations. This district leadership team made sure to share what they learned with teachers along the way, tilling the soil for further inquiry.

We have explored a case of a district at the beginning stage of developing shared understanding. We illustrated the processes we used with the district to support the goal of developing shared understanding as well as new ways of working together as a leadership team. As we continue to work with this district, we will build on their emerging shared understanding about student engagement as well as their capacity to engage in learning walkthroughs and collective inquiry. The habit of routine classroom visits in order to more deeply understand the nature of teaching and learning across the district, the discipline of observing without judging, and their growing capacity to more precisely discuss teaching and learning can now be leveraged in service of more sophisticated orchestration of teachers' professional learning. After a year of sharpening their vision for teaching and learning, developing the practices of observation without interpretation, and talking about their observations in increasingly evidence-specific ways, this district leadership team began to see the through-line from the classroom to their leadership.

ORGANIZING THINKING: A MIDDLE SCHOOL CASE

"There is so much I *could* say," noted Larry, a middle school principal after observing in a sixth-grade classroom, "but what *do* I say? How do I determine what is important to highlight with a teacher after an observation that is not an evaluation?" Similar to most of the principals we work with, Larry wanted to be able to both push teachers' practice and develop trust with his teachers. Additionally, Larry worried that he did not know enough about the content (mathematics, reading, writing, and so on), the teaching of that content, and how students learned that content in rigorous ways. Although Larry was getting smart about the teaching and learning of reading and writing alongside his teachers each time the consultant came to support the school's learning focus of literacy, he was pretty sure he didn't know more than the teachers he was supervising. Larry realized that the school had to do a much better job teaching children literacy than they currently were doing: "At least now I know what I should be thinking about: the rigor of the reading and writing tasks students engage in, the repertoire of strategies a teacher uses, and how students engage in the thinking work and how they communicate their thinking. I know that our schoolwide professional development in literacy will continue, that grade levels are looking at the tasks they assign students along with the resulting student work, and I know I can continue to communicate the urgency of *why literacy, why now* at staff meetings. I just want to figure out how to organize my thoughts right after an observation with a teacher and say something productive! Where should I start? What questions should I ask? How should I offer suggestions for next steps for the teacher?"

In Chapter Six we will lay out a more extensive example of how this principal uses classroom observations to inform his decision making about supporting individual teacher learning, small-group learning, and schoolwide professional learning. For now, we will focus on how Larry could organize his thinking for thoughtful feedback to a teacher he just observed.

Larry entered J.B.'s classroom just as the lesson began. The script shown in Exhibit 5.3 is the set of notes Larry took when he observed the teacher, J.B.,

EXHIBIT 5.3. LARRY'S SCRIPT

[T = teacher; . . . . = could not hear]

[Students are seated together at the front of the room, facing the T, who refers to a chart as he talks to the students.]

T: . . . . and we will work on our conversations. We're not having rich discussions; only a few voices are heard, but you all have great ideas and I want to hear more. We tend to speak in one- to two-word sentences but we've been talking about extending our ideas, stretching them out . . . . want to talk in paragraphs and essays . . . . We have the idea in this class that all ideas are valid or right, that all ideas are equal . . . . Remember last week, when we were talking about Martin Luther King Jr. and arguing about our ideas, the one idea we had. We didn't have a deep conversation . . . . we have a "you have your idea and I have mine" syndrome. Turn and talk about these observations I just made about our class discussions. [All students turn and talk when prompted and the T listens in to a couple of partners as they talk. After a minute, T asks for the students' attention and they quickly quiet down.]

(continued)

T: I heard some interesting things . . . . keep in mind, we want to bring these new discussion habits back to the "you have your idea and I have mine" . . . . Here are some beliefs about interpretation . . . . and where sometimes we go astray. Some people believe there is one interpretation of a story or poem. Others believe there are many interpretations for a poem or story. Today, we are going to find a balance between these two ideas. As a class today we will find out what the most justifiable interpretation is. Interpretation becomes justifiable when we provide evidence for our thinking about what the most justifiable interpretation is. Our goals as readers today are [T reads from a chart]:

- All voices heard

- Invite conversation

- Try on new ideas and determine which interpretation is the most justifiable by evidence, evidence, evidence

[T reads the poem "This is just to Say" by William Carlos Williams, with the text projected onto a large screen.]

---

during his sixth-grade language arts lesson. The notes represent about seven minutes of a twenty-minute observation.

Larry took good notes when he observed in the classroom and in Table 5.3 you will see how this principal's wonderings hold the potential to become

Table 5.3.
Responding to Classroom Observations

FROM OBSERVATION TO RESPONSE	LARRY'S EXAMPLE
Noticing *Specific* data *related to teaching and learning gathered during an observation*	Students seated together, away from their desks, facing the teacher. Students turn and talk when prompted by the teacher (J.B.). J.B. listens in to a student conversation.
Wondering *Based on what I saw and heard, I'm curious about . . .*	What J.B. considers the potential for student conversations? How does he ultimately want students to engage with their own thinking, with the content, and with one another? I *(continued)*

	wonder if J.B. is satisfied with what he hears students saying? What is he listening for? How does the way he listens to student talk allow him to assess student understanding?
Analysis *Using what I know about what student learning would look like in the ideal in relation to what I've noticed and wondered . . .*	I wonder whether engagement in learning through talk is accountable—to the learning community, to knowledge in the discipline, and to rigorous thinking. In J.B.'s class, students knew the routine of turning to a partner to talk and those who shared their ideas seemed comfortable doing so. The students seemed really accustomed to this routine and had things to say to their partners. This tells me that J.B. has supported the level of talk that does exist. I assume J.B. understands that engagement is much more than students staying on task or students having the opportunity to talk and that authentic engagement must provide opportunities for students to engage in academic discourse in order to deepen their thinking and conceptual understanding. I'd like to know more about J.B.'s beliefs about literary analysis in general and his students in particular.
Developing a Theory to Test *Based on my analysis and my plan to learn more about J.B.'s vision for student learning, the potential he envisions for the student conversations, and how he understands the role of talk in student learning, I think that . . .*	J.B. has a long-term goal in mind for his students as thinkers, communicators, and how to engage them in literary analysis. J.B. is intentional and thoughtful about releasing responsibility for students to take on increasingly sophisticated conversations.
Questions I Might Ask the Teacher *Based on the theory I'd like to test, I will ask J.B. . . .*	How do you decide the content of partner talk and how do you decide when to have students talk to partners? What is your long-term plan for your students' partner talk? How would you like your students to be running their own conversations? How do you want them to be pushing each other's thinking by June?

authentic questions and responses to the teacher. Larry might use any of his wonderings as an entry point to engage the teacher in honest conversation about the teaching and learning he observed. Each wondering has the potential to prompt the teacher's thinking and reflection and will allow the principal to learn more about the teacher's beliefs, knowledge, and skills. The principal can then consider how to support the teacher's growth. Larry knows that the immediate next steps for the teacher should align with learning goals that are more long range. For instance, supporting a teacher to respond differently to student comments by suggesting some open-ended questioning techniques connects to the more complex and deep shift in how and why we listen to student responses.

Table 5.3 illustrates a process that will help Larry organize his thinking after classroom observations. You will see how Larry uses what he noticed about teaching and learning as a basis for his thinking. You will also see how Larry frames his questions for the teacher as theories about the teacher's decision making he would like to test. This process for organizing thinking into a response rests on the assumption that the teacher has the best intentions for his students and is doing what he knows how to do.

We have found that when principals can organize their thinking into a process that allows them to make sense of what they observed and that allows them to engage in co-inquiry with a teacher, the conversations are more satisfying for both the principal and the teacher. The process illustrated in Exhibit 5.3 will be revisited in subsequent chapters, including Chapter Seven, where the reader will see how the work of instructional coaching uses a similar process. Indeed, we believe that instructional leaders—no matter if their role is that of coach, principal, or district office personnel—all use this process to organize their thinking.

CONCLUSION

This chapter used two cases to illustrate responses to classroom observations after a walkthrough. In the first case, a newly formed district leadership team came together to make sense of their district's new instructional framework, calibrating their understanding of student engagement and developing new ways of working together in the process. In the second case, we examined how a middle school principal organized his thinking for how he would respond to his classroom observation. In both cases, we explored the idea of taking an inquiry stance in order to foster the kind of responses that will promote collective inquiry. We asserted that responding to classroom observations should take into account both short-term and long-range learning goals and that a response that emanates from an inquiry stance has the potential to nourish a school culture that is hard on the work, respectful with each other. We also asserted that responding to classroom observations encompasses more than feedback to teachers. It should also connect the through-line from a vision for student learning and teaching practices, to observations, to professional learning opportunities that support teachers' professional growth, and finally to cultivate a school culture with honest conversation about the state of teaching and learning. In Chapter Six, we will explore how classroom observations are the basis for leaders' orchestration of professional learning. We will examine more closely the relationship between the short-term and long-term goals of professional learning and how instructional leaders might consider the development of a school's culture alongside teachers' professional development.

DISCUSSION QUESTIONS

- How do your own responses to classroom observations foster honest conversations and the kind of co-inquiry that is hard on the work, respectful of one another?

- To what extent does your feedback explicitly connect the through-line from classroom observations, teachers' professional learning needs, and the school improvement agenda to a vision of student learning?

chapter SIX

Orchestrating Professional Learning

Providing ongoing learning for teachers' continual development is challenging for leaders because it not only requires building enthusiasm and agreement toward a long-term goal, but it also requires positioning resources strategically. We have spoken previously about the Center for Educational Leadership's two-part leadership equation. First, leaders need to understand what powerful teaching and learning looks and sounds like. Leaders cannot lead what they do not know! Second, leaders need to understand how to *lead* for instructional improvement—targeting and aligning resources toward strategic professional development. In 1998 Florio and Knapp asserted that powerful professional development

- Focuses on challenging, standards-based teaching and learning in particular subject areas and is guided by a vision of how all students can engage in that learning
- Embeds professional learning in the context of the school and the needs of each school as a system with its own integrity
- Balances individual and school priorities in determining the content of professional development activities

- Is grounded in principles of adult learning within professional, collegial communities

- Supports and reinforces new roles and responsibilities for teachers and principals as learners, leaders, designers, team players, managers of change, and master coordinators

- Supports educators' learning through an infrastructure that is more peer based than hierarchical and whenever possible at the work site

Although research has told us about the organizational conditions, the qualities of a professional community necessary for continual learning, and the role that vision and standards play in teachers' professional learning, how leaders go about developing the structures, resources, and social context that will engender such learning is often underestimated. Knowing about *what* teachers need in order to improve their practice does not automatically translate into knowing *how* to do it.

This chapter will explore how leaders orchestrate ongoing professional learning and further connect the through-line from their observations of teaching and learning to their leadership actions. We maintain that the onus is on leaders to cultivate and sustain the adult learning opportunities in their schools and districts whereby teachers can develop their practice. Although leaders need to rely on the extant expertise in their schools and districts and leverage this expertise toward increasingly sophisticated practice, if students are not learning it is ultimately the leader's responsibility. Leaders may have the authority and resources to affect teaching and learning but they may not have developed the instructional leadership knowledge and skills necessary for ongoing instructional improvement. Leading for instructional improvement requires its own technical and adaptive expertise. Instructional leaders need a trained eye (and ear) for observing teaching and learning. This presumes some level of subject area and pedagogical content knowledge. They also need to be able to label areas for improvement and to imagine alternative practices that are likely to produce better results. Additionally, instructional leaders must create an environment in which educators are hungry to learn how to improve their work and in which coaching for improvement is accepted as a norm. Collecting data on teaching and learning is moot unless educators have a strategy and a means to improve it. Data alone cannot enlighten practice. Ultimately, instructional leaders need to have an explicit theory of action and be able to create and communicate the theory of action as a narrative for the rest of the people in the organization. Narrating the story line of instructional improvement efforts reinforces the urgency of improvement and connects the dots among the various entry points of improvement efforts. Each teacher in a school has to see herself in the school's story line of improvement or the improvement efforts will be interpreted as disconnected, irrelevant, or a passing fancy. We believe that instructional leaders need to connect all the dots among the theory of action for improvement, the strategies employed, and an illustration of where the school has been and where it is going.

LEADERS AS CONDUCTORS

In a 2008 report on one of CEL's district partnerships, the researchers noted that leading and implementing complex change processes in schools and districts is like conducting an orchestra (Van Lare, Yoon, & Gallucci, 2008). They note that (1) leaders must develop a finely tuned ear for (or have expertise in) instructional practice in order to recognize needs and shape the learning experiences of others in the system and (2) educational leaders are called on to grapple with the nuances of conducting or leading the overall reform effort. The researchers studied the coordination and leveraging of learning and change in a complex setting and described it as *orchestration*. In the first part of this chapter, we will draw heavily from the Van Lare, Yoon, and Gallucci report and use it in conjunction with examples from various CEL partnerships to illustrate the ways in which instructional leaders orchestrate professional learning. Later in this chapter, we will illustrate how one middle school principal thinks about the orchestration of professional learning. Although each school setting is unique, the ideas explored here are transferable to any context.

Van Lare, Yoon, and Gallucci (2008) describe four dimensions of orchestration, adapted from Zander (2000):

- Being a silent conductor
- Strategizing
- Engaging hearts and minds
- Investing in or developing leadership in others

These authors note the parallels between a principal's leadership of a school staff and a conductor's skill at pulling together an orchestra:

> First, the conductor has to have the right players in the orchestra; the conductor needs to know each player's strengths and abilities in order to place them in the right seats and sections. Each musician has a part to play, and each section is essential to the sound of the whole. The conductor's vision for the music needs to be communicated to all of the orchestra members— and the conductor must have that finely tuned ear in order to judge the quality of each player's effort and performance, as well as of the overall music produced. Although it's up to the conductor to engender engagement and excellence from orchestra musicians, the individual members need to practice and master their parts; the material can inspire or bore; the quality of instruments and acoustics in the concert hall also matter. But, for the most part, the dynamics of "orchestrating" the group and the music lie in the hands of the person on the riser, with the baton in hand. (Van Lare, Yoon, & Gallucci, 2008, p. 3)

Being a Silent Conductor

Instructional leaders are not actually silent—in fact, the ways in which they communicate and use their leadership voice are critical—but the silent conductor listens. The silent conductor is reflective and engaging, developing the skills and passion of individual members. The silent conductor can orchestrate because she knows individual members of the school team. Instructional leaders orchestrate when they do the following:

- Coordinate activities and people (with purpose)
- Connect goals of different activities, people, and resources (how different activities, resources, and participants fit together to achieve goals)
- Create platforms for staff members to develop skills and be seen as leaders by peers
- Clarify and follow up on expectations
- Build norms of participation in work
- Encourage staff members toward ownership of work
- Fine-tune goals, expectations, and content of work

A studio-residency example from one of our district partnerships will help illustrate the idea of an instructional leader being a silent conductor. In 2003, we introduced the studio-residency model for embedded professional development for teachers, coaches, principals, and district level leaders, in which a classroom (often more than one) is selected to be used as a learning site with the CEL consultant and several other teachers. The studio teacher's classroom is used on an ongoing basis and the teachers who participate as residents are also consistent. The classroom is not a model but, much like an artist's studio, it provides a place to explore current and best thinking. The theory of action that underlies the studio-residency model is threefold: (1) it allows teachers to try on new ideas and put theory into practice with students right away; (2) the job-embedded learning encompasses content, coaching, and processes for leading the learning in between studio-residency cycles; (3) it creates a space for teachers to be public with their practice, to learn new ways of interacting together as professionals, and to develop collaborative relationship skills and processes. At best, the studio-residency model for professional development is not a series of events that occur during the course of the school year. Rather, it is but one strategic learning opportunity for a school staff and is interconnected with learning walks, coaching, staff, grade and department meetings, and other professional development opportunities.

Table 6.1 shows how this district expected a school to participate if the school was using a studio-residency model. Notice the clarity of expectations for the participants for before, during, and after the studio residency.

This example of the before, during, and after expectations for the studio-residency team participants has some underlying assumptions: that the focus for the studio residency is explicitly linked to the school's improvement goals, that the participants already have a learning stance and will be public with their learning, and that although the CEL consultant brings a great deal of expertise to the studio residency, she or he is supporting the work owned by the school. We should point out here that the column on the far right of the studio-residency expectations does not have to say *CEL consultant*. This column is ultimately about the expertise that is needed in order to lead and guide this job-embedded professional development. This expertise can be provided by internal or external experts—the key being that this person brings a level of expertise necessary to support the teachers' professional learning.

Table 6.1.
Studio and Resident Team Expectations

BEFORE

STUDIO AND RESIDENT TEACHERS	INSTRUCTIONAL FACILITATOR	PRINCIPAL	DISTRICT OFFICE	CEL CONSULTANT

• Meet with your instructional facilitator to discuss the focus of the work for the studio cycle
 	
• Studio teacher to participate in the e-mail conversation or conference call with the consultant and instructional facilitator about what has been tried and results observed (at least five days prior to the studio day)
 	
• Be prepared to engage in a planning conversation about
  • Identifying necessary materials (that is, texts, documents, student work, and so on)
  • Articulating current content focus, needs of students, goals or outcomes of student work, and so on
	• Meet with the studio teacher to discuss the focus of the work
	
	• Initiate and participate in the e-mail conversation or conference call between the studio teacher and the consultant about what has been tried and results observed (at least five days prior to the studio day)
	
	• Communicate and plan with the principal about
	  • Subs
	  • Schedules
	
	• In consultation with the studio teacher, principal, and consultant, prepare an agenda for the day including goals and schedule. Collect any data or evidence the team gathered from their formative assessments
	
	• Communicate with resident teachers about the focus for the day
		• Consult with the studio teacher and instructional facilitator prior to the e-mail conversation or conference call with the consultant
		
		• Remove obstacles and scheduling roadblocks to facilitate the learning of the group
		
		• Communicate and plan with the instructional facilitator about
		  • Subs
		  • Schedules
			• Be knowledgeable of collaboration (receive e-mails) between the school staff and the CEL consultant; contribute to the discussion as appropriate
			
			• Ask clarifying questions
			
			• Communicate with buildings which members will be participating from district office
				• Set up conference call and respond to school e-mails prompting thinking and focus
				
				• Initiate deep reflection in the planning process
				
				• Assist in the completion of the agenda
				
				• Be transparent in thinking
				
				• Prepare articles, protocols, and professional development ideas to share with buildings

STUDIO AND RESIDENT TEACHERS	INSTRUCTIONAL FACILITATOR	PRINCIPAL	DISTRICT OFFICE	CEL CONSULTANT
• Participate throughout the consultation day • Articulate thinking and decision making; share knowledge of students as learners • Bring data and samples of student work to the consultant visit as decided at last studio cycle • Ask questions and ask for support as needed throughout • Develop at the end of the cycle an implementation plan and the evidence that will be gathered to determine effect on student learning	• Participate throughout the consultation day • Model thinking, ask questions • With the knowledge base about the teacher's strengths and skills, facilitate or prompt the teacher around the work • Focus on and identify the coaching moves being modeled by the consultant through job-alike conversations with other instructional facilitators • Analyze the strengths and needs of the teacher to apply to your further coaching work • Develop at the end of the cycle an implementation plan and the evidence that will be gathered to determine effect on student learning • Collect anecdotal notes regarding process, coaching moves, and content of the session for debrief and reflection	• Frame the work (opening and closing—facilitate all voices in articulating their learning) • Participate throughout the studio day • Facilitate the identification of next steps with action plans, timelines, and responsibilities • Help facilitate the group dynamics • Develop at the end of the cycle an implementation plan and the evidence that will be gathered to determine effect on student learning	• Participate throughout the consultation day • Model thinking, asking questions • With the knowledge base of their strengths and skills, facilitate or prompt the instructional facilitator or principal to accomplish the work • Focus on and identify the coaching moves being modeled by the consultant to apply to the work; articulate the coaching moves observed during the visit • Observe for and analyze the strengths and needs of the instructional facilitator and principal to apply to further work	• Demonstrate lessons with the eye on building independence • Provide and support buildings with material suggestions • Be flexible with the choice of materials based on the needs of the building • Work collaboratively with the teacher and instructional facilitator in designing the instruction for the day • Facilitate and guide new learning about the work before, during, and after the lesson • Introduce pertinent reading or resources to further the learning

(continued)

Table 6.1.
(continued)

| STUDIO AND RESIDENT TEACHERS | INSTRUCTIONAL FACILITATOR | DURING | | |
		PRINCIPAL	DISTRICT OFFICE	CEL CONSULTANT
			• Develop at the end of the cycle an implementation plan for how to support the principal and instructional facilitator in between the cycles	• Articulate rationale for the teaching moves and the decisions made with references to other educators in the literacy field • Know and operate under the gradual release model • Be transparent in thinking • Support development of implementation plans

AFTER

STUDIO AND RESIDENT TEACHERS	INSTRUCTIONAL FACILITATOR	PRINCIPAL	DISTRICT OFFICE	CEL CONSULTANT
• Work with your instructional facilitator and principal in designing opportunities to share the work with the staff as appropriate • Be open to having interested teachers observe the work they are learning through this process • Act on the next steps identified during the process • Work with the instructional facilitator to plan for upcoming consultant visits • Meet with studio and resident team and instructional facilitator for one hour per week in between cycles • Communicate with the consultant as needed regarding questions, reflections, or challenges and successes in between cycles • Monitor and reflect on work (through anecdotal notes and reflections) in between cycles to be able to share with team	• Collaborate with the studio teacher and principal in designing opportunities to share the work with the staff • Act on the instructional next steps identified during the process with district coach and teacher • Try out and approximate coaching moves identified • Work with the teacher and principal to plan for upcoming consultant visits • Collaborate with the principal in connecting the studio work with other school initiatives	• Collaborate with the instructional facilitator and studio teachers in designing opportunities to share the work with the staff • Act on the next steps identified during the process • Ensure that systems are in place to continue the work in between cycles (classroom observations, walkthroughs) • Apply learning • Collaborate with the instructional facilitator in connecting the studio work with other school initiatives	• Act on the next steps identified during the process • Ensure that systems are in place to continue the work (classroom observations, meet with principals, instructional facilitators, and so on) • Give feedback to the principal and instructional facilitator based on strengths and needs observed • Work with administrative team to make connections with the CEL consultant	• Act on the next steps identified during the process • Be transparent in thinking • Continue dialogue with teacher, coach, and principal to carry on the learning

Helping leaders develop their instructional leadership expertise means helping them understand what it means to apply learning, to act on next steps, and to ensure systems are in place. Although leaders are participants in the studio residency—learning the content and processes side by side with teachers—they also need to engage as leaders. One of our CEL colleagues is fond of saying that when leaders participate in professional development with teachers, they have to think in terms of the "double word score," as in the game of Scrabble. Leaders need to learn the content and processes teachers are learning while simultaneously learning about the teachers as learners and potential leaders. The astute instructional leader is (1) observing teachers' participation in order to make sense of teachers' current understandings and (2) observing how teachers interact with one another. The instructional leader is judicious about when and how she or he participates, knowing that listening to teachers and making sense of what they are learning and how they engage as colleagues is crucial. Instructional leaders need to listen deeply and also take responsibility for opening and closing the studio-residency sessions and setting the context for the work in order to put the professional development into the context of the school's teaching and learning goals. For example, the norms for studio-residency sessions as shown in Exhibit 6.1 were initiated by

EXHIBIT 6.1. STUDIO-RESIDENCY NORMS FOR CREATING AND SUSTAINING A COLLABORATIVE CULTURE

In order to create this culture we are committed to

- Ensuring that all voices are heard
- Setting focused, achievable goals
- Actively participating in the studio work (before, during, and after)
- Being present
- Learning and participating
- Engaging in dialogue around both content and process
- Following through on our commitments
- Maintaining a positive approach to change

one school principal and developed by the studio-residency team prior to their first session.

Instructional leaders understand that creating and sustaining a collaborative culture ensures a professional learning environment in which teachers can collectively learn from and with their practice. The development of such a culture is not something that is done first and then followed by the collective examination of practices. Instructional leaders pay attention to the development of school culture as both a *vehicle* and an *outcome* of collective examination of practices. There are various entry points to the collective examination of practices. A school staff might focus on lesson planning and implementation, assessment of student learning, or the use of shared materials and resources. These could all become focal points for schoolwide professional development or grade-level or department meetings—but only if instructional leaders support the quality of the professional community, according to Gallimore, Ermeling, Saunders, and Goldenberg (2009):

> Reorienting existing settings to support teacher inquiry means changing an adaptation that has evolved over time including taken-for-granted assumptions about the purposes of the commonplace, such as grade-level or department meetings. . . . Even in schools and districts committed to continuous improvement through inquiry, including those that have seen achievement gains, maintaining that focus in grade-level/ departmental settings remains a constant challenge. (pp. 550–551)

Teachers need "intensive, focused opportunities to experiment with aspects of practice" (Grossman & McDonald, 2008, pp. 189–190) in order to understand a causal connection between their instructional practice and student outcomes; leaders need to ensure that such opportunities exist.

Notice in Exhibit 6.2 what this high school principal does with the studio-residency agenda and memo she wrote for the teachers participating in a math studio residency, the school's instructional coach, and the three consultants who had various opportunities to work with the staff. You will see that the principal is not silent but that she has learned the strengths and needs of the teachers in relation to the teaching of mathematics and she seizes on the consultants' expertise. As the principal reiterates expectations about participation in the studio residency, she also names teachers' strengths and needs—which are public and articulated in relation to the content and process of the

EXHIBIT 6.2. MATH STUDIO-RESIDENCY AGENDA MONDAY AND TUESDAY, MARCH 3 AND 4

Purpose

- To develop the conditions that promote students' mathematical understanding

Outcomes

- To know how to assess what students are learning
- To learn how to plan instruction that promotes student thinking and discourse
- To know how to anticipate expected student responses and identify questions or statements that will elicit those responses

Schedule

	Monday: Periods 1, 3, 5, 7	Tuesday: Periods 2, 3, 4, 6
7:25–9:05	• Kathy (consultant), Max (district's high school director), and Stacy (principal) observe • Gloria, Paul, and Mary to use analyzing trends in student thinking data recording tool. Debrief to identify progress and needs.	• Algebra 1: Gloria to try modeled lesson from yesterday • Coaching from Kathy • Paul observing • Two substitute teachers needed to cover Gloria's and Paul's classes
9:10–9:50	• Studio-residency goal setting with three math teachers: Gloria, Paul, and Antonio	• Plan subsequent unit with Gloria, Paul, and Antonio
9:55–11:35	• ELL Algebra: Modeled lesson in Gloria's class with Gloria and Paul observing	• Plan subsequent unit with Paul, Gloria, Antonio, and Mary
11:35–12:15	• Duty-free lunch	• Duty-free lunch
12:20–2:05	• Algebra I: Modeled lesson in Gloria's class with Gloria and Paul observing	• Continue planning subsequent unit with Gloria and Paul
2:15–3:15	• Debrief modeled lessons • Plan for Gloria to do the teaching for Tuesday	• Debrief studio residency and plan next steps with the team

Memo to Consultants and Studio-Residency Teachers from the Principal

Thank you again to our three math consultants, Wilma, Linda, and Kathy, for the smart and thoughtful energy you place on the embedded coaching work with our school's math team.

In this memo, I want to establish a context for our work next week and be clear in communicating our needs and outcomes so that there is a seamless transition in our work from consultant to consultant.

Our math culture is stronger in Gloria's room, progressing in Antonio's, and fragile in Paul's. Thus, we are tweaking our studio residency to build on the strengths of Gloria's math culture, Paul's content knowledge, and Antonio's seniority at our school.

Let me start by sharing what we have worked on so far this year. Wilma worked with the team this summer and early fall on three main areas:

- To develop competencies that demonstrate a cohesive build through each math level based on Conley's *College Knowledge,* grade-level expectations, and our state's essential academic learning requirements to co-construct these outcomes

- To identify gaps in students' mathematical understanding and build in skill development and daily routines into the curriculum (especially for Gloria's work)

- To use probing questions to develop student's sociomathematical discourse and to assess students' mathematical understanding (for Paul specifically; Wilma also worked on classroom norms of thinking and learning together)

Kathy and Linda worked with the team in early fall as well and focused on two main areas:

- To know what strategies were essential to the trajectory of the math unit in the long run and that will affect how we inquire with students in order to listen for the strategies they currently use

- To leverage students' understandings and misconceptions in order to build them into the subsequent lesson

(continued)

Anna, our instructional coach, worked in a coaching cycle with Paul on two main areas:

- To develop a culture of mathematical thinking through clear, consistent directions and follow through in holding students accountable to the group's thinking and talk
- To develop ways for students to navigate their learning based on mathematical thinking and learning, not on affective behaviors

Based on the work to this point, we will focus on four main areas:

- To help hone our listening ear and to further develop curiosity about student thinking; to interview students focusing in on assessing before moving to advancing questions and statements. This needs to be modeled but not using exhaustive protocol sheets.
- To assess students' skill gaps and develop daily routines that support skill acquisition while exploring the ideas and concepts from the unit
- To continue to identify the essential learnings for each unit and prioritize and identify areas for differentiation and possible misconceptions
- To develop authentic cooperative groups that navigate mathematical discourse and learning with one another

Knowing that we work with several consultants and coaches we need to keep processes and protocols simple and easily accessible and replicable in our own school context. Therefore, I think we need to simplify the amount and types of protocols we use to organize our thinking and conversations. For example, to assess student thinking we will simply use a T-chart, as follows:

Student Gets/Does Not Get	Evidence and Implications

It is essential that we also use similar language to articulate our thinking and work. Our team needs to calibrate using a language that is comfortable and authentic for us. Here, we use terms similar to those from our literacy work to describe our math work. We talk in the meeting area for the *launch,* we *explore* in groups and during independent work time and often just come back together for a *share* versus a *plenary.* When we listen in and script students' talk, we say we are *listening in* or *pushing in* to conversation. When working one-on-one, we *confer* rather than *probe.* Yet, when we question we probe, so it's all pretty relative.

I am excited to continue this journey together. I look forward to learning about and thinking together as we explore math.

See you Monday and Tuesday.
Stacy

---

studio-residency agenda. In her memo, she also addresses an issue that surfaced as staff worked with the various consultants. When an instructional leader is a silent conductor, she pays close attention to the state of student learning, listens to teachers, and creates the connective tissue among activities, people, and expectations for adult learning.

In Exhibit 6.2, the principal, Stacy, not only made connections among goals, activities, resources, and people, but she also reiterated expectations for participation as well as for the content of the work. In the truest spirit of the silent conductor she was able to do this because she had deep knowledge of teachers' strengths and needs and she understood the nature of the professional development. Next we will explore how an instructional leader's understanding of teachers' strengths and needs allows her to be strategic.

Strategizing

A significant part of orchestration is strategic thinking and action, which is an integral part of being able to support people through guiding them to a proper use of time, collaboration, and other resources. For example, one aspect of strategizing to improve the quality of teaching across a school is to understand when social relationships can deepen or hinder professional learning.

A principal needs the ability to build relationships with staff members and to leverage relationships among staff members, for example, in these ways:

- Select key people as emerging leaders
- Use resources to support activities that are most productive for staff members
- Make use of social capital
- Place coaches or instructional facilitators strategically

In the studio-residency example, district and school leaders needed to think through who was ready for this sort of learning opportunity. One team of school leaders we worked with developed the criteria shown in Table 6.2 from which to consider who might be considered as a studio-resident teacher.

Instructional leaders need a clear rationale as to *why* people are being invited to participate in professional development as well as a clear vision as to the *capacity* they are building (what is the intellectual and social capital being developed and for what purpose?). Without a well-developed rationale, the expectations for participation in the studio-residency structure will likely feel like "one more thing to do" instead of a plan for collective learning in order to improve practice. To help leaders think strategically about who they might first consider to participate in a studio residency—especially for the first time this job-embedded professional development structure is being used—we might ask them questions such as the following:

- Currently, how do teachers see and listen to their students' thinking, ideas, and learning experiences?
- To what extent is teachers' work autonomous versus collaborative?
- To what extent is there a culture of continuous, ongoing learning?
- How is teaching expertise distributed and shared among teachers and the principal?
- To what extent are there established and shared expectations for the quality of student work?
- To what extent are there organized, targeted opportunities for teachers in the school to learn the specifics of teaching their subject matters well?
- To what extent do teachers trust, depend on, and learn from each other?

Table 6.2.
Criteria for Selection of Studio and Residency Teachers

A STUDIO-RESIDENCY TEACHER IS . . .	A STUDIO-RESIDENCY TEACHER IS NOT . . .
• A teacher who has (or is developing) strong instructional practice in terms of purposeful planning and instruction, student engagement, classroom environment and culture, or assessment • A teacher who has a stance of continuous professional inquiry; a teacher who strives to develop and grow as a professional through such avenues as attending state and national conferences, subscribing to and reading current professional journals, maintaining a membership in professional organizations such as NCTE, ASCD, IRA, and so on and reads current book publications • A teacher who has the collaborative and interpersonal skills necessary to gain the trust and respect of his or her colleagues; a teacher who not only seeks out his or her colleagues for collaboration but is someone his or her colleagues seek out and trust as well • A teacher who is willing to engage in difficult conversations in service of student achievement but who would never jeopardize the trust of colleagues, administrators, students, or parents; a teacher who knows how to be hard on the work, respectful with each other • A teacher who understands the importance of reflection and what can be learned from results—good or bad; a teacher who continually plans with the strengths and needs of students in mind as well as the rigor of the task or activity	• A teacher in need of fixing or one who is worrisome to administrator, peers, or parents • A teacher who takes the stance of "I have arrived" or "I already know or do that" • A teacher who isolates or insulates from peers; a teacher who sees him- or herself as an island of knowledge or expertise • A teacher who is judgmental or evaluative • A teacher who is unwilling to honestly and frankly reflect on results or engage in some form of inquiry around his or her work

Knowing teachers as individuals helps with mapping out the strengths and needs of a school staff as a group—and its multiple sources of knowledge, expertise, social influence, and other resources. Principals who orchestrate place financial and professional learning supports strategically throughout the staff and school building in order to spread the instructional work, develop teachers' expertise, and deepen conversations and trust. In scholarly literature, this is described as making use of social capital (Coburn & Russell, 2008). The idea of social capital emphasizes the resources that are available to a teacher through social interaction with colleagues and creating a normative environment that enables change in classroom practice. In other words, instructional leaders build *intellectual capital* in their schools by establishing a vision and expectations for the quality of teaching and learning and in organizing targeted opportunities for teachers in the school to learn the specifics of teaching their subject matters well. Instructional leaders also pay attention to the development of the *social capital* that allows people to trust, depend on, and learn from each other.

Engaging Hearts and Minds

This third dimension of instructional leadership as orchestration refers to keying into individuals' passions and interests. Engaging hearts and minds addresses the need for principals, teachers, and staff members to experience ownership and authenticity in the instructional initiative. Engaging hearts and minds is not about putting structures in place or making sure teachers participate in activities. Rather, it means building relationships so that leaders can accurately assess what strengths, needs, and interests will serve and spark staff members. Instructional leaders engage hearts and minds by the following activities:

- Using formal structures (for example, staff meetings or grade level or department meetings) to carry messages and set vision
- Painting the picture of a vision for student learning and teaching practice across formal and informal activities and settings
- Building relationships and a school culture and climate for learning

We have already seen how instructional leaders might use their leadership voice in instructional letters to staff or to open or close professional development sessions in order to communicate a rationale, convey urgency, or nourish a vision of possibility for student learning. Leadership voice can also engage hearts and minds as the instructional letter from a high school principal to his staff in Exhibit 6.3 illustrates. Notice how the principal, Max, simultaneously paints a picture of teaching and learning and taps into the interest and good will of his staff as he continues to convey a visionary message.

EXHIBIT 6.3. A GOOD DESCRIPTION OF EQUITY AND EXAMPLES OF TEACHING THAT SUPPORT IT

A Good Description of Equity

I know that we as a staff have struggled with finding a working definition of equity. We have had a number of intellectual and sometimes passionate discussions of what we mean by equity. Last Thursday evening, Colleen and I had the pleasure of meeting with eight mothers of Somali students. We met at the Sands apartment complex and even though we needed an interpreter to bridge our language gaps, these women made it very clear to me what a working definition of equity might be for us. When asked what they hoped for their children, all eight women clearly and adamantly agreed that they want their children to graduate and go to college. Colleen and I asked them again what they wanted and again they repeated they wanted their children to go to college.

As we delved deeper into this conversation the women shared that many of them had not gone to school in Somalia and they struggled with how to help their children, but they expected their children to graduate and go to college. Of equal importance, they asked for our help as educators in seeing to their children's success. They have many assets that they offer their children but they felt they were not able to help with the academic side of high school. They made it clear that if we were willing to help they would make any family sacrifices necessary to help their kids. For example, these women dismiss their children from family chores and taking jobs so they can focus on staying after school and doing homework. During my drive home, I could not get over how easy and clearly these women were able to give me a working definition

(continued)

for equitable outcomes. As we discuss the appropriateness of having all students college ready, I will hold the voices and expressions of these women in mind.

Examples of Teaching That Will Help Us Achieve Equitable Outcomes

I hope that some of you noticed that I did not mention *planning, purpose, and questioning strategies* in my last letter. However, I still spent my time in classrooms last week looking for *planning, purpose, and questioning strategies* that support *intellectual rigor for all students.* Here is a composite description of what I saw in three ninth-grade literacy classrooms, all of which are inclusive.

Purpose

Students will look closely at a piece of text in order to understand or hypothesize about the choices the author made.

Thinking Questions for Independent Reading

1. How would the text change if a different character told the story?

2. Why did the author choose the narrator that he or she did? What was his or her intent?

3. How reliable is the narrator in being able to convey information to the reader?

Conferring

In one classroom I observed the teacher conferring with one student who reads well below grade level and one honors student. In both instances the teacher asked each student rigorous questions that forced them to support the answer with evidence from their text. Without the teacher telling me which student was a low-level reader, I would not have been able to discern who had a higher reading level.

Rigor

Since being in these three classrooms, I have been trying to answer the same questions about the book I am reading. I can attest to the fact that these are difficult questions that make you think deeply about what you are reading.

ELL Reading Classroom

As soon as I entered this room I was struck by the fact that class was going to end soon but that every student was reading an independent reading book with their reading logs open. Each student I spoke with was tracking the big ideas in their text. While this was going on the teacher was conferring individually with a student.

Conferring Questions

1. What would you do in this situation?
2. Which reading strategies are you using?
3. How are you keeping the story straight in your mind?
4. What is your reading goal for today?

What is striking to me in these examples is the teachers' focus on intellectual work, personalization, and their steadfast belief that every student in the room must be challenged. In these rooms, student success is aided by clear purpose and individualized teacher support.

It is the work we are doing as educators that will help our students meet the dreams of the Somalian parents Colleen and I met with. I know we are all working toward the same goal. Let's not get so caught up on our definition of equity and whether or not our students and their families want to succeed. Let's continue to improve what we do and be surprised by the results we will get. Have a great week!

Peace,
Max

Although Max constantly uses memos to staff to name the teaching practices he would like to see across the school, he also uses these memos to restate the vision of equity of outcomes for students. In so doing, Max engages hearts and minds when he reminds staff about their collective discussions about equity, the shared goal they are all working toward, and how their work will help fulfill the dreams of their students' parents. Max reinforces a vision for student learning that the staff cares about. In the letter shown in Exhibit 6.4, Max continues to remind staff of the efficacy of their efforts on behalf of their students. He

I know that for most, if not all of us, this year is turning into a blur of activity, excitement, and sometimes anxiety. Personally, I am finding it difficult at times to keep a clear focus on the goals we set at the beginning of the year. On my bad days, I get caught up in the rush and stress of everything that needs to be completed. Unfortunately, on those days I find myself being less visible, less accessible to others and in general not a great guy to be around. However, on my good days (which are no less busy than my bad days) I am able to center and focus on what is best for our students and staff. Thankfully, on these days I am emotionally present, productive, and available to those who need me. Although both types of days are equally busy, I think my better days are better because I understand why I have taken on this job and believe in the work we are doing and the challenges we face. In this spirit of keeping us all focused and centered, I offer this reminder of our strategic goals for this year.

We Will Focus on Helping Our Students Grow as Critical Thinkers and Embrace the Metaphor of Student as Worker

As the primary aspect of this goal we have chosen to improve our instruction with better *planning, purpose,* and *questioning strategies.* Additionally, our literacy teachers are implementing readers' workshop to ensure that all students are working with text they can access. Throughout our school and in all departments I have seen greater student thinking and engagement as a result of our efforts. On December 15 you will have a chance to collaborate with others in your department on the classroom environment and teaching strategies necessary for students to willingly engage each other. If you get confused about what we are doing, remember that each day we are trying to improve instruction so that all of our students have opportunities for critical thinking and intellectual work. For me, this goal means that I need to be observing in classrooms and supporting teacher professional development on a daily basis.

We Will Create a Safe, Civil, and Productive Culture with a Tone of Decency for All

Our primary work to achieve this goal is creating classroom cultures conducive to purposeful learning and student talk. I am amazed each day at the progress we have made in creating respectful and productive classrooms. So many of you have taken on the challenge of *bell-to-bell learning, cooperative learning,* and *student talk.* With our early success in this area we need to keep working hard to ensure that our campus and classrooms get safer and more civil each day. Please continue to do tardy sweeps and be visible between classes. Our students love seeing us as much as possible.

I hope the common thread in these goals is that we are doing all of this because we believe we have the ability to improve learning outcomes for our students while creating learning environments that are healthy and productive for students, staff, and community. The big answer to the question of why we are working so hard is that our community deserves the best education possible and we are up to the challenge of providing this. Please remember that when you get confused, anxious, or stressed (no doubt we are all going to experience this) that we have chosen a path that will serve our students better and create better places for us to work.

Peace,
Max

---

reminds everyone of why they engage in such hard work, names their collective values, and ties their collective values directly to their instructional improvement efforts.

Investing in or Developing Leadership in Others

A final dimension of orchestration includes the development of leadership among staff members other than the building principal. Investing in others implies taking time to build relationships in order to know in whom and what to invest. The principal creates concrete ways for emerging leaders to participate in the instructional initiative and to begin to take ownership for its goals.

The work that is handed over or opened for participation needs to be valued and genuinely important for participants as much as for the principal. Some ways to invest meaningfully in others might be to do the following:

- Build relationships to get to know staff members' interests and strengths
- Invite staff members to set their own goals
- Work with individuals and small groups
- Give others opportunities to display knowledge or skill
- Ask others to take on concrete leadership roles

Investing in or developing leadership in others can turn into a set of isolated activities versus a purposeful instructional improvement plan if leaders are not vigilant. Leaders need to see the connections and relationships in their instructional leadership work so that they can reflect on their effort and effectively create an ongoing plan that supports the biggest shifts in teaching, learning, and a school culture. If leaders are clear about their long-term goals then they can be more responsive and flexible in their short-term work. Having both short-term and long-term plans helps leaders anchor their daily work to their broad goals. Without a long-term plan, day-to-day work can get lost. Leaders may find that they're unable to follow up on previous coaching or professional development sessions or be able to thoughtfully connect the dots and narrate the story line of instructional improvement so that it is relevant for teachers. At its best, instructional leaders create a plan that is carefully crafted *and* responsive, well thought through *and* spontaneous.

Organizing for intentional planning toward both short-term and long-term goals requires a consideration of the seen and the unseen. What are the most tangible and immediate outcomes of your leadership? What are the less immediately tangible outcomes but could be seeds to plant? Consider the short-term and long-term goals for professional learning outlined in Table 6.3. Expert instructional leaders consider the following elements as they invest in individuals in order to develop shared leadership toward common goals: (1) the content, structures, or strategy that they want teachers to learn; (2) teachers' habits of mind or big shifts in thinking and practice; and (3) the culture of the school.

Earlier in this chapter, we mentioned the idea of social and intellectual capital and how instructional leaders plan for the development and sustenance of both. We showed how the studio-residency model for professional learning

Table 6.3.
Considering Short-Term and Long-Term Goals

CONTENT, STRUCTURES, OR STRATEGY	TEACHERS' HABITS OF MIND (BIG SHIFTS IN PRACTICE)	THE CULTURE OF THE SCHOOL
Individually conferring with students to assess learning	Helping teachers see and listen to their students' thinking, ideas, perceptions; helping teachers pay closer attention to their students' learning experience; growing teachers' capacity to consider what they want their students to know and be able to do	Creating opportunities for students to articulate their strengths and needs and to advocate for their learning Shifting the nature of teachers' work from autonomous to collaborative

illustrated instructional leadership as strategizing and being a silent conductor. The reality is that being a silent conductor, strategizing, engaging hearts and minds, and investing in or developing leadership in others are complementary ideas. Each of these ideas could be considered when analyzing the studio-residency model for job-embedded learning or other acts of instructional leadership, such as writing letters to staff in order communicate the story line of capacity building. The following case of a middle school principal planning for schoolwide professional development illustrates the interrelated concepts of instructional leadership as orchestration.

ORCHESTRATING PROFESSIONAL LEARNING

Let us return to Larry, the middle school principal we met in Chapter Five, who during a twenty-minute observation focused in on one aspect of a sixth-grade language arts lesson. During the observation, the principal noticed and wondered about student talk because the school focus for the year was to develop students' academic language. Larry thought through how he would respond to what he observed based on assuming the teacher's best intentions, what Larry knew about teaching and learning language arts, and testing theories about the teacher's decision making. We noted several questions Larry thought about that emerged from his observation, all of which had the potential to engage the teacher, J.B., in an honest conversation about the teaching and learning in his classroom. We noted that Larry's consideration for how to support J.B. with immediate next steps he could take to improve his practice needed to align with long-range goals for J.B. In this example, we will see how Larry's response to J.B. is part of the connective tissue of schoolwide capacity building. We will see how Larry thinks about J.B. as an individual learner, how to use the current expertise of the school staff, how to leverage the time and people resources he has for professional learning, and how to further develop the intellectual and social capital in his school. We will see how Larry considers the current capacity in his school alongside his plan for capacity building.

Before we take the reader through Larry's capacity-building planning processes, let's take a look at what this middle school was working toward in terms of increasing student learning and the development of teaching practices to meet the student learning goals. Based on the collective and thorough examination of summative assessment data, teachers' formative assessment and anecdotal data, and the principal's regular classroom observations, the school staff agreed that in order to improve their students' ability to access rigorous content standards they would need to develop the students' ability to think and communicate in each content area. The staff also understood that their own clarity of standards and the thinking demands in their content areas had to be explicit enough for students to know *what* they were going to learn and *how* they would learn it. Thus, for the last year, the entire staff has had professional development on designing and implementing more purposeful instruction (see Chapter Two for a thorough discussion of the dimension of *purpose* and what purposeful instruction entails). The entire staff also collectively learned about the role of talk in student learning and each department has met in order to flesh out what talk should sound like in their respective content area (see Chapter Two for a discussion of talk as a dimension of *student engagement*).

After Larry observes in teachers' classrooms, he includes his observations in a "teacher next steps inventory" he maintains (see Table 6.4). Such an inventory allows Larry to be thoughtful and systematic about the nature of professional development that might be needed—for individual teachers, departments, or for the entire staff. The inventory also allows Larry to notice

Table 6.4.
Teacher Next Steps Inventory

TEACHER	STRENGTHS	AREAS OF IMPROVEMENT	NEXT STEPS
A.M.—Social Studies (fifteen years experience)	• Assignment for day posted • Essential question posted • Lesson plan—outline of period activities • Student work posted (changed regularly) • Step Up to Writing implemented with fidelity • Beginnings of a leveled resource library • Meeting space created	• Post purpose with learning target daily • Lesson plans with clear learning target, minilesson, and independent activities for each class • Rework minilecture to become minilesson with modeling • Create opportunities for students to talk and respond to each other • Post rubrics with student work	• Review daily lesson plans with feedback weekly—focus on learning target and minilesson script (with modeling) • Attend monthly student engagement professional development seminars—peer observation with feedback on implementation of seminar strategies
J.B.—Language Arts (one year experience)	• Clear purpose statement with essential question and learning target • Leveled library sorted by genre with student recommendations • Minilessons with modeling • Lots of turn-and-talk attempts • Transitions to independent work time efficient	• All student-to-student talk teacher generated • Provide students with more opportunities to respond to each other's thinking • Relate learning targets more clearly to state standards and a college-going trajectory	• Refer to standards for each lesson in lesson plans • Script a few talkworthy prompts for each lesson • Focus minilessons specifically on student discourse—for example, how to extend a conversation, how to respond to peer thinking • Focus coaching cycles specifically on releasing discourse to students • Attend monthly student engagement professional development seminars—peer observation with feedback on implementation of seminar strategies *(continued)*

Table 6.4.

(continued)

TEACHER	STRENGTHS	AREAS OF IMPROVEMENT	NEXT STEPS
H.C.—Math (department chair, ten years experience)	• Daily agenda (activities), problem sets, and homework clearly posted • Lots of enthusiasm and teacher talk when reviewing homework and problems • Very active in tutoring students during work time; focused on helping them get right answer • Always willing to help students at lunch and after school	• Develop purpose statements with learning targets daily • Give students opportunities throughout the period to think and share thinking with peers • Student seating conducive to talking with each other • Student conferring as formative assessment rather than just helping to get an answer	• Post purpose statements with learning targets daily • Create a meeting space and table groups for student seating • Attend monthly student engagement professional development seminars—peer observation with feedback on implementation of seminar strategies

Note: Partial example from the first week of October after at least three walkthrough observations in each classroom trends in and patterns of student learning and teaching practice. Although Larry and his staff examine summative assessment data (for example, state test outcomes) and closely monitor any achievement gaps, he also uses his regular classroom observations and frequent conversations with teachers as another data point for the state of teaching and learning in the school.

At the same time, Larry understands that his classroom observations, analysis, and conversations with teachers following his observations will support the development of a school culture of public practice. Table 6.5 describes three benchmarks related to a principal's classroom observations and subsequent conversations with teachers. You will note that benchmark one is all about the principal practicing classroom observations and responding to them on a consistent basis. Benchmark two is about how the practice of classroom observations informs the leader's subsequent strategies and actions. Benchmark three is about how observations of student learning and teaching practices become deeply embedded in the culture of the school. Larry is intentionally working toward benchmark three in both areas. Although Larry's regular classroom observations inform his instructional leadership decision making and serve as a data point for decisions about professional development, he knows that as an entire staff, they are still in the midst of honing their shared understanding about the state of teaching and learning in the school. Teachers' understanding and public conversations about their own and others' practice are still emerging. For example, conversations about teaching share a common language but still tend to focus on giving advice to one another based on what teachers are doing in their own classrooms. Practices that get implemented do not get studied and adjusted based on student need. Conversations among staff that are characterized by concrete and honest dialogue about student learning and the race, class, and language issues that emerge are not yet present.

As Larry thinks about the learning needs of students, the extant teaching practices in the school, and the culture of shared and public practice he wants to develop, he considers what he knows about the strengths and needs of each teacher, the functioning of each department's professional learning community (PLC), and his goal of cultivating a schoolwide culture of ongoing, collective scrutiny of teaching practices. He also thinks about what the school is focused on as well as the structures and resources he has at his disposal. Larry created Table 6.6 to help him think all these things through.

Table 6.5.

Benchmarks for Principal's Classroom Observations and Subsequent Conversations with Teachers

INSTRUCTIONAL LEADERSHIP PRACTICE	BENCHMARK ONE	BENCHMARK TWO	BENCHMARK THREE
Classroom observations of student learning and teaching practices	Classroom observations are done on a regular, intentional basis to observe student learning and teaching practices.	Observations of student learning and teaching practices inform instructional leadership decision making (for example, what to communicate to students, staff, and other stakeholders; what to consider in planning for professional development). Observations of student learning and teaching practices are intentionally used to hone shared understanding about teaching and learning and to calibrate schoolwide understanding of the state of teaching and learning in the school. Observations of student learning and teaching practice are a data point for instructional and professional development decision making.	Observations of student learning and teaching practices are part of the fabric and culture of the school, used in a continuous cycle of reflection and improvement. Observations of student learning and teaching practices continuously inform leader's analysis of the quality of student learning. Observations of student learning and teaching practices are routinely reflected in the school's professional development and capacity building plan.

| Analysis and debrief conversations of classroom observations of learning and teaching | Analysis of classroom observations of learning and teaching are descriptive (not evaluative) and authentic questions for inquiry are noted.

Conversations to debrief with teachers are one-on-one, by department, and whole staff. Leaders share their classroom observations, what they noticed, and what they wondered. | Analysis of observations of learning and teaching are part of an ongoing conversation among staff, reflected in the professional learning community (PLC), and form the basis for professional development plans. | Regular analysis and debrief conversations are part of the fabric and culture of the school, used in a continuous cycle of reflection and improvement.

All staff are comfortable discussing and analyzing their own and others' practice as it relates to student learning and are able to discuss the race, class, and language issues that emerge.

Regular analysis and debriefing conversations use classroom observations of learning and teaching as data for decision making. |

Table 6.6.
Structures and Resources for Teacher Learning

Who Participates?	Structure and Resource for Professional Development: Whole School	Structure and Resource for Professional Development: Departments' PLCs	Structure and Resource for Professional Development: Coaching Cycles for Individual Teachers
Entire staff	Monthly student engagement professional development seminars—peer observation with feedback on implementation of seminar strategies (led by the principal)	Professional learning community focused on (1) the study of student work, practices, and refinement of practice; (2) developing teachers' ability to publicly discuss and critique teaching practice (led by teachers within the department)	
Departments: Social Studies Mathematics Language Arts		*Department Focus: Social Studies* Looking at student work to calibrate definitions of *quality* and to develop fluency in the use of protocols to structure their time effectively	

Individual teachers: J.B. (Language Arts) B.C. (Mathematics)	*Mathematics* Studying justifiable explanations *Language Arts* Studying academic language during book conversations	Coaching cycles with a focus on refining particular aspects of teaching practice. The instructional coach spends approximately two days per week at the school. Coaching cycles span four days over two weeks. Releasing discourse to students Setting up group work in which students have more opportunity to justify their answers

Larry will use collective staff meeting time to work with the whole staff in shared learning about student engagement. Although he needs to carve out this collective time from the time shaved off from various, short staff meetings, this once-a-month session allows Larry and his staff to wrestle with ideas together, developing knowledge and community in the process. The focus for the collective staff meetings align with the individual coaching cycles that certain teachers, such as J.B., will participate in. In J.B.'s case, the specific coaching he will receive will help him acquire the strategies he needs to develop and release more of the responsibility for academic discourse to his students. Because Larry noted that each department's PLC had certain strengths and needs, he wanted to shore up the ones that still needed basic processes to work together (such as the Social Studies department) as well as support the development of more sophisticated processes that allowed departments to continuously study and adjust their practices based on student need. Table 6.7 illustrates the study cycle the Math and Language Arts departments used across six PLC sessions. As noted earlier, PLCs are one resource that is leveraged in order for teachers to have an ongoing venue for learning. Because it takes expertise to build expertise (Chapter One) and because the assistant principal has extensive knowledge and experience as a math teacher, he participates in the math department's PLC. Not only does the assistant principal's participation in the PLC allow him to engage as a learner with the Math department, but his expertise in the teaching of mathematics also will support the development of knowledge and skills within the PLC. The Language Arts department's PLC cycle followed a reading comprehension workshop in which they all participated. Larry, the principal, has a clear understanding that the PLCs need to have access to expertise that will continue to raise the bar for a vision for student learning.

In Table 6.7, you will note that the PLC cycle is the same for both the math and language arts departments, that both departments are working on some aspect of student discourse, that student discourse is a characteristic of *student engagement*—the focus for the entire school—and that the teachers are simultaneously learning how to be public with their practice.

We have seen how Larry uses his regular classroom observations to assess the state of student learning and teaching practices. He has a system for tracking the strengths and needs of each teacher and uses this information to plan for professional development. He thinks about the resources of time and

Table 6.7.

PLC Cycles for the Math and Language Arts Departments

MATH DEPARTMENT PLC CYCLE	LANGUAGE ARTS DEPARTMENT PLC CYCLE
The team of math teachers is joined by the assistant principal to build shared understanding of a *justifiable explanation*. They start by reading professional texts on this topic and forming a tentative definition.	The team of language arts teachers want to understand what it might look and sound like when students really practice using academic language in their book conversations. The group meets and writes a beginning definition of this idea and seem to agree right away.
They then visit one another's classrooms sometime during the next week to observe how students are justifying their answers. The teachers take careful notes; one teacher tape records a few student conversations. Several teachers collect student work with example explanations.	The teachers return to their classrooms and take notes about their own students' book conversations. The teachers are careful to gather student data from as many groups of learners as possible.
The teachers and assistant principal get together and study their notes from observation and student work. Together they describe how students are currently justifying their answers in the classrooms. The group works hard to just *describe* what they see and hear, not judge or evaluate. They attempt to describe the qualities of a student justification right now.	The group comes together to compare their notes. They take their time to read each others' notes carefully and jot down their impressions. As they read, several teachers realize that students are using academic language quite differently from class to class and that perhaps the teachers themselves have different understandings of *academic language*. The group decides to return to defining this idea. They decide that this time they will ask the principal to help them arrange an opportunity to visit one classroom and take notes about the same student conversations. This shared experience then helps the group come to a tentative clarification about what their students are currently doing with academic language.
The teachers then describe what they think is next for their students. What will a strong justification sound like	The teachers work together to write a book conversation they would love to hear from their students by the end of the school

(continued)

Table 6.7.
(continued)

MATH DEPARTMENT PLC CYCLE	LANGUAGE ARTS DEPARTMENT PLC CYCLE
in a month? What about June? What are the characteristics of these stronger justifications?	year. The group is careful to define the qualities together. This involves at least one more research experience in a classroom and a clarifying debrief session of that shared experience.
The teachers decide to invite the district math coach to their next PLC meeting to offer practical suggestions to shift their teaching practices to promote the kind of justifications they want to see from their students. One teacher volunteers her classroom as a lab site—the coach will work with her while the others observe. The assistant principal decides to secure video equipment to tape the coaching and share the tape with the rest of the staff at an upcoming schoolwide seminar.	The teachers then discuss which teacher practices they think are promoting the kinds of talk they consider the most academic. They discuss which teacher practices seem to support student risk taking the most. The group agrees to one particular practice to all try for the next common unit of study.
The teachers spend ten minutes reflecting individually on their new understanding of justification, including what is possible in the future. One teacher raises a new question about teaching the language of justification explicitly, particularly to English language learners.	The teachers reflect as a group about the phases of the process that helped them reach new clarity about *academic language*. They articulate the link they now understand between teacher practice and student dialogue.
One teacher leads the group through a writing process to write a new shared definition of *justifying an answer*. The new definition is posted in their staff room. The teachers continue to research their own students, with careful attention to ELLs.	The teachers write individual definitions of *academic language use in book conversations*. The group then works together to build a shared definition. The teachers continue to research their own students and their use of academic language during book conversations.

people he has access to and considers what can be accomplished in whole-staff sessions, department level PLCs, and with coaching for individual teachers. Larry also thinks about the development of teachers' expertise and the development of a school culture that will allow the ongoing scrutiny of practices alongside student achievement. This requires him to simultaneously plan for intellectual and social capacity building. Larry also uses his regular classroom observations as an opportunity to reflect on the quality of the professional development afforded teachers and as a continuous data point to include in the narrative he constantly constructs so that teachers can also see the through-line from their vision for student learning, the improvement of their teaching practices, to their participation in the professional development. Larry wrote the letter shown in Exhibit 6.5 to his staff in early October. It illustrates how he weaves together his classroom observation reflections, vision for student learning, how he will support the development of teachers' practice, and his expectations for the implementation of professional learning.

EXHIBIT 6.5. LARRY'S LETTER TO STAFF

Dear Staff,

Once again, I am at my computer late at night, unable to phrase a clever opening for an instructional letter about questioning strategies and student talk. In my heart and mind I know how important it is and the immediate need we have to intellectually engage our students. I need look no further than the recent presidential press conferences staged as debates to know we can't let our students out of here without the ability to think with a discerning mind about current issues, math, science, and literature. I think, however, that we have not been as aggressive as we need to be in engaging our students as thinkers. Have no fear, help is on the way.

Our strategic plan speaks of helping students to use their minds well and for us to promote the metaphor of student as worker. Now that we have all been refreshed on the importance of *daily planning* and *purpose* we need to take our next step in engaging our students and helping them grow intellectually. Beginning with our late arrival this Wednesday, we are going to turn our attention to improving our questioning strategies and use of student talk.

(continued)

Improved questioning strategies and student talk are logical next steps in all of our classes. Regardless of how good we might be at this, there is always a need to ask better questions and figure out new ways for students to engage with each other. Think about some of the best questions you were asked as a student or professional. Try to remember that feeling of uncertainty and challenge of being asked a question with no correct response but needing sufficient evidence to answer. We need for our students to have these feelings on a daily basis. We can no longer have students think that they can get by using lower-order thinking skills.

Toward this end, we will spend our late arrival this week discussing how to ask questions that require students to think, feel, and support their thoughts. You will have an opportunity to work within your departments to customize a plan that will address your needs in improving your ability to ask questions and engage students with each other. The goal of each of your plans will be to improve the level of intellectual vibrancy in your classes.

As we move forward with our work on questioning and student talk, please remember this is just the next step toward helping students use their minds well and their doing the intellectual work in the classroom. Your work on having a daily purpose and plan must continue as we move into more sophisticated strategies for student engagement. What we do this week will be a great addition to your toolkit of strategies to help students meet your daily purpose.

I look forward to our ongoing work together.
Larry

CONCLUSION

In this chapter, we illustrated that the expertise instructional leaders need in order to improve the quality of teaching is akin to conducting the orchestra, which requires leaders to know teachers' strengths and needs and develop a plan for intellectual and social capacity building. Instructional leaders need to create the conditions necessary for ongoing learning and *leverage* their formal and informal authority toward strategic and humane action. They need to be clear that as they learn about the strengths and needs of the staff, they are thinking about the simultaneous development of teachers' practice and a school culture conducive to the ongoing critique and analysis of teaching and learning. We illustrated how instructional leaders use existing structures and resources to develop teachers' practice and think through how to best leverage resources for individual or small groups of teachers and an entire school staff. The level of instructional leadership expertise required to orchestrate professional learning as fluently as an accomplished conductor of a professional symphony cannot be learned in a preservice principal preparation program. Although preparation programs can certainly be useful—and are a necessary foundation—instructional leadership expertise requires many years to develop the required knowledge and skills. We will return to the complexity of developing instructional leadership expertise in Chapters Eight and Nine. First, in Chapter Seven, we will explore the expertise required for instructional coaching. Although instructional coaching to improve teaching practice has taken off across the country, many school districts do not consider the depth of knowledge and skills that instructional coaches need if they are to support the improvement of teachers' practice. We will see how expert instructional coaches use their knowledge and skills about teaching and learning, coaching, and adult learning to support teachers in the improvement of practice.

DISCUSSION QUESTIONS

- How do you currently orchestrate professional learning? What is the intellectual and social capacity you are intentionally developing and how do you intend to leverage this developing capacity? For example, how do you currently leverage the structural resources you have (such as staff meetings or PLC time)? How might these resources be leveraged further in order to support teacher learning?

- What is your evidence that the resources for professional learning (such as instructional coaching or time spent in PLCs) affect teacher learning?

chapter SEVEN

Coaching to Improve Practice

The following vignette describes part of a job-embedded instructional coaching cycle. We use it to help us illustrate the various forms of coaching that might take place in job-embedded instructional coaching.

INSTRUCTIONAL COACHING

It's the first coaching cycle of the new school year for the language arts teachers at this high school in the Rainer School District. Three of the five teachers sitting together this morning have already engaged in two years of classroom-embedded coaching with their literacy consultant, Jennifer. One of the teachers in today's session is brand-new to the profession; another is an experienced teacher with twelve years under her belt but new to the department. Two of the women are the English as a Second Language (ESL) teachers and the remaining three teach ninth- through twelfth-grade English.

Prepared with notebooks to record their observations, thinking, and questions, the group enters their colleague's classroom to observe Alexis's first period ninth-grade language arts class. Alexis is in her third year of participating in classroom-embedded coaching with Jennifer. Jennifer sidles up next to Alexis, who is sitting with her students in a half-moon cluster surrounding a large easel at the front of the room. The easel reads, "Ways We Respond to Texts." As teachers engage in this learning process, their principal joins them to observe and learn. Stacy, the principal, notes, "I spend a significant amount of time with the teachers so that's helped me to develop a better understanding of what literacy work with our students needs to look like, which helps when I need to support the teachers."

Once the students are reading independently, Jennifer and all the teachers sit down in a small circle with Juan, a student, who suddenly has six adults focused on him. As Juan begins to talk about his book, *Always Running*, by Luis Rodriguez, he explains, "I like stories about Latinos and how they kinda make their lives better. You know, like when they get out of gangs sometimes."

This vignette draws from data collected by Beth Boatright as part of ongoing research on the district partnership work of the Center for Educational Leadership at the University of Washington. Rainer School District is a pseudonym.

The five teachers and principal featured in the chapter-opening vignette are engaged in a particular form of professional development called *coaching*. Although schools across the nation have adopted coaching as a strategy to improve teaching and learning, different districts employ and envision the work of coaching differently. This chapter will examine the broad field of coaching, situating its various forms in education research and our experience. We will then elaborate on one kind of coaching—*content coaching*—that we find most successful in shifting teacher practice and boosting student learning. Our aim is to highlight the kind of expertise that content coaches need most in order to be most successful in their work. Throughout, we offer practical tools to guide principals and coaches in leveraging coaching as a strategy for instructional improvement. We will frequently revisit Jennifer and the teachers at this high school—as well as other coaches and teachers we know—to help illustrate the demanding and promising practice of coaching.

WHAT IS COACHING?

Similar to many researchers, we have noted that coaches occupy a variety of roles and have a range of titles around the country. Some coaches are called *mentors* and others are called *lead teachers, math coaches*, or *content specialists*. Many researchers note that these can be highly ambiguous roles that depend on contextual requirements, agreements, and resource constraints (see Mraz, Algozzine, & Watson, 2008). Coaches might perform widely varying kinds of work, including not only classroom observations and feedback, but also test data interpretation, curriculum design, and facilitation of teams.

Nonetheless, although districts and researchers define coaching differently, most definitions include several commonalities. First, coaches are nonsupervisory educators with no positional authority (Taylor, 2008); generally, coaches are contractually designated as *teachers*. This is not to say that supervisory instructional leaders cannot coach and develop teachers but people who are designated *coaches* typically cannot rely on supervisory authority to move teacher practice. Research and practice indicate that the work of coaching is

- Focused on instructional practice
- Embedded in teachers' classrooms
- Intensive and ongoing
- Grounded in partnerships
- Facilitated through respectful communication (Knight, 2009)

In our experience, we see that more and more districts frequently link coaches to instructional improvement initiatives. Sometimes researchers or districts describe coaches as *change agents* positioned between a standards-based reform initiative and the classroom (Tung, Ouimette, & Feldman, 2004). The Rainer School District hired CEL consultants (such as Jennifer) to work as coaches in the context of a small high school conversion process and a literacy initiative. In other districts, coaches might find themselves coaching for elementary math instructional improvement in light of a math initiative.

WHY DOES COACHING MATTER?

Our experience tells us that coaching changes teacher practice and amplifies student learning. Yet, coaching is a resource-intensive model of professional development and districts want to know that their investment will pay off in teacher and student learning. For several decades, researchers have called for rigorous studies that examine the effect of coaching on teacher practice and student learning (Neufeld & Roper, 2003). In response to this call, researchers have started examining the influence of coaching on teacher beliefs, vision, standards for students, and the practice of coaching as an inquiry stance. (Boatright, 2008; Gibson, 2005). Some studies compare districts with coaches to districts without coaches, examining differences in test scores (Marsh et al., 2005).

MODES OF COACHING

So, we have a general definition of coaching, an understanding that it is defined differently in different places, and research and anecdotal data that says coaching helps teachers shift their practices and improve student learning. How might a district start to implement and train coaches? How might other districts examine their current use of coaches? In light of all the different understandings of coaching, how do we advise districts to proceed? First, we want to help our readers understand some of the terms they will hear in the field and read in the research on coaching. Our first task is to differentiate among the different types of coaching.

This chapter will adopt the term *modes* to describe the various approaches to coaching in today's schools. The term *mode* comes from the study of writing, dating back to ancient Greek references to rhetorical *approaches* or *forms of imitation*. In modern composition theory, the word *mode* refers to the *method* or *approach* a writer assumes in a piece of writing. A political commentary writer, for example, may move back and forth among modes in a single piece of writing, shifting from narrative to persuasive to expository modes in service of convincing a reader of a point.

Some districts choose to adopt a particular mode of coaching (such as *literacy coaching*) for its instructional improvement work across a system. In these cases, coaches might operate mainly in that mode. In other cases, regardless of formal title or designation, we believe that individual coaches tend to operate in different modes at different times, depending on teacher or school needs. A coach might shift among modes of coaching within a department or even a single coaching session. We suggest the term *mode* best conveys these categories because it suggests that a coach's approach can be fluid, depending on purpose and context. Furthermore, we do not want to define coaching by the specific titles a person might hold (such as *district coach, school-based specialist,* and *mentor*) because school districts vary widely in their coaching philosophy, assumptions, and definitions. As such within these titles and roles, a range of actions and approaches are possible.

PEER COACHING AND MENTORING

You might be most familiar with the terms *peer coaching* and *mentoring*. Although these words might seem ordinary today, at first they represented a dramatic shift from the once ubiquitous, one-size-fits-all, "sit-and-get" teacher professional development workshops where teachers gather and passively receive information. Beverly Showers (1985) had become increasingly frustrated with weak teacher implementation of ideas from professional development workshops. She thought teachers would be more successful with one-on-one support from a colleague who could help them solve real classroom problems and apply ideas from professional development. Showers believed that teachers needed to implement a new practice twenty-five times with peer feedback before mastering it (Denton & Hasbrouck, 2009). Over time, districts have adopted different versions of peer coaching to increase teacher implementation of reform ideas and increase teacher efficacy. Peer coaching does not require any particular expertise outside of some general collegial conversational strategies and of course the ability to create trust with the teacher being coached.

Let's imagine that the high school in our opening vignette had adopted a peer-coaching model. Four of the teachers had a planning period during Alexis's ninth-grade English class. All five of the teachers had recently attended a district training on helping students respond to text. However, the four teachers would have entered Alexis's classroom without support from a person designated as *coach*. So Jennifer would not have been present. The teachers would have observed Alexis's minilesson and after the class would have given Alexis some kind of feedback on her implementation of ideas from the professional development workshop. Alexis would have reflected on the feedback and perhaps made some changes the next day. Then again, she may not have made any changes or the changes she would make may not be the highest leverage changes in terms of affecting student learning. This is similar to the example of the skiers' study group from Chapter One when we determined it takes expertise to make expertise.

The term *mentoring* generally refers to experienced teachers supporting novice teachers in their first few years in the profession (Hobson, Ashby, Malderez, & Tomlinson, 2009). Perhaps when you first started teaching you were assigned a new-teacher mentor from your district or your grade level.

Typically, mentors focus on beginning teachers' general needs such as classroom and time management, basic teaching strategies, and understanding of school policies, regardless of content area of focus (Koballa & Bradbury, 2009). Studies have shown that having a mentor significantly helps new teachers support diverse student populations and develop their own identities as ongoing professional learners (Barrera, Braley, & Slate, 2010). Coaches of any designation might operate in the mentoring mode when supporting new teachers with these familiar start-up concerns. Mentoring requires general expertise in multiple content areas and an understanding of typical new teacher development.

If the high school placed its emphasis primarily on mentoring new teachers, the vignette at the start of the chapter would have looked quite different. The coach, Jennifer, would have worked primarily with the new teacher in the department, likely one-on-one. Jennifer might have taken the new teacher to visit Alexis's class to observe how she sets an academic tone, how she organizes her library, or how she maintains notes about her students. Otherwise, Jennifer would have spent most of her time with the new teacher in that teacher's classroom, observing lessons and co-teaching lessons, with an emphasis on general instructional issues such as how to help students enter the classroom and get right to work. It is possible that Jennifer might have not even had expertise in the new teacher's content area.

COGNITIVE COACHING

Cognitive coaching is a specific mode of coaching that requires prompting deep reflection on teaching practice. The approach assumes that teachers will figure out for themselves what to change in their practice if prompted to reflect. As it was originally imagined, any teacher could receive training in cognitive coaching and then coach his or her peers while still working as a classroom teacher. Cognitive coaching has a predictable cycle. The coach has a planning conversation with the other teacher about an upcoming lesson, gathers information about that teacher's goals and strategies, and sets a focus for data collection. The coach observes the lesson and gathers the requested data. Finally, the coach asks the teacher to reflect on the lesson and they together examine the data. Then, if both teachers are trained as cognitive coaches, the roles are reversed (Costa & Garmston, 2004).

The fictional transcript in the next vignette illustrates a cognitive coaching conversation that could have occurred between Jennifer and Alexis prior to, during, and after the opening vignette.

Before the Class

Jennifer: So, Alexis, I am looking forward to observing your lesson today. What are your goals for the students?

Alexis: Hmmm. I have lots of goals for all the students as readers. We are all working on reading stamina—that's a semester-long goal. But, I guess specifically, today, I am really hoping that a few of the students can tell me about how they respond to texts. So, the goal is for students to be able to describe how they like to respond to their books.

Jennifer [writes down what Alexis said]: OK, so I hear you want your students to be able to articulate how they respond to books. That makes sense. What kinds of instructional strategies do you plan to try?

Alexis: I plan to practice conferring one-on-one with the students I am most curious about.

Jennifer [writing]: OK, so you are working on conferring. What kinds of information would you like me to gather? Think of me as another set of eyes.

Alexis: Hmmm. Could you take notes on what students say during the conferences? I could use that information. It would help to see if we notice the same things.

Jennifer: Yes, I can script what students say during the conferences. Are there particular students you want me to watch even during the minilesson?

Alexis: Definitely Juan. Take notes on Juan. I will confer with him but sometimes he seems tuned out during the minilesson.

Jennifer: OK, I will take notes on all the students you talk to in conferences but I will pay special attention to Juan throughout the class.

During the Class

During the minilesson on responding to text, Jennifer sits close to Juan and takes descriptive notes on his actions, comments, and what he writes down. During the conferences, Jennifer sits right next to Alexis. She does not intervene or talk to anyone. Instead, she writes furiously to capture as much as possible of what the students say.

After the Class

Jennifer: So, you told me that your goals for the students were for them to keep working on their reading stamina and to articulate how they respond to texts during the conferences. How well do you think the students met those goals?

Alexis: Well, some of them did much better today with reading for a long time without stopping. I think some of the lessons we did on strategies for staying engaged in a text are finally paying off. Whew! Some of them could probably use more support for how to keep reading when I am conferring with someone else. Hmmm. Students are really all over the place with how they talk about responding to texts.

Jennifer: So, it sounds like you think most of them met the goal of improving stamina but only some of them met the goal of talking about how they respond to texts well?

Alexis: I think so.

Jennifer: How do you think your conferences went?

Alexis: I think they went well. For instance, Juan was very articulate about how he likes to respond to text.

Jennifer: I took notes on that conference, too. I also have lots of notes on Juan from the minilesson. Should we look at all those notes now and then you can talk about what you think you could do tomorrow?

Alexis: Sounds good.

Note how Jennifer, acting as a cognitive coach, helps Alexis focus on goals for the lesson, collect data on the goals, and then reflect on the data and how the lesson went. The cognitive coaching mode requires an ease with prompting reflection and facility with observing classroom practice without interpreting. Alexis did most of the work of reflection herself. Over time, Alexis would not need prompting from a cognitive coach—she would be asking herself those questions on a regular basis.

INSTRUCTIONAL COACHING AND CONTENT COACHING

An instructional coach is someone "whose primary responsibility is to bring research-based practice to classrooms by working with adults, not students" (Kowal & Steiner, 2007, p. 2). Many definitions of instructional coaching do not reference a specific content area, implying that instructional coaches are primarily responsible for just that—instructional practices—across the disciplines. Instructional coaching emerged in the context of the standards movement and is aimed at helping teachers implement standards-based instructional practice. We have observed instructional coaching most frequently in secondary schools. In these cases, coaches work with teachers across the content areas, perhaps in order to support student habit-of-mind development, regardless of subject matter.

If Jennifer were operating as strictly an instructional coach, she might have provided side-by-side feedback to Alexis on general instructional practices like using turn and talk in the minilesson or prompting a quick write, asking students to jot down their thinking before sharing it out loud, to help Juan talk more in the conference. Such strategies might apply across content areas.

Other researchers link instructional coaching with specific content areas, reflecting an assumption that instructional practices and reasoning are content specific and require content-specific support (Gallucci, Van Lare, Yoon, & Boatright, 2010). Typically, instructional content coaches focus on English language acquisition, math, literacy, or science, and most content coaches work with teachers regardless of their years of experience. Instructional and content coaching generally involve preconferences, observations, and postconferences (West & Staub, 2003).

Although all these modes of coaching have merit and, in fact, an experienced coach might draw on all of them, this chapter will examine in greater depth *content instructional coaching* or, simply, *content coaching*. In our work with districts and teacher leaders we have witnessed a lack of appreciation for the coaching expertise needed to support both teacher training implementation and the long-range shifts in teachers' habits of mind that support teacher decision making, understanding student needs in relationship to high academic standards, and beliefs about student capacity to learn. We also note that this expertise parallels that of an instructional leader engaged in the inquiry-based Habits of Thinking for Instructional

Leadership, which will be detailed in Chapter Eight. Most important, we want to underscore once again that improving practice is a matter of expertise. Before we elaborate on content coaching we will offer you a vision for what it could look like in practice. Following, we resume the vignette so you can see how the coach actually intervened in the classroom. Jennifer is, in fact, a content coach. Keep in mind how the other modes of coaching—peer, mentoring, cognitive, and instructional—could have played out in this story. As you read, consider how Jennifer's choices have the potential to influence teacher learning in ways that peer coaching, mentoring, cognitive coaching, or instructional coaching could not. Notice especially how Jennifer uses her knowledge of high school literacy learning and a vision for Alexis's students and her classroom to guide her decisions.

Once the students are reading independently, Jennifer and all the teachers sit down in a small circle with Juan, a student, who suddenly has six adults focused on him. As Juan begins to talk about his book, *Always Running*, by Luis Rodriguez, he explains, "I like stories about Latinos and how they kinda make their lives better. You know, like when they get out of gangs sometimes." Jennifer explains to Juan (and the teachers) that because he is particularly attracted to books about successful Latinos, he could become a resident expert on this genre for the class. Juan smiles shyly in approval. As Alexis prompts him to talk about his responses to this text, using the terms from the day's lesson, Jennifer comfortably jumps in. "See, here is what I'm thinking for Juan to develop as a reader." She continues, suggesting that Juan could use one of the bins in the classroom to start a book collection of this genre for other ninth-graders or give a presentation on Latino success stories and invite people in from his community to talk about how they left their gangs. Alexis agrees that this is a great idea and she and Juan come up with some next steps. As Juan leaves the circle, Jennifer says to Alexis and the group, "So what you saw here is a kid who can really do more. We want to be leveraging kids' responses for a bigger purpose, not just the day's lesson."

EXPERTISE IN CONTENT COACHING

Many new coaches we know are hesitant to assert that they have a particular expertise. We frequently hear coaches say, "I am not an expert but . . . " This tendency is common in the culture of teaching in general, possibly because traditionally teachers have worked in isolation without a shared language for teaching practices (Lortie, 1975). Nonetheless, we assert that strong content coaches do develop particular areas of expertise that both encompass and are distinctly different than those of strong teachers. We believe that coaches must be strong content teachers themselves but that strong teachers do not automatically become strong coaches. The skill sets are different. This section will examine three main dimensions of content coach expertise: expertise in content, expertise in instructional practice, and expertise in adult professional learning.

Before we proceed, we would like to acknowledge that although much of our discussion of expertise comes from our experiences in the field, we are also grounded in a larger theoretical orientation toward learning. We take a constructivist, sociocultural view of learning. In this view, ideas and understandings are not simply transmitted from the head of an expert to the head of a learner. Instead, we view learning as the active construction of understandings and processes in light of existing experiences and understandings, often guided and supported by a more experienced other (Vygotksy, 1987). We also assume that learning occurs in social contexts—distinct national, regional, district, school, and classroom cultures—as well as within larger discourse communities of education, mathematics, science, or language arts (Rogoff, 1995).

Expertise in Content

Content coaching is distinct from other modes of coaching, precisely because it is anchored in specific disciplines. A content coach might have general knowledge of and experience with multiple content areas, but we believe strong content coaches know the areas in which they are coaching quite well. For literacy coaches, for example, this means knowledge of the composition process, literary interpretation, and reading theory. Although there are many ways to develop this depth of content knowledge over time (university programs, self-studies, professional development), coaches work hard to stay current regarding new understandings and developments in their field. We know coaches who take advanced coursework in their content area well into their careers and who read new articles and publications in math, literature, or science extensively.

When we say *content*, we mean both the academic discipline itself *and* how children come to learn and think in that discipline. In 1986, researcher Lee Shulman coined the term *pedagogical content knowledge* to describe the kind of content knowledge that teachers should develop to support their students' understandings. He argued that elementary school teachers did not necessarily need to have deep understanding of calculus, they needed specific understanding of how students come to understand place value and common misconceptions that develop along the way. He also argued that teachers need the ability to recognize and interpret evidence of student understanding. In other words, teachers should develop their pedagogical content knowledge in the subject areas they teach.

We believe that content coaches ideally need both kinds of content knowledge—deep and extensive knowledge of the discipline itself *and* of how children come to learn it. Why is this the case? Take for example a math coach working in a third-grade classroom. That coach can certainly draw on her knowledge of how students learn number concepts to help the teacher understand why her students are struggling with multiplication, but she can also help that teacher develop a long-term vision for mathematical thinking in general. This larger vision for a trajectory of math learning, for how mathematicians think, act, and communicate in their discipline, may or may not become explicit in the coaching relationship but will guide and inform how the coach works with the teacher.

This deep and wide content understanding also helps content coaches work across the grade levels. For instance, high school English teachers often have read lots of canonized fiction and know the work of literary analysis quite well, but they might know less about how children learn to read. A strong content coach can apply her own knowledge of literary theory and her understandings of early literacy to help a secondary teacher assess, describe, and support the range of students in her classroom.

For example, consider the agenda in Exhibit 7.1 from some coaching work at a different high school. A content coach, Dianna, has been supporting one of the teachers, Ronda, in her ability to model her thinking when reading challenging texts. Ronda, similar to many high school English teachers, has a wide knowledge of historically significant books and has high standards for her students' ability to read and think about them. She knows less about the reading process or how to model her thinking. Margaret, the principal, invited Dianna to support two other English teachers and a social studies teacher in similar work. This agenda frames an afternoon in which these three teachers and Margaret will observe Ronda trying on some new learning about reading instruction.

EXHIBIT 7.1. HARMONY HIGH SCHOOL

Goals

- Continue to build literacy teacher leadership and collaboration
- Begin a classroom intervisitation process to make practice public
- Consider how to organize our instruction so we prepare all students to engage in rigorous classes, particularly in the upper grades
- Hone our abilities to model and think aloud about reading and writing
- Practice observing student learning objectively

Agenda

1. Opening and goals for the day (11:45–11:55) (Margaret, principal)
2. Setting up the observation (11:55–12:05) (Dianna)

   Reflect: How have you been practicing modeling your thinking when reading challenging texts?

   Reflect: What are your questions about modeling your thinking with reading challenging texts?

   Observing, not interpreting student learning and teacher practice
3. Context for the lesson and students selected (12:05–12:20) (Ronda)

   Here's what we're working on . . .

   Here's what I am trying out today in my lesson and modeling . . .

   Here are the students I am curious about . . .

   (continued)

4. Observation in Ronda's classroom (12:20–1:15, approximately)

   Observing, not interpreting

   –Student learning in the meeting area

   –Teacher modeling

5. Sharing our observations of students (1:15–1:45)

6. Sharing our observations of the teacher modeling (1:45–2:15)

7. Implications for our own practice and next steps (2:15–2:45)

In order to design this agenda and the learning experience, Dianna, the content coach, had to draw on several kinds of expertise, for instance, recent research on secondary literacy and how students develop the ability to think in different disciplines. She also drew on her experience working with younger readers to consider the role of immersion in a wide range of complex texts in learning to read. This deep expertise allowed her to create an agenda that infuses new content learning alongside the goals of teacher leadership and collaboration.

Expertise in Instructional Practice

Shulman (1986) defines expertise in instructional practice as a subcomponent of pedagogical content knowledge. A teacher with strong science pedagogical content knowledge understands how students typically come to understand why we have seasons and furthermore understands how to structure interactive, social-learning experiences to shape student conceptual mastery of the seasons. This ability to design flexible, supportive learning experiences represents one form of content-specific knowledge of instructional practices. Some instructional practices (such as setting clear objectives or thinking aloud) apply across content areas but strong content area teachers and content coaches understand how and why even these general practices shift in particular disciplines.

Content coaches have a flexible, wide-ranging understanding of instructional practices in their content area across the grade levels as well as a deep understanding of why certain practices might make more sense than others in certain situations. Content coaches are furthermore guided by their visions of literate practice in a given discipline. They understand that instructional practices are tools for scaffolding students' independent skill and knowledge development toward these visions. These instructional practices are not end points in and of themselves for teachers to master.

For example, let's imagine a literacy coach working in Brenda's language arts class. The coach might know that Brenda's department has been working hard on the practice of partner talk as a tool to develop student thinking and independence. The coach visits Brenda's classroom to prepare for a coaching cycle, knowing that this cycle will do more than just help Brenda do turn and talks right. The coach will certainly take note of the partner talk in the classroom in order to consider how the teacher is currently thinking about its role and how the talk is currently helping the students become truly independent thinkers.

During this observation, imagine the coach notes that all the students in the class seemed very excited to talk with each other and further notes that most partners spoke very generally about their writing. The coach might recognize that all the students had lots to say and could benefit from academic language support. She might think about other instructional strategies or ways to augment this one to support student language development, including the following:

- Modeling a turn and talk about her own writing and writing identity using the terms *revise* and *develop ideas*
- Presenting a graphic organizer showing the writing cycle with academic language and sample sentences
- Asking students to self-assess as writers and put a sticky note on the part of the writing process showing where they think they are, then telling a partner about how they knew where they were
- Asking students to turn and talk about their writing using the terms *revise* and *develop ideas* rather than simply saying, *turn and talk about your writing*
- Revising ideas or drafts publicly along with students (*guided writing*) using posted sentence stems to prompt discussion

Content coaching requires a flexible understanding of a range of instructional approaches from across the grade levels and also a flexible ability to decide why to use given approaches as a means to a certain vision for student learning. In these ways, content coaching is different from general instructional coaching, cognitive coaching, or peer coaching. We assert that strong content coaches do indeed have particular expertise in their content areas and that these content-based understandings guide the coaching work.

Expertise in Adult Professional Learning

We acknowledge that the writing lesson vignette highlights a coach with significant pedagogical understanding and reasoning. However, we also believe that strong content coaches incorporate even more complex decision-making processes. So far, the coach in our example has not considered Brenda's unique set of beliefs, experiences, goals, issues, and her particular trajectory as a learner. In this section, we will address some general principles of adult professional learning and some specific considerations when working with individual teachers. We believe that coaches draw on expertise about adult learners to plan and enact their work.

Researchers and practitioners have written extensively about adult professional learning from a range of theoretical orientations. Much of this literature overlaps with research on effective professional development in general (Valli & Hawley, 2003). Effective adult professional learning should accomplish the following:

- Engage participants in personal short-term and long-term goal setting
- Assess what teachers already know and understand
- Be relevant to teachers' work, examining concrete problems of practice and practical solutions
- Involve teachers in posing questions, seeking data, and drawing conclusions, in other words, involving teachers in cycles of inquiry (for example, Nelson, Slavit, Perkins, & Hawthorn, 2008)
- Immerse adults in the content area of focus, such as reading, writing, or math, and reflecting on the skills and strategies required
- Become anchored in student work and student outcomes
- Acknowledge predictable teacher-learning trajectories in a content area

Effective content coaches embrace these principles of adult learning. They assume that teachers come to their work with unique experiences and goals and seek to uncover and leverage these resources. Content coaches also work in the teacher's work context—generally right there alongside her in the classroom—but also in the context of student work and curriculum materials. A content coach also assesses the teacher's larger work context, the department, grade-level, school, or district as a whole, assuming that this environment affords distinct opportunities and problems of practice. Content coaches often start with a teacher's expressed needs and dissatisfactions in the classroom—such as low student participation or inconsistent student work habits—providing both concrete strategies and scaffolding changes in teacher thinking or beliefs about students. In many cases, content coaches model taking an inquiry stance toward students and their learning. Furthermore, when appropriate, content coaches engage teachers in content-based experiences in the discipline.

Refer back to the agenda from Harmony High School in Exhibit 7.1. The agenda includes time for all the teachers to reflect on their implementation of and questions about modeling their thinking. During this time, the coach can assess how teachers are currently thinking about their practice and gather a larger context. This time also allows teachers to set some goals for their own learning. The work is embedded in a concrete problem of practice—helping Ronda model her reading work—and allows time for teachers to debrief the experience and consider implications for their own classroom practices. The coach also prompted the teachers to observe student learning and offered parameters for this observation. In other sessions, this group of teachers read challenging texts together to discuss their own thinking processes.

However, in addition to these general principles of adult learning, we have noted that successful content coaches also approach individual teachers with a constant stance of inquiry. Successful content coaches are not driven exclusively by their knowledge of content or desire to support implementation of a particular instructional practice or reform initiative. Content coaches always seek to understand who that teacher is as a learner, a thinker, a teacher, and a person and use this understanding to guide choices about coaching strategies. To do this, coaches develop and test *theories*.

The following section describes the process of theory formation and offers a few tools to guide new coaches in forming a theory and making a plan for coaching.

RESEARCH-DECIDE-COACH

Strong content coaches are strong practitioner researchers. Content coaches assume that teachers are complex human beings on a life-long learning trajectory. Uncovering a teacher's assumptions, understandings, goals, beliefs, and strengths is the ongoing work of a coach. If we lose sight of who the teacher is, then we also risk losing the coaching relationship and any possibility of change in practice. Many content coaches describe their work as helping a teacher reach his or her vision for the ideal classroom. In order to do this, a coach must figure out what this vision is, possibly help a teacher develop an even more nuanced and powerful version of it, and figure out what is in the teacher's way of reaching this vision. From this understanding, a coach can start to experiment with carefully selected coaching strategies to focus the teacher's work on specific instructional practices and habits of mind. However, this work begins with a theory.

Literacy specialist Lucy Calkins (2001) coined the construct *research-decide-teach* as the typical structure of a one-on-one conference with a young reader. This cycle incorporates gathering information about the reader, making a decision about what to teach him or her, then actually choosing a teaching method and teaching. A similar cycle might be applied to coaching, though it would be reimagined as *research-decide-coach*.

Research

To form a theory, a content coach uses two main research skills: observation and conversation. These skills can be employed inside or outside the classroom.

Observation   A coach is constantly gathering information while watching a teacher interact with her students and with other teachers. But, although our tendency at first might be to judge or reach quick conclusions about what is happening, a skilled content coach focuses on separating observation from interpretation and forms questions before forming conclusions. (See Chapter Five for more on separating observation from interpretation.) Coaches look for patterns of behaviors that might suggest a tendency or common issue. The sum of these observations becomes a tentative theory. This observation never stops—even after a coach and teacher start experimenting with changes in practice. A coach will still ask herself how the teacher seems to be making sense of the learning and why that might be the case. Here are some questions a coach might ask herself during a classroom observation to gather information and form a theory:

- What do I see? What am I curious about?
- What do I think is important to this teacher? How do I know?
- What do I notice might be frustrating to this teacher? Why?
- What do I think this teacher really wants for her students?
- How do the students talk about their learning?
- What is in the way of this teacher having her ideal classroom?

Taken together, questions of this type guide a coach to form a theory about a teacher as a learner and practitioner. These questions focus a coach's attention on the teacher and students—and a long-term vision for their growth—rather than on discrete instructional practices. A coach, similar to any instructional leader, thinks extensively and analyzes practice while it is occurring.

As an illustration, notice in Table 7.1 the difference between notes a coach might have taken in Brenda's language arts classroom from a theory-forming perspective versus from a prematurely conclusive perspective.

As previously explored in Chapter Five, notice how the notes in the left column include low-inference observations about the classroom, including direct quotes from students. The left column also includes the coach's questions about the teacher's thinking and beliefs. In the right column, the coach has already formed conclusions and judged what is happening, for example, stating, "they were so bored!" There are no low-inference notes to examine and study. A coach reading over these notes on the right-hand side would not be able to plan a coaching conversation to investigate teacher thinking, beliefs, and vision—there is nothing to investigate!

Conversation   Observation is only one tool a coach might use to form a theory. In and of themselves, observational notes do not constitute a theory. A strong content coach expects that she might be wrong about any or all of her inferences or preliminary theories. She uses her observational notes to guide her planning for a debrief conversation with the teacher. This conversation might help her test her theory and start to decide on a coaching plan with the teacher. However, it also might not. Experienced content coaches take time to make sure they have a solid working theory and remain open to revising these theories as the work progresses.

Table 7.1.
Classroom Observation Notes

THEORY-FORMING NOTES	CONCLUSIVE NOTES THAT DO NOT LEAD TO A THEORY
Brenda just asked the students to turn and talk and the students immediately starting talking. Everyone had a partner. The students seem to know the routines well. *How long has this teacher been using this practice? What role does she want it to serve for students? What does she believe about student talk and the resulting learning?*	The teacher should have had the students turn and talk earlier. They were so bored! They seemed really unengaged until right now.
Brenda is getting close to students while they talk. *What is she noticing? What does she tend to do with that information? Does she know what to do with it?*	This teacher clearly did not understand the part of the professional development about taking notes during turn and talks! She has no information.
Tan, "I am putting my words in this part in a different order. I like it better this way."	
Matt, pointing to Tan's paper, "Yours is really good! I like how it sounds when you have pictures not talking first." *These two students seem to be listening to each other. They are talking about their writing and seem quite excited about it, based on their vocal volume and their use of the writing itself. I wonder if they want to have other, more specific words to use? Does the teacher want this, too? Does she know to listen for it? What are possibilities for the quantity and the quality of partner talk in this classroom because it already seems so enthusiastic?*	These two ELL students had a great conversation but did not use any of the language from the lesson. They must need more visual support.

New coaches often think the coaching conversation is purely organic and spontaneous. It is true that over time, coaches become more flexible and intuitive in their debriefs. However, especially at first, coaching conversations require considerable intentionality on the coach's part. They have the potential to provide a coach with significant information about the teacher's thinking and beliefs. Generally, coaches look over their observation notes to plan a coaching conversation. During this process, these kinds of questions help support a coach's ability to plan a coaching conversation:

- What am I really curious about? What strikes me in my notes?
- What do I think is this teacher's vision for her classroom? How can I verify that theory?
- Which parts of the class that I observed seemed the most typical for the teacher?
- What do I want to understand about this teacher's understanding of the content or instructional practice?
- Taken together, what do my notes so far suggest about this teacher's goals and beliefs? What do I want to know more about?
- Which moments in the class might represent habits a teacher has that I want to understand?
- What might be in this teacher's way? What worries her in her practice? How could I find out?
- How does this teacher seem to learn best? How does this teacher think she learns best?
- Does this teacher seem likely to admit dissatisfaction in her classroom? If not, why? If so, how might I prompt her to discuss it?

A coach cannot necessarily address all these theory-building questions in one conversation. Furthermore, she must leave space for probing or follow-up questions based on what the teacher says. In practical terms, most coaches rely on a teacher's thirty- to forty-five-minute planning period to hold conversations. For these reasons, content coaches usually go into a conversation with a few carefully selected questions. Consider the previous example from Brenda's classroom and the questions we might plan to ask in a debrief in Table 7.2. We

Table 7.2.
From Theory-forming Notes to Theory-testing Questions

THEORY-FORMING NOTES	POSSIBLE QUESTIONS WE MIGHT PLAN TO ASK TO TEST THE THEORY
Brenda just asked the students to turn and talk and the students immediately starting talking. Everyone had a partner. The students seem to know the routines well. *How long has this teacher been using this practice? What role does she want it to serve for students? What does she believe about student talk and the resulting learning?* Brenda is getting close to students while they talk. *What is she noticing? What does she tend to do with that information? Does she know what to do with it?* Tan, "I am putting my words in this part in a different order. I like it better this way."	What already excites you about turn and talks in your room? **How is planning for turn and talks different from how you used to plan for lessons?** **How do you want students to be talking about their learning by the end of the year?** **What did you notice today when your students turned and talked?**
Matt, pointing to Tan's paper, "Yours is really good! I like how it sounds when you have pictures not talking first." *These two students seem to be listening to each other. They are talking about their writing and seem quite excited about it, based on their vocal volume and their use of the writing itself. I wonder if they want to have other, more specific words to use? Does the teacher want this, too? Does she know to listen for it? What are possibilities for the quantity and the quality of partner talk in this classroom because it already seems so enthusiastic?*	I want to ask you about one specific moment in the partner talk today. I noticed you leaning in to listen to Matt and Tan. What did you notice? How would you like to hear them talking about their work?

bolded the questions we would be sure to ask because we suspect they might provide the most information about the teacher's thinking.

Notice that the questions the coach plans to ask are genuine, sincere, open-ended questions. See the Habits of Thinking for Instructional Leadership guidelines in Chapter Eight for other questions to ask the teacher. Some of the questions are ones the coach might want Brenda to ask herself as a reflective practitioner (for example, What did I notice about my students when they turned and talked today?) but all the questions are designed to inform the coach's developing theory. They are not leading questions or questions designed to trick the teacher into saying something the coach already has in mind. Teachers can generally tell when they are being lead and such questions tend to feel manipulative and can damage a coaching relationship.

Table 7.3 shows a further illustration of the difference between a leading question and a theory-building question.

Sometimes questions could fall into either category. In these cases, it is the coach's stance or intent that determines how the teacher perceives the question.

Decide

After reviewing the data a coach collects during classroom observations and conversations, she starts to form a theory about the teacher and from that theory she starts to form a coaching plan. Both the theory and the coaching

Table 7.3.
Leading Questions Versus Theory-building Questions

LEADING QUESTIONS IMPLY THAT COACH HAS ANSWER IN MIND	NONLEADING QUESTIONS DESIGNED TO INFORM A THEORY AND COACHING PLAN
What will you do differently tomorrow to make the turn and talks better?	What did you notice about your students' language in the turn and talks?
What did you learn about ELL issues in the staff professional development that you could have used today?	How do you want your students to be talking by the end of the year?

plan can be negotiated and adjusted along the way. In this part of the coaching work, a coach considers the teacher as a learner, the school and district instructional context, principles of adult learning, understandings of the way teachers tend to learn to teach that content area, and her own pedagogical content knowledge. To start to craft this theory and then coaching plan, a coach might ask herself these questions:

- What am I learning about this teacher?
- What do I now think she really wants for her students? What else could I help her see?
- What seems most in her way?
- What is the biggest shift this teacher could make in her practice that would help her get closer to her vision?
- What will be hardest for her in this shift?
- What content area instructional practices might she try that would help her reach that vision?
- What habits of mind do I want her to develop?
- What coaching strategies seem most appropriate to help this learner?

Questions such as these direct a coach's attention to the teacher's beliefs and goals as well as keep coaches grounded in general best practices in a content area. They also keep the idea of the teacher as a learner firmly in focus—teachers are not empty recipients of someone else's best practices or reform ideas. Furthermore, they anchor the work in both short-term (instructional strategies) and long-term (habits of mind) goals that will set up a teacher to make deep shifts in the classroom—not just superficial changes or quick-fix strategies.

Returning to Brenda's language arts class example, let's imagine that the coach asked her some theory-building questions. A brief excerpt from their coaching conversation is on the following page.

Based on several conversations and sets of observational notes, the coach formed the following working theory about Brenda and possible short-term and long-term goals for the coaching work (see Table 7.4).

Notice that the theory shown in Table 7.4 encompasses a larger vision for a language arts classroom, the teacher's goals, where she is in her learning, her learning needs, and her understanding of the work. The short-term goals are

COACHING CONVERSATION EXCERPT

Coach: So, tell me, how do you hope you will hear your students talking about their writing by the end of the year?

Brenda: Hmmm. That's a good question. I guess I hadn't thought about that. I want them to be comfortable sharing their writing with each other during their turn and talks. But they already seem comfortable doing that, so I don't know. They seem to trust each other.

Coach: How do you know?

Brenda: Well, whenever I say, "turn and talk!" they do it and they stay on task. No one seems scared they will be put down. Like today. Did you see that?

Coach: I did notice. They seemed really excited to share their work with each other. It sounds like they do that fairly consistently. [Teacher nods.] Great! Getting students to trust one another sounds like it is very important to you, and it is very important to building a strong community of writers. [Teacher nods again.] This is a strength I think you can really leverage. What do you think got them to this point?

Brenda: I don't know. [Pause] It might be because I always tell them they are smart and do good work. They seem to really like hearing that and I hear them telling each other that, too.

Coach: So, you model for them providing positive feedback. What else?

Brenda: I think they just came that way. They are a nice group. [Pause] When I listen to them, though, I know I am supposed to write things down, but I don't because I don't know what to write down. I am just so happy that they are talking. I don't want to interrupt them or hurt their feelings. It seems really good already!

Coach: So, it sounds like you are satisfied with the amount of talking they are doing and the level of trust between them in the classroom. But, it sounds like you want to know what more is possible for them to talk about. It sounds like you are open to finding out what else they can do but you are also a little nervous about shutting them down.

Brenda: Yes! What do we do about that?

Table 7.4.

Working Theory to Inform Short-term and Long-term Goals

THEORY	SHORT-TERM GOALS	LONG-TERM GOALS
A strong classroom culture is very important to Brenda. She really wants students to feel safe enough to take risks. She probably also needs to feel safe and supported with positive feedback herself. She might be fearful of pushing students if she is worried they won't succeed. She also does not always see the link between her own instructional actions and student learning. She underestimates herself!	Increase student specificity during partner talk, small-group talk, and whole-group talk Brenda will increase the scaffolding during talk opportunities. Brenda will give increasingly specific feedback to students (this might require some writing content study—possible new theory about Brenda's content knowledge?).	Help Brenda connect her instructional actions with student learning Help Brenda develop an assessment lens and understanding of the range of possible student learning

concrete, measurable, and observable. The coach will be able to check in and monitor progress toward them in this cycle and during the year. The coach will assess progress toward the long-term goals by listening to and watching Brenda talk about and interact with students and her practice. All goals are situated in the context of the department's work on accountable talk.

Coach

After initial consideration, a content coach then engages the teacher in a conversation about a possible direction for the coaching work. The coach asks for the teacher's feedback on the work and also proposes a strong rationale for her short-term and long-term goals and strategies. Keep in mind that this proposed coaching strategy encompasses the coach's working theory and important contextual factors such an instructional initiative's aims. Once the coach and teacher have reached an agreement about the work itself, the coach can start to plan how she will work with the teacher.

Many new coaches plan for coaching much in the way they planned for teaching. They help the teacher plan the next day's lesson. For example, in this case, a coach might co-plan a lesson in which the turn and talks have additional visual support. This strategy will likely change the instruction in the class the next day but it may or may not change the following day's lesson or address long-term goals, such as changing the way the teacher thinks about and assesses students. Strong content coaches gain the most traction with teachers when they plan for *coaching* strategies not only for teaching.

Once a coach and teacher have agreed on a coaching point or goal, the coach might ask herself questions like these to plan for coaching:

- What do I still have to figure out to plan for my coaching work with this teacher?
- Based on the coaching point, the teacher as a learner, and the context, what coaching strategies might I use inside the classroom? Outside the classroom?
- What questions or habits of mind do I want this teacher to develop? What strategies will I use to help her start developing those habits?
- How will I gradually release responsibility for the new instructional practices to the teacher?

Many coaches think of a coaching cycle or set of coaching goals in terms of a gradual release of responsibility to the teacher. After some initial scaffolding, we plan ways to help the teacher take on more and more of the work (both instructional practice and habit of mind). We also remember that habit-of-mind goals will likely take longer than instructional practice goals. The coach also recognizes that the teacher will continue to experiment after the coaching cycle ends, and we must plan for this, too. Table 7.5 shows an example of a template that might guide a coach's planning in this coaching situation.

This template is meant just as a guide or suggestion for how a coach might plan a coaching cycle with a teacher. Often, truly long-term coaching points extend across several coaching cycles and they can evolve along the way. The coach continues to engage in a cycle of assessment (research-decide-coach) throughout the coaching relationship.

Table 7.5.
Short-term and Long-term Instructional Practice Goals

INSTRUCTIONAL PRACTICE GOALS (SHORT TERM)
1. Brenda will increase the scaffolding during student talk opportunities. 2. Brenda will give increasingly specific feedback to students about their work and learning.

HABIT-OF-MIND GOALS (LONG TERM)
1. The teacher will connect her instructional actions with student learning. 2. The teacher will develop an assessment lens and understand the range of possible student-learning processes.

PLANNING FOR THE GRADUAL RELEASE OF RESPONSIBILITY

To:	With:	By:
Inside the classroom, I will *model* setting up students for partner talk using visual supports with key academic language. I will ask Brenda to follow me around and watch how I prepare the students for talk and how I respond to them during the talk by giving specific feedback. I will think aloud to Brenda before I offer the feedback to students. We will debrief these experiences right after they happen so it will be fresh in Brenda's mind. She might be nervous about what to do when students don't know what to say.	Inside the classroom, I will *co-teach* the set-up for the partner talks with Brenda. She will probably be nervous about the parts when she has to give them feedback. I will model some of those and we will talk to each other to process what we are hearing and I will help her figure out what to say. I will have to reassure her that she might not know what to do with some of the information she gathers, and that's OK. Outside the classroom, we will debrief what we heard the students say and I will ask Brenda how she is thinking about organizing for student talk tomorrow. I	Inside the classroom, I will *observe* Brenda setting up the partner talk. If she gets stuck, she can ask me to jump in. I will make a point of pushing her to give the students feedback even if she is not 100 percent sure what to say. I will narrate for her how her actions changed the way the students are talking. Outside the classroom, we will debrief how she is thinking about partner talk and giving specific feedback. We will set some agreements around how she will practice setting students up for talk and gathering information.

In a coaching conversation after this in-class experience, I will ask Brenda for examples of language I used that she wants to try tomorrow. We will plan to set up the turn and talks together tomorrow. I will ask her which parts she wants me to lead.	will support her planning as needed.	

CONCLUSION

This chapter offered some general context for the increasingly widespread professional development strategy called *coaching*. We also placed our stake in the ground at content coaching, a form of coaching we have observed to have the greatest effect on teacher and student learning. That said, we also have attempted to detail the complexity of the work of content coaching. Content coaching requires deep and wide expertise in content areas, instructional practice, and adult learning. We offer the construct of research-decide-coach as a possible tool for thinking through the work of content coaching, complementing our discussion in Chapter Eight of Habits of Thinking for Instructional Leadership.

Much of the research on coaching describes it as highly relational, person-to-person, work. We do not disagree—we know that without strong relationships with teachers, coaches will not experience success in changing instructional practice. However, this chapter helps clarify the type of relationship work that content coaching entails and the extent of expertise that grounds such relationships.

DISCUSSION QUESTIONS

- How do you use coaching to improve practice?
- What is the further expertise your coaches may need in order to improve their ability to support teaching practice?

PART FOUR

Embracing New Opportunities for Leading and Learning

chapter EIGHT

The Leader's Role in Improving Teacher Practice

The previous chapters have provided a variety of case examples, illustrations, and tools for school leaders in their effort to improve the quality of teaching. The purpose of this chapter is to examine more broadly the roles and responsibilities of school and district leaders in their collective work to improve teaching practice. Specifically, we will revisit the concept of reciprocal accountability as it relates to an instructional improvement agenda and then introduce a final framework to help leaders at all levels of the organization engage in the kind of ongoing inquiry practice necessary to improve teaching and learning for all.

RECIPROCAL ACCOUNTABILITY

The idea of reciprocal accountability provides a particularly useful construct for school and district leaders who are intent on improving the quality of teaching and learning. Reciprocal accountability simply means that if we are going to hold you accountable for something, we have an equal and commensurate responsibility to ensure you know how to do what we are expecting you to do (Elmore, 2000; Resnick & Glennan, 2002). Practically speaking, this important concept means that accountability must go hand in hand with organizational capacity building with a specific focus on ensuring that teachers and leaders have the expertise necessary to ensure high achievement for all students. Let's examine how the concept of reciprocal accountability should play out from the classroom to the district boardroom.

Reciprocal accountability has usually (not always) been taken for granted in the classroom. The whole idea of schooling implies that teachers are responsible for ensuring that students learn prescribed subject matter. This means that teachers must know deeply each of their students as individual learners, differentiating their instruction accordingly so that each student meets the stated standard regardless of the student's starting place. As we discussed in previous chapters, this sophisticated and complex art and science of teaching requires a clear through-line linking together the five dimensions of *purpose, student engagement, curriculum and pedagogy, assessment for student learning*, and *classroom environment and culture*. Implicit in the act of teaching is that we cannot hold students accountable for something that has not been taught. Of course this is where the breakdown often occurs. Teaching something once, in one way, to all students is usually not sufficient to then hold students accountable for learning. To ensure that students learn, we need to do more than disseminate content. The truth is that reciprocal accountability in the classroom exists only to the extent that subject matter is taught well as embodied by the vision statements in the Five Dimensions of Teaching and Learning framework. Excellent teachers know and understand that student learning is ultimately a measure of their own teaching.

Although the lion's share of attention is focused on the relationship between teachers and students as the critical variable in student learning, the concept of reciprocal accountability provides the same useful lens to examine the relationship between teachers and principals. To start this examination, it is instructive to contrast prevailing expectations of teachers and principals. As we discussed previously, it is generally expected and assumed that teachers will get to know their students as individual learners. Teachers will use a variety of assessment tools and techniques to know students' strengths, weaknesses, learning styles, and needs. Again it is assumed that excellent teachers will use their thorough assessment of student learning needs in relation to state and national standards to shape their teaching point and instructional strategies. Although principals don't take this relationship between teachers and students for granted, they often fail to recognize the similar reciprocal nature of their role with their own teachers.

Just as teachers need to know their students as individual learners, principals need to know their teachers as individual learners. Excellent principals also use a variety of assessment tools and techniques to know teachers' strengths, weaknesses, learning styles, and needs. We have illuminated a variety of strategies, frameworks, and tools in previous chapters to help principals with this effort. However, it starts with a fundamental awareness and understanding that as a school leader, if I am to hold my teachers accountable for high-quality teaching, then I need to ensure they have the knowledge and expertise necessary to do what I am expecting them to do. In our experience the extent to which principals understand and practice the reciprocal nature of their role as an instructional leader varies widely. Many principals indeed embody the essence of reciprocal accountability in their daily practice, yet some principals do not know their teachers as individual learners, engage in pro forma classroom visits at best, and are generally absent in the important work of improving teaching practice.

Even in cases in which principals try to provide relevant feedback, it is often isolated from any kind of strategic improvement effort. For example, we have observed this typical interchange between principals and teachers dozens of times. A principal observes a portion of a ninth-grade language arts teacher's class during a formally scheduled observation visit. During the course of the observed portion of the lesson the principal notes that the teacher's questioning strategies of students requires a rather low level of student thinking. Specifically, the principal notes that the teacher asks eleven questions during a twenty-minute review of the novel *To Kill a Mockingbird*. Each one of the eleven questions required students to only recall information or retrieve information from their text. The principal then seizes on this insightful observation to provide written feedback to the teacher complementing the teacher on several aspects of the lesson, provides feedback about the low level of questioning, and suggests that the teacher begin to use higher-level questions that require the students to infer, analyze, and synthesize information and ideas. Absent is any kind of connection between the feedback and what the principal is or has been doing to support teachers' professional learning—in this case how to develop a repertoire of questioning strategies that require much higher levels of student thinking. The more expert instructional leader might go back to the dimensions of purpose (standard and teaching point) and curriculum and pedagogy to question the purpose of teaching a whole class novel in the first place. However, with respect to questioning strategies in particular, the truth is that if the teacher knew how to employ higher-level questions and help scaffold students' thinking in order to answer higher-level questions, the teacher would already be doing it. Teachers work at the limits of their pedagogical and subject matter content understanding every single day. Simply providing written feedback to teachers pointing out something they should improve on without actually teaching them how to do so generally falls short of actual improvement. If principals want teachers to teach differently—in any way, shape, or form—then they must guide, support, and nurture teacher learning just like we expect teachers to do for students.

Let's imagine school principals approaching their instructional leadership work as one would expect a teacher to do so for his or her students. We should expect the principal to have a detailed assessment and accounting of each teacher including but not limited to the following criteria:

- How each student is progressing in the teacher's class along with particular problems of student learning that have emerged
- What the teacher is doing to address problems of student learning
- What the teacher does well as measured by an instructional framework for high-quality teaching such as the Five Dimensions of Teaching and Learning
- Where the teacher needs to develop more expertise according to the same instructional framework
- What the principal is doing to develop that teacher's expertise including the trajectory of improvement and benchmarks by which the principal will measure the improvement

Imagine this kind of detailed assessment and accounting for each teacher as an individual learner and performer in contrast to the typical school improvement plan that is commonplace in schools across the country. In the typical school improvement plan process, principals lead their staff in a careful review of data designed to surface specific improvement goals for the school. Although this process is not bad in so much as the review of data is an important component of inquiry work, it's that the resultant goals tend to lack the granularity necessary to improve individual teaching practice. For example, a typical school improvement goal, after months of data review and hours of staff discussion and consensus building, may read something like this:

- Third-grade students will show a 15 percent gain in mathematics as measured by the state test of academic proficiency by the end of the academic school year.

The school improvement plan may go on to link specific professional development strategies such as a common book study in inquiry-based math teaching or lesson analysis and so on. Again there isn't anything inherently wrong about this process except that it stops far short of getting to the heart of the matter, which is how each individual teacher is supposed to go about improving his or her own teaching practice. Just as with students, teachers are also at different starting places in the depth of their subject matter and pedagogical expertise. Improvement of individual teaching practice requires the same kind of differentiated instructional leadership as improvement of student learning requires differentiated instruction. This is the nature of reciprocal accountability in the school.

If principals are to know their teachers as individual learners and to orchestrate professional learning in ways that help each of them improve their teaching practice, then it is equally important to examine the role of central office leaders in support of school principals. As long as school districts continue to be an instrumental unit under the governance of an elected board of directors or a local mayor, then it is critical to create a coherent system that actively supports high-quality teaching practice in every school. This is the difference between a true school system, responsible for systemwide improvement, versus a system of individual schools left on their own to figure out how to improve. Some continue to argue that school systems as we know them are largely incapable of supporting high-quality teaching practice for all students, thus the only sensible reform effort should be to use prevailing market forces to create private school choice in the form of independent and other types of charter schools. Although we are not opposed to a thoughtful integration of charter schools into a larger system of public schooling we believe deeply that there is a fundamental role for school district central offices in support of high-quality teaching and learning. The fact that so many school district central offices have not risen to this role is not necessarily an indictment of the school district or central office as a critical unit in support of teachers and leaders. We believe that the historic inability of central offices to ensure high-quality teaching for all is less of a structural issue and more of a paradigm issue. The very idea of a central office in the early history of public education in the United States was to provide material support—goods and services—and basic management functions for schools. Central offices were never designed to provide instructional leadership. Even by today's higher accountability standards many central office leaders fail to recognize the reciprocal nature of their role as instructional leaders. However, a growing body of educational research has noted the important relationship school district central office leaders play in supporting student learning across the system (Copland & Knapp, 2006; Honig, 2008; Wahlstrom, Seashore, Leithwood, & Anderson, 2010). Looking at it through the lens of reciprocal accountability our question is, "What do central office leaders need to know and be able to do in order to help principals improve their instructional leadership practice so that teachers in turn improve their teaching practice?" Just as we noted in Chapter Four when we introduced the three types of observations, there must be a clear and purposeful connection among the work of central office leaders, principals, and teachers in service of improved practice.

Although we believe that central office leaders must play a role in improved teaching and learning, there is a question of what this should actually look like in terms of their daily leadership practice. University of Washington researchers sought to answer this exact question (Honig & Copland, 2010). Studying several prominent school district central offices that fundamentally transformed its leadership role in support of schools and situating these findings in the larger body of school district instructional improvement efforts Honig and Copland captured actual practices that central office leaders employed in service of improving teaching and learning. In short they noted that true central office transformation must be measured not by organizational structures, reporting relationships, managerial titles, and functions but by the actual practices central office leaders engage in every day to support teaching and learning.

In CEL's growing work with school district central office transformation, Honig and Copland have expanded on this research in the development of the Five Dimensions of Central Office Transformation found in Table 8.1. We use the framework to help central office leaders examine their practices and ensure that their daily work is measured ultimately against the standard of improved teaching practice as evidenced by improved student learning.

Just as the Five Dimensions of Teaching and Learning framework serves to develop a shared vision of high-quality instruction and prompt specific instructional leadership actions, the Five Dimensions of Central Office Transformation serves to identify and prompt specific central office leadership

Table 8.1.
Five Dimensions of Central Office Transformation

FIVE DIMENSIONS	SPECIFIC PRACTICES
1. Learning-focused partnerships with school principals to deepen principals' instructional leadership practice	Dedicated central office administrators (instructional leadership directors, or ILDs) engage principals one-on-one and in networks or learning communities around principals' instructional leadership. Specific practices in these relationships include the following: • Differentiating supports for principals' instructional leadership consistently during the entire academic year • Modeling instructional leadership thinking and action • Developing and using tools to support principals' engagement in instructional leadership • Brokering external resources to help principals focus on their instructional leadership • Engaging all principals in the network as instructional leadership resources
2. Assistance to the central office–principal partnerships	• Professional development for ILDs that provides them with regular opportunities for challenging conversations about the quality of their work with school principals and how to improve it • Taking issues and other demands off ILDs' plates, freeing up their time to work with principals on principals' instructional leadership • Leading through—rather than around—the ILDs and otherwise supporting the leadership of ILDs, vis-à-vis principals' instructional leadership *(continued)*

Table 8.1.

(*continued*)

FIVE DIMENSIONS	SPECIFIC PRACTICES
	• Developing and using an accountability system in which ILDs do not act as the sole agents holding principals accountable for improvements in student performance
3. Reorganizing and reculturing of other central office units to support teaching and learning improvement	• Shifting the practice of central office administrators across central office units to personalize services through case management and focus on problem solving through project management • Developing the capacity of people throughout the central office to support teaching and learning improvement • Holding central office administrators accountable for high-quality performance
4. Stewardship of the overall central office transformation process	• Ongoing development of the theory of action for central office transformation • Ongoing communication about the work of central office transformation and its underlying theory of action • Strategically brokering external resources and relationships to support the overall central office transformation process
5. Use of evidence throughout the central office to support continual improvement of work practices and relationships with schools	• Ongoing intentional search for various forms of information, especially evidence from central office administrators' experience about how to support teaching and learning improvement • Deliberate efforts to incorporate that information into central office policies and practices

practices. These practices embody the concept of reciprocal accountability. Note that there is nothing hierarchical about these practices. In fact the very nature of *learning-focused partnerships*, for example, conveys the very opposite of hierarchy. It conveys that the improvement of instruction is not just the work of teachers or principals but also the work of everyone in the school system. The degree to which central office leaders understand and practice this level of joint work is the extent to which they can seize on these important reciprocal relationships to improve instructional practice and student learning. For a thorough examination of the research findings and analysis that led to the creation of CEL's Five Dimensions of Central Office Transformation framework (Honig & Copland, 2010) go to the actual study and final report, which can be downloaded from the CEL Web site at www.k-12leadership.org.

Implicit in the central office transformation work is that the superintendent, too, plays a critical reciprocal accountability role. It is the superintendent who must envision, advocate for, and sponsor the work of instructional improvement. It is the superintendent who must help the entire organization focus its efforts on instructional improvement and ensure that appropriate accountability measures are in place to support this work. It is the superintendent who understands that his or her primary role is to ensure that central office leaders, principals, and teachers have clear expectations for their performance and that the entire organization coalesces to ensure all have the necessary expertise to do their jobs well. Finally, it is the superintendent who understands that although his or her leadership will be measured against many standards and diverse expectations, in the final analysis the ultimate measure of leadership success is the improvement of instruction and student learning.

In those school districts that have elected school boards, board members also play a reciprocal accountability role in instructional improvement. In school districts in which reciprocal accountability is present from the board-room to the classroom, school board members understand that their role is first and foremost about setting policy not engaging in management. Second, school board members must set policy that is consistent with the tenants of reciprocal accountability. Although school board policy must cover the gamut of organizational needs including health, safety, facilities, operational, and fiduciary responsibilities, board members must pay special attention to their policies and spending pertaining to increasing student learning. Those policies and concomitant allocation of resources must embody the understanding that students will learn more when they receive higher-quality teaching, and it is the responsibility of the district to ensure that teachers have the expertise necessary to teach all students well.

LEADING WITH AN INQUIRY STANCE

We discussed what it means for instructional leaders to develop a learning stance alongside teachers. The development of expertise necessary to improve teaching practice requires learning at all levels of the organization. Here we want to introduce one final tool that helps school leaders in their learning work by formalizing a process of classroom inquiry necessary to bring to the surface problems of teaching and leadership practice. We call the following tool the *Habits of Thinking for Instructional Leadership,*[*] although this kind of inquiry process can be used as effectively at the classroom, school, or district level (see Figure 8.1). This tool is rooted in the belief that a foundational skill for all successful instructional leaders is the ability to lead a rigorous inquiry process designed to bring to the surface problems of student learning and teaching practice and identify specific leadership strategies and actions that can be put into place to address these problems.

Let's examine how instructional leaders can use this tool to improve teaching and learning. The first step in the process is what we call *noticing and wondering*. In the inquiry process, noticing is the act of gathering data. We found that on entering a classroom, expert observers of instruction suspend judgment; instead, they focus their efforts on *noticing* as much as possible about the activity the students are engaged in, what the teacher is doing and saying, and what the students are doing and saying. Just as scientists carefully observe and log data as the first step in scientific inquiry, instructional leaders do the same thing through the kind of detailed lesson scripting discussed in Chapter Four. Based on what they are observing, instructional leaders may begin to wonder about specific teaching choices and strategies employed by

---

[*] You have seen this tool in various forms throughout this book. In the early chapters we talked about the importance of staying in the descriptive mode by *noticing* and *wondering*. We provided examples of school leaders engaged in analysis, testing *theories,* and taking specific leadership actions. In fact we thought about formally introducing this tool in its entirety as early as Chapter Two. However, we decided to withhold the formal introduction until the end of the book so that our readers had the opportunity to engage in the various steps of this inquiry process without having to worry about naming all of the parts.

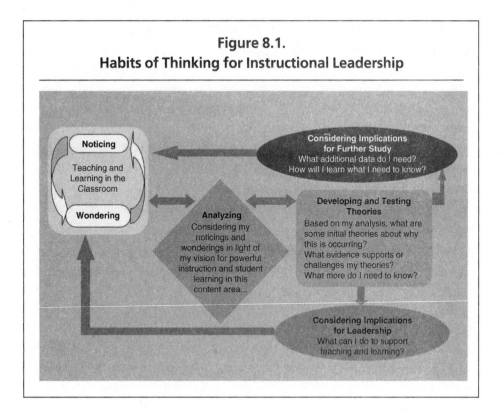

Figure 8.1.
Habits of Thinking for Instructional Leadership

Noticing

Teaching and Learning in the Classroom

Wondering

Analyzing
Considering my noticings and wonderings in light of my vision for powerful instruction and student learning in this content area...

Considering Implications for Further Study
What additional data do I need? How will I learn what I need to know?

Developing and Testing Theories
Based on my analysis, what are some initial theories about why this is occurring? What evidence supports or challenges my theories? What more do I need to know?

Considering Implications for Leadership
What can I do to support teaching and learning?

the teacher. In this case, *wondering*, is just that—an open and honest question without preconceived notions or judgment. For example, we may enter a ninth-grade algebra classroom and notice that students are working together in groups of four to solve a particular problem. We may notice that some students are doing most of the talking in these groups. We may *wonder* how the teacher went about setting up these groups and whether the teacher intentionally grouped certain students together to support each other's learning. Remember in Chapter Three how the principal (in her analysis of Jacob's math lesson) had detailed noticings that led to genuine wonderings.

From noticing and wondering the next step in the inquiry process is *analysis*, which requires the observer to situate the noticings and wonderings within his or her vision of powerful instruction. This part of the process gets tricky because it assumes the observer of instruction has a deep enough knowledge of powerful instruction to begin testing theories, which is the next step in the process. We found that expert instructional leaders are able to ground their noticings and wonderings to a deep understanding of subject matter content knowledge and powerful pedagogical practice in order to analyze thoroughly their observation in the context of the stated lesson purpose. In the ninth-grade algebra classroom, an expert instructional leader with a strong mathematics subject matter understanding may discern that students in this classroom were struggling with problems that should have been mastered earlier in the year in terms of the curricular sequence. This curricular knowledge provides the instructional leader more to posit in terms of wonderings than someone who did not have the same curricular knowledge. This further informs this leader's analysis in terms of generating problems of student learning and teaching practice. From here the expert instructional leader is able to generate plausible *theories* about why these students are struggling. Those theories may have to do with the teacher's own understanding of the ninth-grade algebra curriculum and his chosen instructional strategies. Again, we refer the reader back to Chapter Three to see how the principal's subject matter and pedagogical expertise enabled her to engage in a deep analysis of Jacob's lesson and develop plausible theories that would help Jacob improve his teaching practice. This level of analysis and theorizing leads to the final two steps. In some cases those theories may prompt the instructional leader to gather more evidence to further illuminate the problem of practice being studied. In other cases those theories may lead to specific steps the leader will take to support the teacher's learning.

The unique aspect to this type of inquiry process is that each one of the steps not only can be learned, but in fact also must be mastered, hence the title *habits of thinking*. This is a disciplined cycle of inquiry requiring instructional leaders to develop *habits* that eventually become part of their daily leadership repertoire. As such, each one of the habits requires practice and refinement over time. This practice can be facilitated using any of the three types of classroom observations discussed in Chapter Four.

Let's look at how leaders can use the Habits of Thinking for Instructional Leadership to inform their leadership moves. Table 8.2 shows one example of the inquiry process through the eyes of a middle school principal. In this case the principal was observing a seventh-grade social studies class in which students were studying early civilizations.

In this example, the principal began with her noticing—in this case with one specific noticing that students only had their textbook as the primary source

Table 8.2.
Principal's Inquiry Cycle: Seventh-Grade Social Studies

HABITS OF THINKING FOR INSTRUCTIONAL LEADERSHIP	EXAMPLE
Noticing *Specific facts related to teaching and learning that I've recorded during an observation*	Each student had one textbook open on his or her desk to look up information about early civilization.
Wondering *Based on what I saw (or didn't see), I'm curious or would like to know . . .*	Are there other resources available for students to access core content learning?
Analysis *I'm using what I know about what learning would look like in the ideal in relation to this context I've observed. I will now think about this information as it compares with my noticings and wonderings.*	My knowledge of readers and the reading process is that there are a variety of readability levels in our classrooms. Also, the process of reading is a complex one that entails syntax (structure of language), phonographic understanding (letter-sound correlation), and semantics (comprehension). What I'm seeing in the classroom is that students in this classroom have one textbook to access information. And given the wide range in students' reading abilities I know that all students cannot access the subject content from the textbook.
Theories *Based on multiple observations across all classrooms and a preponderance of data, this is one theory about why student learning is as I've observed . . .*	Teachers may not have the reading content knowledge or skill set to know how to teach reading within the content areas.
Leadership Implications *Using this theory as a guide, this is one implication for professional development and my decisions as a*	What do we, as a staff, need to learn about reading content knowledge and pedagogy that is pertinent to promoting student understanding *(continued)*

Table 8.2.

(continued)

HABITS OF THINKING FOR INSTRUCTIONAL LEADERSHIP	EXAMPLE
leader. As I implement next steps, I realize that I'll need to gather additional information and data to measure effectiveness.	(for example, text features of nonfiction to navigate any text)?

document. This led to the principal's wondering whether or not students had access to other information sources. As you can see in the principal's analysis, she drew on her knowledge of reading and her students as learners to recognize that not all of the students were able to access the information due to their reading level. Furthermore, she knows enough about good teaching practice to know that if students cannot access the text, and if there are no other sources for them to access, then they would not be able to understand the information they were asked to research. Notice that when the principal began testing theories, she did so by placing this one classroom observation alongside multiple other observations to generate even more data in the inquiry process. This led her to the theory that more than just this one teacher lacked expertise in teaching reading across the content area. From here the principal began to generate possible next steps to support teachers' professional learning.

To illustrate how principals can use this inquiry process to examine different aspects of instructional practice, let's return in Table 8.3 to the example from Chapter Five from the sixth-grade language arts class in which the teacher is in the middle of a poetry unit. At this point in the unit the teacher is expecting students to justify their interpretation of a given poem.

In this example the principal began the inquiry process with noticing and wondering focused specifically on student talk, which we know from Chapters Two and Three is a critical subdimension of student engagement. Notice how the principal's analysis required a deep understanding of the role of student talk beyond simply the routine of turning and talking with one another. Just

Table 8.3.
Principal's Inquiry Cycle: Sixth-Grade Language Arts

HABITS OF THINKING FOR INSTRUCTIONAL LEADERSHIP	EXAMPLE
Noticing *Specific* data *related to teaching and learning gathered during an observation*	Students seated together, away from their desks, facing the teacher. Students turn and talk when prompted by the teacher (J.B.). J.B. listens in to a student conversation.
Wondering *Based on what I saw and heard, I'm curious about* . . .	What J.B. considers the potential for student conversations? How does he ultimately want students to engage with their own thinking, with the content, and with one another? I wonder if J.B. is satisfied with what he hears students saying? What is he listening for? How does the way he listens to student talk allow him to assess student understanding?
Analysis *Using what I know about what student learning would look like in the ideal in relation to what I've noticed and wondered* . . .	I wonder whether engagement in learning through talk is accountable—to the learning community, to knowledge in the discipline, and to rigorous thinking. In J.B.'s class, students knew the routine of turning to a partner to talk and those who shared their ideas seemed comfortable doing so. The students seemed really accustomed to this routine and had things to say to their partners. This tells me that J.B. has supported the level of talk that does exist. I assume J.B. understands that engagement is much more than students staying on task or students having the opportunity to talk and that authentic engagement must provide opportunities for students to engage in academic discourse in order to (*continued*)

Table 8.3.

(continued)

HABITS OF THINKING FOR INSTRUCTIONAL LEADERSHIP	EXAMPLE
	deepen their thinking and conceptual understanding. I'd like to know more about J.B.'s beliefs about literary analysis in general and his students in particular.
Developing a Theory to Test *Based on my analysis and my plan to learn more about J.B.'s vision for student learning, the potential he envisions for the student conversations, and how he understands the role of talk in student learning, I think that . . .*	J.B. has a long-term goal in mind for his students as thinkers, communicators, and how to engage them in literary analysis. J.B. is intentional and thoughtful about releasing responsibility for students to take on increasingly sophisticated conversations.
Gathering More Information **Questions I Might Ask the Teacher** *Based on the theory I'd like to test, I will ask J.B. . . .*	How do you decide the content of partner talk and how do you decide *when* to have students talk to partners? What is your long-term plan for your students' partner talk? How would you like your students to be running their own conversations? How do you want them to be pushing each other's thinking by June?

as in the prior example, the principal must have enough instructional expertise in order to test plausible theories and help the teacher examine his or her own instructional strategies. The deeper the principal's instructional expertise, the more sophisticated is his or her theories and next steps.

Keep in mind that in both examples each step in this inquiry process was based on one specific noticing. The utility of the habits-of-thinking inquiry process is that leaders can focus their noticing on any relevant aspect of classroom instruction. In the first example the principal built the inquiry from noticing that each student had one textbook to retrieve information about early civilizations. In the second example the principal built the inquiry from noticing what was happening during student talk. When we think about just how much we can notice in a thirty- to forty-five-minute classroom observation, applying the habits of thinking steps can become a rather daunting instructional leadership process. Again this is why we refer to this inquiry process as *habits*. Once something becomes a habit, it doesn't require the same level of overt thinking. It is in the deepening and refinement of these habits that instructional leaders can draw on an ample reservoir of expertise to support teachers' professional learning. And it is in the rigorous application of these habits that instructional leaders seek first to establish evidence before making premature judgments. Remembering that teaching is indeed a sophisticated and complex endeavor helps us remember that the instructional leadership necessary to improve the quality of teaching is also complex and sophisticated. Developing these habits of thinking alongside a thorough understanding of the 5D framework will go a long way to support leaders' efforts to improve the quality of teaching.

Accountability with an Inquiry Stance

The Habits of Thinking for Instructional Leadership provides a useful lens from which to view accountability for school improvement. Learning to lead with an inquiry stance is in fact the bedrock of reciprocal accountability. It is the very nature of reciprocal relationships guided by the goal of developing expertise that requires everyone to be a serious student of inquiry. Increasing student learning requires improving the quality of teaching practice and the process of improving practice involves careful study (inquiry) designed to build expertise.

Contrast this notion of accountability with prevailing national and state level accountability policies rooted in traditional market-driven concepts of incentives and rewards. The idea of extrinsic motivation is rooted in tenants of behavioral psychology, a mainstay of American business enterprise for the last two centuries. The idea is that by incentivizing workers through increased compensation or other benefits, productivity will increase. And conversely by threatening or punishing workers with sanctions, productivity will maintain or increase. Merit pay for teachers along with monetary rewards for schools that show student achievement gains are gaining more widespread acceptance among public policy circles. Conversely, reconstituting poorly performing schools, removing the principal or half of the teachers, full take-overs by charter management entities, and so on also are gaining in policy circle popularity as the stick to use on underperforming schools.

We believe there is in fact an important body of psychological research indicating that the long-term effect of extrinsic motivation is to erode intrinsic motivation. However, this is neither the time nor place for expounding on this argument. Regardless of one's philosophical beliefs about the power of extrinsic versus intrinsic motivation, we make the following argument: the idea behind incentives and rewards assumes implicitly that there is enough expertise among teachers and principals to improve dramatically the quality of teaching, if we can only find a way to incentivize teachers and principals. Implicit in this thinking is that somehow our teachers and principals are showing up to work every day and only giving the students their "B" game, all the while holding their "A" game back waiting for some kind of external incentive. And once that incentive is bestowed then the teachers will take the "A" game out of the closet. Of course, this all assumes there is an "A" game in the first place. The truth is that whether their game is "A" quality or "B" quality is not the issue. We know the vast majority of teachers and school leaders are giving their "A" effort every day on behalf of students in their care. If they have not been able to elevate the quality of their "game," then that is an issue of expertise not desire or motivation.

In order to understand the current level of instructional expertise among school leaders, our own faculty and researchers at the University of Washington have been assessing leaders' ability to observe and analyze instruction and provide feedback to teachers using a sophisticated, research-based instrument designed to measure leaders' knowledge of instruction through the lens of the Five Dimensions of Teaching and Learning framework. Participants log onto a secure Web site, watch a twenty-minute language arts or math lesson, and write in response to three questions:

1. What do you notice about teaching and learning in the classroom?

2. Based on this observation, what feedback would you give the teacher?

3. If this were a pattern of teaching in your school, what are the implications for teacher professional development?

Researchers developed a four-point rubric that runs from novice to expert: 1.0 = novice; 2.0 = developing expertise; 3.0 = emerging expertise; 4.0 = expert. Participants are rated on each of the five dimensions and thirteen sub-dimensions. As of October 2010 approximately eighteen hundred principals and central office leaders from thirty-one school districts in ten states had participated. Figure 8.2 illustrates the average scores for the five general dimensions.

According to the chart, the average placement on the four-point rubric runs from 1.47 to 2.03 for the five general dimensions—somewhere between *novice* and *emerging expertise.* This important research clearly demonstrates that too few leaders charged with leading the improvement of instruction have developed sufficient expertise to identify really good teaching and explicate what makes that teaching "really good." Without developing this expertise, all of the incentives, rewards, and accountability systems in the world will not improve at scale the quality of teaching and learning necessary to educate all students well and to eliminate the pernicious achievement gap that continues to divide our nation's children along the lines of race, class, and language.

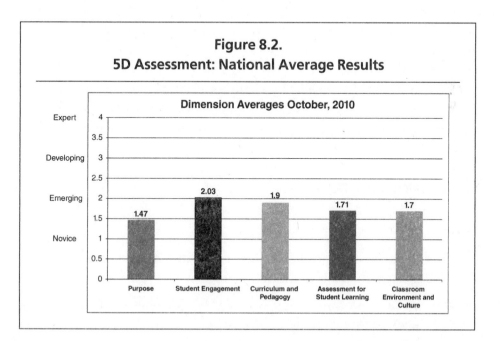

Figure 8.2.
5D Assessment: National Average Results

CONCLUSION

The purpose of this chapter was to focus once again on the leader's role in improving teaching practice. We reintroduced the concept of reciprocal accountability, which we believe is critical if district and school leaders are to improve the quality of teaching practice in their district and schools. We explained what it means to be reciprocally accountable for student learning.

We introduced a useful inquiry cycle called the Habits of Thinking for Instructional Leadership. Although this inquiry cycle was developed specifically to guide school leaders in their work with teachers, the inquiry cycle is suitable for any type of teaching or leadership problem of practice that requires evidence gathering, analysis, and the development of theories that lead to specific actions. For example, from Chapter Seven on instructional coaching, we introduced the construct of *research-decide-coach*. Thinking about this construct using the habits-of-thinking inquiry cycle we find that the research phase is akin to the noticing and wondering and the decide phase is akin to the analysis, developing a theory to test, and questions parts of the habits of thinking.

Finally, we offered a view of accountability that stands in stark contrast to many of the prevailing views and policies guiding teacher and school accountability. Accountability *through an inquiry stance* recognizes that developing expertise is the ultimate marker for school leaders who are intent on improving teaching and learning. This accountability stance is not an apologist view that forgives poor teaching practice or is it intended to shift the burden of responsibility from the teachers and school leaders to some larger social unit or dynamic. It is just a stark reminder that district and school leaders must ensure that teachers have the knowledge and expertise necessary to ensure quality learning for all students.

DISCUSSION QUESTIONS

- To what extent is your leadership reciprocally accountable, that is, specifically builds the expertise capacity of those whom you supervise or support?
- To what extent do you lead with an inquiry stance in order to engage colleagues in collective, ongoing learning?
- How do you as a school or district leader think about incentives and rewards as a way to improve the quality of teaching?

chapter NINE

A New Vision for Improving Learning for All

In this concluding chapter we offer a new vision for improving learning for all students. Rather than a vision that overlays aged and flawed assumptions of incentives, rewards, and quick program fixes on an educational system that has proved inherently unable to make at-scale improvements to teaching and learning, we offer a different view that is predicated on the idea that lack of expertise is the central issue that precludes dramatic improvement in student achievement across the country. We believe we have made a compelling argument about the importance of expertise as well as offer strong case examples of how educators can go about the task of developing expertise. As such our view calls into question the very structural and economic model that contributes to the current expertise crisis among teachers and school leaders.

To elaborate let's compare two critically important professions for citizen health and welfare—medicine and teaching—in terms of the professional preparation and ongoing training for teachers and physicians. Both of these professions require some kind of state licensure with oversight by a type of professional standards board. The typical medical school preparation for a doctor involves four years of undergraduate work with a heavy emphasis in the physical and biological sciences, four years of medical school with a blend of classroom and clinical experience, and a two- to six-year residency depending on the medical student's preferred subspecialty. This means from the time the student enters medical school until the time he or she can practice medicine with no direct oversight ranges from six to twelve years. And of course once the doctor is out practicing independently he or she must still be involved in ongoing training as new information and techniques become part of the medical mainstream.

The typical education school preparation for teachers involves either a fifth year beyond the undergraduate experience (although in some cases it becomes part of the four-year undergraduate degree) or in some cases a one- to two-year master's degree program beyond the four years of undergraduate experience. In terms of clinical experience, the time students actually spend in classrooms practicing their teaching under the supervision of an experienced teacher may range from an academic quarter of approximately ten weeks to a semester of eighteen weeks. In some cases students may serve two rotations in classrooms for a total of twenty to thirty weeks of practice. There is in fact a growing range of program options and offerings for prospective teachers including more clinical and alternative paths for state licensure, all aimed at increasing the knowledge and skills of newly certified teachers. However in all cases, the amount of preparation a teacher receives before practicing (independently) the craft of teaching is nowhere near the kind of preparation a doctor receives before seeing patients without oversight.

Can you imagine sending yourself or a loved one to a doctor who has only completed one year of medical school? Or perhaps placing the delivery of your first child in the hands of a medical resident who has had one ten-week rotation in obstetrics? Or perhaps scheduling surgery with someone who has only completed two courses in anatomy along with several hours of cadaver dissection? Of course not! There is a widespread understanding that the level of expertise required to practice medicine well necessitates a long and arduous training regimen before one is deemed worthy of being licensed as a medical doctor and an even longer training regimen before one is deemed worthy of being a board-certified subspecialist. Yet each year we place teachers to work with our most precious commodity—our children—without the background knowledge and expertise necessary to ensure that all students will experience quality teaching and learning. And when we get a product (in this case teaching quality) that is entirely consistent with the degree of training in this complex and sophisticated profession, we jump to blame.

Here is another excerpt from Deborah Ball's (2010) testimony to the U.S. House of Representatives that poignantly illuminates our expertise argument:

. . . . There is a difference between reading about how to put in an intravenous line and the first time one tries to do it on a patient. Or landing an airplane in the fog, rain, or blowing snow using only the instrument panel. These skills take both head knowledge and hand knowledge, and they take time to develop. In no other profession in this country do we presume that people who are trying something for the first time, or second, or third, can be given full responsibility for the task or left alone to figure it out. Many people have ideas about improving teacher quality. . . . Not one of these is sufficient to solve the core problem: that of ensuring that every teacher, in every classroom, can do the work we are asking of him or her. What we need is quality *teaching*. This is a problem of training, both initial and continuing, and not merely one of sanctions, rewards, or other incentives. . . .

It's interesting to note that teacher education programs are under increasing attack for producing teachers incapable of teaching all students well. In fact education schools are in peril as states contemplate and put into force alternative means of teaching certification, at least in part motivated by the frustration among policy makers and school district officials that schools of education remain incapable of reforming to the changing needs of the public school system. Although we believe that schools of education in general, and some in particular, need to undergo major transformation in order to better educate prospective teachers, let's be clear about the basic structural and economic model at play.

It is understood and accepted that doctors need to invest ten to sixteen years (inclusive of undergraduate study) of their lives to develop the expertise necessary to practice medicine well. And the prevailing economic model is such that doctors are financially rewarded for this investment. Teachers, however, must invest somewhere between four and six years of their time with low to modest financial reward. We need to be honest about this. Either we believe that the expertise required to teach well is not nearly as complicated as the expertise necessary to practice medicine well or we just care less as a society about the educational welfare of our children than we do about our own physical welfare. We believe that contrary to popular perception, the practice of teaching so that *all* students learn at high levels is every bit as sophisticated and complex as the practice of medicine. Hence our vision for improving learning for all students begins with a major revamping—structurally and economically—of the preparation pathway for prospective teachers.

The preparation pathway for school leaders is no more extensive or arduous than it is for teachers. The typical preparation program for school principals involves one or no more than two years consisting largely of individual courses covering topics such as school leadership, law, finance, change, and so on. There is typically some kind of internship that may run for a school quarter or semester; however, in many cases the internship manifests mainly in activities such as leading school level committees and developing a specific improvement project. In most cases principals receive little to no further instructional training in either their preparation courses or internship. Yet somehow we think they are capable of the deep instructional improvement work that we described in preceding chapters.

In the face of increasing impatience among the public, business community and policy makers there are now alternative routes to leadership licensure as well as teaching licensure. The idea for leaders flows from an argument that goes something like this: Good leadership is just good leadership so it is important to find good leaders regardless of their industry. Whether it be former military officers or corporate or nonprofit leaders there is a prevailing belief among some that the future of our children's education should be entrusted to someone whose domain expertise may be how to command a naval battle group. This is not a criticism of any particular school or district leader. In truth the early evidence suggests that there is no measurable difference between traditional and alternative pathways to teaching licensure (Committee on the Study of Teacher Preparation Programs in the United States, 2010), which we suspect will be true of leadership licensure as well on further study. This actually makes good sense because none of the current pathways lead to the kind of expertise development we see in other fields such as medicine or law. Nothing short of a major revamping of the preparation pathways for teachers and school leaders is going to yield the expertise necessary to improve learning for all students.

Because a revamping of this type is likely just a pipe dream, perhaps no more than a glimmer of light several galaxies away, we need to wrestle with the very real challenge of how to build dramatically the expertise of teachers and principals in the course of their daily practice. As we have seen, this work is challenging to say the least and perhaps just plain daunting on a daily basis. However, make no mistake: we cannot wait for the day when the initial preparation of our teachers is more consistent with the deep body of knowledge necessary to teach all students well. We cannot wait for the day when the initial preparation of school leaders is more consistent with the deep body of knowledge necessary to lead the improvement of teaching and learning. We can and must be working every day to build the expertise of our teachers and principals. We need to acknowledge and accept the current level of knowledge and skills among our teachers and school leaders and work with all of our adults from where they are at now with an eye toward building their individual and collective expertise. We know how to do this work and we trust the prior chapters have provided insights, tools, and strategies that will be useful in this endeavor. However, tools and strategies are only as useful as the investment we are willing to make into developing the expertise of our teachers and school leaders. This is not an inexpensive venture. It will require the courage of policy makers to allocate the necessary funding and the wisdom of school district leaders to use that funding wisely.

In conclusion, we are faced with an interesting conundrum. On the one hand, we have argued that students will learn more when teachers provide students higher-quality learning experiences. This is a leadership issue that requires teachers and principals to deepen their instructional expertise. We have demonstrated how to go about building this expertise with the recognition that this cannot be done overnight. On the other hand, we live every day with the reality that too many of our students are not getting the kind of quality education they need to be successful citizens of the twenty-first century. As we relegate legions of poorly educated students every year to a permanent economic underclass, the cry to do something now resonates louder and louder. There is great urgency to act. Every time we go into classrooms and see students languishing in low-level, irrelevant seat work that contributes to their disenfranchisement, we bleed for those students. It is a sobering experience. At the end of the day it is a social justice and equity issue for our students and families. And it is an issue for the economic and democratic well being of our country.

In the final analysis the conundrum we face is how to act with urgency when we know the development of expertise necessary to improve teaching is a long-term process requiring a long-term commitment. It is this very conundrum that continues to spawn an endless plethora of quick-fix programs, policies, and strategies. Yet in the end deepening one's expertise to improve practice takes time. That said, we believe the answer lies in approaching the development of expertise—both teaching and leadership—with the urgency and seriousness that the current educational situation demands. School leaders need to be acting with a singularity of focus measured by the extent to which practice improves every day—not every month or every year. Leaders can do this work with the urgency our students deserve. We have seen it happen in dozens of schools and school districts. And when this happens it sets up a kind of self-fulfilling prophesy in which teachers and leaders believe in the efficacy of their hard work and actions and in which students believe they are expected to and capable of learning to the highest standards. This can happen today in schools anywhere. We hope you will use the tools and strategies we have offered in this book to seize the moment and make it happen in your school, too!

DISCUSSION QUESTIONS

- What systems, structures, and strategies does your school and school district have in place to increase the instructional expertise of teachers and principals?
- How will you go about assessing the effectiveness of these efforts?
- How do you and your colleagues reconcile the urgency to act now to improve quality learning for all students with the understanding that building the necessary teaching expertise takes time?

5D Framework

5D	SUBDIMENSION	THE VISION	GUIDING QUESTIONS
Purpose	Standards	• The lesson is based on standard(s) that are meaningful and relevant beyond the task at hand (e.g., relate to a broader purpose or context such as problem solving, citizenship, etc.) and helps students learn and apply transferable knowledge and skills. • The lesson is intentionally linked to other lessons (previous and future) in support of students meeting standard(s).	• How do the standard and teaching point relate to content knowledge, habits of thinking in the discipline, transferable skills, and students' assessed needs as learners (in terms of language, culture, learning styles, etc.)? • How do the standard and teaching point relate to the ongoing work of this classroom? To the intellectual lives of students beyond this classroom? To broader ideals such as problem solving, citizenship, etc.? • What is the teaching point of the lesson? How is it meaningful and relevant beyond the specific task or activity? • Is the task or activity aligned with the teaching point? How does what students are actually engaged in doing help them to achieve the desired outcome(s)? • How are the standard and teaching point communicated and made accessible to all students? • How do students communicate their understanding about what they are learning and why they are learning it? • What will students know and be able to do as a result of the lesson? What will be acceptable evidence of student learning?
Purpose	Teaching Point	• The teaching point is based on knowledge of students' learning needs in relation to standard(s). • The teaching point is clearly articulated, linked to standard(s), embedded in instruction, and understood by students. • The teaching point is measurable. The criteria for success are clear to students and the performance tasks provide evidence that students are able to understand and apply learning in context.	

5D	SUBDIMENSION	THE VISION	GUIDING QUESTIONS
Student Engagement	Intellectual Work	• Students' classroom work embodies substantive intellectual engagement (reading, thinking, writing, problem solving, and meaning making). • Students take ownership of their learning to develop, test, and refine their thinking.	• What is the frequency of teacher talk, teacher-initiated questions, student-initiated questions, student-to-student interaction, student presentation of work, etc.? • What does student talk reveal about the nature of students' thinking? • Where is the locus of control over learning in the classroom? • What evidence do you observe of student engagement in intellectual, academic work? What is the nature of that work? • What is the level and quality of the intellectual work in which students are engaged (e.g., factual recall, procedure, inference, analysis, metacognition)? • What specific strategies and structures are in place to facilitate participation and meaning making by all students (e.g., small group work, partner talk, writing, etc.)? • Do all students have access to participation in the work of the group? Why or why not? How is participation distributed? • What questions, statements, and actions does the teacher use to encourage students to share their thinking with each other, to build on each other's ideas, and to assess their understanding of each other's ideas?
	Engagement Strategies	• Engagement strategies capitalize and build upon students' background knowledge, experience, and responses to support rigorous and culturally relevant learning. • Engagement strategies encourage equitable and purposeful student participation and ensure that all students have access to, and are expected to participate in, learning.	
	Talk	• Student talk reflects discipline-specific habits of thinking and ways of communicating. • Student talk embodies substantive and intellectual thinking.	

5D	SUBDIMENSION	THE VISION	GUIDING QUESTIONS
Curriculum and Pedagogy	Curriculum	• Instructional materials (e.g., texts, resources, etc.) and tasks are appropriately challenging and supportive for all students, are aligned with the teaching point and content area standards, and are culturally and academically relevant. • The lesson materials and tasks are related to a larger unit and to the sequence and development of conceptual understanding over time.	• How does the learning in the classroom reflect authentic ways of reading, writing, thinking, and reasoning in the discipline being studied? For example, how does the work reflect what mathematicians do and how they think? • How does the content of the lesson (for example, text or task) influence the intellectual demand (for example, the thinking and reasoning required)? • How do lesson content and instructional strategies provide all students with access to the intellectual work and to participation in sense making? • What does the instruction reveal about the teacher's understanding of how students learn, of disciplinary habits of thinking, and of content knowledge? • How is student learning of content and transferable skills supported through the teacher's intentional use of instructional strategies and materials? • How does the teacher differentiate instruction for students with different learning needs?
	Teaching Approaches and Strategies	• The teacher makes decisions and utilizes instructional approaches in ways that intentionally support the instructional purposes. • Instruction reflects and is consistent with pedagogical content knowledge and is culturally responsive in order to engage students in disciplinary habits of thinking.	
	Scaffolds for Learning	• The teacher's use of instructional approaches balances the interplay of explicit teaching, scaffolding for the gradual release of responsibility, and for student choice and ownership. • The teacher uses different instructional strategies based on planned and/or in-the-moment decisions to address individual learning needs.	

5D	SUBDIMENSION	THE VISION	GUIDING QUESTIONS
Assessment for Student Learning	Assessment	• Students are able to assess their own learning in relation to the teaching point. • The teacher creates multiple assessment opportunities and expects all students to demonstrate learning. • Assessment methods include a variety of tools and approaches to gather comprehensive and quality information about the learning styles and needs of each student (e.g., anecdotal notes, conferring, student work samples, etc.). • The teacher uses observable systems and routines for recording and using student assessment data (e.g., charts, conferring records, portfolios, and rubrics). • Assessment criteria, methods, and purposes are transparent and students have a role in their own assessment to promote learning.	• How does the instruction provide opportunities for all students to demonstrate learning? How does the teacher capitalize on those opportunities for the purposes of assessment? • How does the teacher gather information about student learning? How comprehensive are the sources of data from which he or she draws? • How does the teacher's understanding of each student as a learner inform how the teacher pushes for depth and stretches boundaries of student thinking? • How does assessment help students to become more metacognitive and to have ownership of their learning? • How does the teacher's instruction reflect planning for assessment? • How does assessment inform the teacher's instruction and decision making? • How does the teacher adjust instruction based on in-the-moment assessment of student understanding?
	Adjustments	• The teacher plans instruction based on ongoing assessment and an understanding of students, standards, texts, tasks, and pedagogical content knowledge. • The teacher makes in-the-moment instructional adjustments based on student understanding.	

5D	SUBDIMENSION	THE VISION	GUIDING QUESTIONS
Classroom Environment and Culture	Use of Physical Environment	• The physical arrangement of the room e.g., meeting area, resources, student seating, etc.) is conducive to student learning. • The teacher uses the physical space of the classroom to assess student understanding and support learning (e.g., teacher moves around the room to observe and confer with students). • Students have access to resources in the physical environment to support learning and independence (e.g., libraries, materials, charts, technology, etc.).	• How does the physical arrangement of the classroom and the availability of resources and space to both the teacher and students purposefully support and scaffold student learning? • How and to what extent do the systems and routines of the classroom facilitate student ownership and independence? • How and to what extent do the systems and routines of the classroom reflect values of community, inclusivity, equity, and accountability for learning? • What is the climate for learning in this classroom? • How do relationships (teacher-student, student-student) support or hinder student learning? • What do discourse and interactions reveal about what is valued in this classroom? • What are sources of status and authority in this classroom (for example, reasoning and justification, intellectual risk taking, popularity, aggressiveness, etc.)?
	Classroom Routines and Rituals	• Classroom systems and routines facilitate student responsibility, ownership, and independence. • Available time is maximized in service of learning.	
	Classroom Culture	• Classroom discourse and interactions reflect high expectations and beliefs about all students' intellectual capabilities and create a culture of inclusivity, equity, and accountability for learning. • Classroom norms encourage risk taking, collaboration, and respect for thinking.	

Source: Copyright © 2010 Center for Educational Leadership, University of Washington. www.k-12leadership.org.

Appendix B: Types of Classroom Observations

TYPES OF OBSERVATIONS	PURPOSE(S)	SUPPORTING THEORY	LOGISTICAL CONSIDERATIONS	POSSIBLE LEADERSHIP ACTIONS FOR CONSIDERATION
Learning Walkthrough District administrators, principals, and teacher leaders focus on one or more dimensions of instruction (for example, student engagement, curriculum, and pedagogy) connected to an identified problem of leadership practice.	• To develop a shared vision for high-quality teaching and student learning based on an instructional framework (for example, 5D) • To calibrate and deepen understanding of the dimensions of an instructional framework (for example, student engagement and classroom environment and culture) • To calibrate understanding of best practices in a particular content area • To provide principals and teacher leaders a tool to assess their own classrooms against an emerging vision of instruction • To begin to use the language of an instructional framework to communicate learning to staff • To develop a school and district culture of public practice • To gather data necessary to identify relevant problems of practice • To observe and analyze the effect of teacher practice on student learning	• If we (as school and district leaders) spend regular and focused time in classrooms observing and describing teaching practice with the support of an instructional framework, then we will develop a common vision and shared understanding of high-quality instruction and how it affects student learning. • If we develop a common vision and shared understanding of high-quality instruction, then we will be able to identify and lead with greater clarity the improvement of teaching practice. • If we are open and transparent about our own learning, then we will be able to model the kind of reflective learning culture necessary to support improved practice for all.	• Who will participate? • Which classrooms will we visit? • How much time will we spend in classrooms? • What protocols, tools, or processes will we use in classrooms • What data will we collect? • What protocols, tools, or processes will we use after the walkthroughs to gather feedback and to inform the next steps? • What and how will we communicate to staff?	How will leaders • Communicate with staff about the walkthrough? • Model what it means to be a learner? • Highlight and celebrate what they want to reinforce? • Use teacher expertise to build collective learning? • Use their deepened understanding of quality instruction to inform critical problems of leadership practice? • Strategically plant seeds for future dialogue and reflection? • Articulate their vision for teaching and learning? • Consider revisions to professional development plans for individuals and groups? • Provide an avenue for feedback and conversation on both the process and subsequent learning?

TYPES OF OBSERVATIONS	PURPOSE(S)	SUPPORTING THEORY	LOGISTICAL CONSIDERATIONS	POSSIBLE LEADERSHIP ACTIONS FOR CONSIDERATION
Goal-Setting and Implementation Walkthrough *District level:* central office leaders, principals, teacher leaders *School level:* principal, instructional coaches, teachers	• To determine the level of implementation of curriculum materials and guidelines along with the amount of further support and professional development needed to implement the curriculum with fidelity • To determine the extent to which new learning(s) resulting from specific professional development offerings are being applied in actual practice • To determine additional supports and professional development needed to implement learning(s) • To establish the school instructional improvement goals • To determine schoolwide patterns across grade levels and subject areas to inform professional development • To determine individual goals and supports for teachers • To monitor student progress • To help identify a problem of leadership practice	• If we carefully monitor the expected level of implementation of new curriculum and professional development learning(s), then we will be able to measure the level of implementation across the district or school. • If we are able to identify the level of implementation of new curriculum and professional development learning(s), then we will be in a position to bring focused and differentiated support when necessary to improve the implementation and application of new practices. • If we examine our teaching practices in light of our deepened understanding of powerful instruction, then we will be able to establish specific improvement goals (district, school, or individual) along with the professional development necessary to improve practice.	• Who will participate? • Which classrooms will we visit? • How much time will we spend in classrooms? • What data will we collect? • What and how will we communicate to staff? • What protocols, tools, or processes will we use in classrooms? • What protocols, tools, or processes will we use after the walkthroughs to gather feedback and to inform the next steps?	How will leaders • Communicate with staff about the walkthrough? • Highlight and celebrate what they want to reinforce? • Create and communicate new expectations if necessary? • Use teacher and principal expertise to build collective learning? • Modify professional development as needed? • Strategically consider providing new or additional supports, for example, professional development, coaching, study groups, readings, and so on, if necessary? • Articulate their vision for teaching and learning? • Provide an avenue for feedback and conversation on both the process and subsequent learning?

TYPES OF OBSERVATIONS	PURPOSE(S)	SUPPORTING THEORY	LOGISTICAL CONSIDERATIONS	POSSIBLE LEADERSHIP ACTIONS FOR CONSIDERATION
Supervisory Walkthrough Supervisors and principals	• To examine the teaching and learning process as it relates to the school's and district's instructional goals • To examine relevant student performance data and monitor student progress • To focus on progress made since the last walkthrough visit and the best type(s) of professional development to meet teachers' needs • To identify specific leadership actions necessary to support the improvement of teaching practice • To assess leader's understanding of new learning • To hold leaders accountable for agreed-on leadership actions	• If we carefully examine and monitor student performance data and the quality of teaching and learning in light of our deepened understanding of powerful instruction, then we will be able to identify specific leadership actions necessary to improve practice. • If we carefully examine and monitor the extent to which agreed-on leadership actions are enacted, then we can hold leaders accountable for the improvement of teaching and learning.	• What student performance data will we examine? • Which classrooms will we visit? • How much time will we spend in classrooms? • How often should we visit specific classrooms? • What other school structures will we observe, for example, department meetings, PLC meetings, and so on? • What will we communicate to staff? • What protocols, tools, or processes will we use in classrooms?	How will leaders • Communicate with staff about the walkthrough? • Highlight and celebrate what they want to reinforce? • Create and communicate new expectations if necessary? • Provide new or additional supports, for example, professional development, coaching, and so on, if necessary? • Articulate their vision for teaching and learning? • Hold leader(s) accountable for agreed-on actions? • Assess the implementation of agreed-on actions using student learning as a measure?

Source: Copyright © 2010 Center for Educational Leadership, University of Washington.www.k-12leadership.org.

REFERENCES

Ball, D. (2010). Summary of testimony to the United States House of Representatives Committee on Education and Labor. May 4, 2010. Available from http://edlabor .house.gov/documents/111/pdf/testimony/20100504DeborahBallTestimony.pdf.

Barrera, A., Braley, R., & Slate, J. (2010). Beginning teacher programs: An investigation into the feedback from mentors of formal mentoring programs. *Mentoring & Tutoring: Partnership in Learning, 18*(1), 61–74.

Boatright, B. (2008). *Teachers' professional learning in the context of high school reform.* Saarbrucken, Germany: VDM Dr. Müller.

Bransford, J., Brown, A., & Cocking, R. (Eds.). (2000). *How people learn: Brain, mind, experience, and school.* Washington, DC: National Academy Press.

Bransford, J., & Schwartz, D. (2008). *It takes expertise to make expertise. Some thoughts about why and how and reflections on the themes in chapters 15–18.* Seattle: LIFE (Learning in Informal and Formal Environments) Center, University of Washington.

Brophy, J., & And, O. (1983). Relationships between teachers' presentations of classroom tasks and students' engagement in those tasks. *Journal of Educational Psychology, 75*(4), 544–52.

Calderon, M. (1996). *TLC's: Teachers learning communities.* El Paso, TX: International Academy for Cooperative Learning.

Calkins, L. (2001). *The art of teaching reading.* New York: Longman.

City, E., Elmore, R., Fiarman, S., & Teitel, L. (2009). *Instructional rounds in education.* Cambridge, MA: Harvard Education Press.

Coburn, C. E. & Russell, J. L. (2008). District policy and teachers' social networks. *Education Evaluation and Policy Analysis, 30*(3), 203–235.

Committee on the Study of Teacher Preparation Programs in the United States (2010). *Preparing teachers: Building evidence for sound policy.* Washington, DC: Center for Education, National Research Council, National Academy Press.

Copland, M., & Knapp, M. (2006). *Connecting leadership with learning: A framework for reflection, planning, and action.* Alexandria, VA: Association for Supervision and Curriculum Development.

Costa, A., & Garmston, R. (2002). *Cognitive coaching: A foundation for renaissance schools.* Norwood, MA: Christopher-Gordon.

Danielson, C. (1996). *Enhancing professional practice: A framework for teaching.* Alexandria, VA: Association for Supervision and Curriculum Development.

Denton, C., & Hasbrouck, J. (2009). A description of instructional coaching and its relationship to consultation. *Journal of Educational and Psychological Consultation, 19,* 150–175.

Dufour, R., & Eaker, R. (1998). *Professional learning communities at work: Best practices for enhancing student achievement.* Bloomington, IN: National Education Service.

Elmore, R. (2000). *Building a new structure for school leadership.* Washington, DC: The Albert Shanker Institute.

Elmore, R., & Burney, D. (1997). *Continuous improvement in Community District #2, New York City.* High Performance Learning Communities Project. Available from www.lrdc.pitt.edu/hplc/hplc.html.

Fink, E., & Resnick, L. (2001). Developing principals as instructional leaders. *Phi Delta Kappan, 82,* 598–606.

Florio, D., & Knapp, M. S. (1998). *Investment in professional learning: Options for the reauthorization of the Elementary and Secondary Education Act.* Seattle: Center for the Study of Teaching and Policy, University of Washington.

Gallimore, R., Ermeling, B. A., Saunders, W. M., & Goldenberg, C. (2009). Moving the learning of teaching closer to practice: Teacher education implications of school-based inquiry teams. *Elementary School Journal, 109*(5), 537–553.

Gallucci, C., Van Lare, M., Yoon, I., & Boatright, B. (2010). Instructional coaching: Building theory about the role and organizational support for professional learning. *American Educational Research Journal, 47,* 919. Originally published online 9 June 2010.

Gibson, S. A. (2005). Developing knowledge of coaching. *Issues in Teacher Education, 14*(2), 63–74.

Gladwell, M. (2008). *Outliers.* New York: Little, Brown.

Grossman, P., & McDonald, M. (2008). Back to the future: Directions for research in teaching and teacher education. *American Educational Research Journal, 45*(1), 184–205.

Haycock, K. (1998). *Good teaching matters: How well-qualified teachers can close the gap.* Washington, DC: The Education Trust.

Hobson, A., Ashby, P., Malderez, A., & Tomlinson, P. (2009). Mentoring beginning teachers: What we know and what we don't. *Teaching and Teaching Education, 25*(1), 207–216.

Honig, M. I. (2008). District central offices as learning organizations: How sociocultural and organizational learning theories elaborate district central office administrators' participation in teaching and learning improvement efforts. *American Journal of Education, 114*, 627–664.

Honig, M., & Copland, M. (2010). *Central office transformation for district-wide teaching and learning improvement.* Final Report to the Wallace Foundation. Seattle: Center for the Study of Teaching and Policy, University of Washington.

Hord, S. (1997). *Professional learning communities: Communities of continuous inquiry and improvement.* Austin, TX: Southwest Educational Development Laboratory.

Johnson, S., & Donaldson, M. (2007). Overcoming the obstacles to teacher leadership. *Educational Leadership, 65*(1), 8–13.

Knight, J. (2009). Coaching. *Journal of Staff Development, 30*(1), 18–22.

Koballa, T., & Bradbury, L. (2009). Leading to success. *Educational Digest: Essential Readings Condensed for Quick Review, 75*(2), 39–42.

Kowal, J., & Steiner, L. (2007). *Instructional coaching. Issue brief.* Washington, DC: Center for Comprehensive School Reform and Improvement.

Leithwood, K., Louis, K. S., Anderson, S., & Wahlstrom, K. (2004). *Review of research: How leadership influences student learning.* Minneapolis: Center for Applied Research and Educational Improvement, University of Minnesota.

Little, J. W. (1982). "Norms of collegiality and experimentation: Workplace conditions of school success." *American Educational Research Journal, 19*(3), 325–340.

Lortie, D. (1975). *Schoolteacher: A sociological study.* Chicago: University of Chicago Press.

Machado, A. (1982). *Selected poems* (Alan Trueblood, trans.). Cambridge, MA: Harvard University Press.

Marsh, J. A., Kerr, K. A., Ikemoto, G. S., Darilek, H., Suttorp, M., Zimmer, R. W., et al. (2005). *The role of districts in fostering instructional improvement.* Santa Monica, CA: Rand.

Marzano, R., Pickering, D., & Pollock, J. (2001). *Classroom instruction that works: Research-based strategies for increasing student achievement.* Alexandria, VA: Association for Supervision and Curriculum Development.

Mooney, M. (1990). *Reading to, with, and by children.* Katonah, NY: Richard C. Owen Publishers.

Mraz, M., Algozzine, B., & Watson, P. (2008). Perceptions and expectations of roles and responsibilities of literacy coaching. *Literacy Research and Instruction, 47*, 141–157.

Natriello, G. (1984). Managing the culture of the school. *Educational Leadership*, *42*(2), 80–82.

Nelson, T. H., Slavit, D., Perkins, M., & Hawthorn, T. (2008). A culture of collaborative inquiry: Learning to develop and support professional learning communities. *Teachers College Record*, *11*(6), 1269–1303.

Neufeld, S. B., & Roper, D. (2003). *Coaching: A strategy for developing instructional capacity: Promises & practicalities.* Boston: Education Matters.

Peske, H., & Haycock, K. (2006). *Teaching inequality: How poor and minority students are shortchanged on teacher quality.* Washington, DC: The Education Trust.

Pintrich, P., & De Groot, E. (1990). Motivational and self-regulated learning components of classroom academic performance. *Journal of Educational Psychology*, *82*(1), 33–40.

Reeves, D. (2002). *Making standards work: How to implement standards-based assessments in the classroom, school and district.* Denver: Center for Performance Assessment.

Resnick, L., & Glennan, T. (2002). *Leadership for learning: A theory of action for urban school districts from* School Districts and Instructional Renewal. New York: Teachers College Press.

Rogoff, B. (1995). Observing sociocultural activity on three planes: Participatory appropriation, guided participation, and apprenticeship. In J. V. Wertsch, P. Del Rio, & A. Alvarez (Eds.), *Sociocultural studies of mind* (pp. 139–164). Cambridge, MA: Cambridge University Press.

Rowan, B., Correnti, R., & Miller, R. (2002). What large-scale survey research tells us about teacher effects on student achievement: Insights from the prospects study of elementary schools. *Teachers College Record*, *104*(8), 1525–1567.

Saphier, J., & Gower, R. (1997). *The skillful teacher: Building your teaching skills* (5th ed.). Acton, MA: Research for Better Teaching.

Schlechty, P. C. (2002). *Working on the work: An action plan for teachers, principals, and superintendents.* San Francisco: Jossey-Bass.

Schmoker, M. (2001). *The results fieldbook: Practical strategies from dramatically improved schools.* Alexandria, VA: Association for Supervision and Curriculum Development.

Showers, B. (1985). Teachers coaching teachers. *Educational Leadership* (April), 43–48.

Shulman, L. S. (1986). Those who understand: Knowledge growth in teaching. *Educational Researcher*, *15*, 4–14.

Stein, M. K., & D'Amico, L. (1999). *Leading school- and district-wide reform: Multiple subjects matter.* Paper prepared under the sponsorship of the High Performance

Learning Communities Project at the Learning Research and Development Center. Pittsburgh: University of Pittsburgh.

Stein, M. K., & Nelson, B. S. (2003). Leadership content knowledge. *Educational Evaluation and Policy Analysis, 25*(4), 423–448.

Stigler, J., & Hiebert, J. (1999). *The teaching gap: Best ideas from the world's teachers for improving education in the classroom.* New York: The Free Press.

Stronge, J. (2002). *Qualities of effective teachers.* Alexandria, VA: Association for Supervision and Curriculum Development.

Taylor, J. E. (2008). Instructional coaching: The state of the art. In M. M. Mangin & S. R. Stoelinga (Eds.), *Effective teacher leadership: Using research to inform and reform* (pp. 10–35). New York: Teachers College Press.

Tung, R., Ouimette, M., & Feldman, J. (2004). *The challenge of coaching: Providing cohesion among multiple reform agendas.* Boston: Center for Collaborative Education.

Valli, L., & Hawley, W. (2003). Designing and implementing school-based professional development. In W.D.E. Hawley (Ed.), *The keys to effective schools: Educational reform as continuous improvement* (pp. 86–96). Washington, DC: National Education Association.

Van Lare, M. D., Yoon, I. H., & Gallucci, C. (2008). *Orchestration as an aspect of leadership in district-wide reform.* Seattle: Center for the Study of Teaching and Policy, University of Washington.

Vygotsky, L. S. (1987). *The collected work of L. S. Vygotsky: Problems of general psychology including the volume thinking and speech.* New York: Plenum.

Wahlstrom, K., Seashore, L. K., Leithwood, K., & Anderson, S. (2010). *Learning from leadership: Investigating the links to improved student learning.* Final Report of Research to the Wallace Foundation. Minneapolis: University of Minnesota.

West, L., & Staub, F. (2003). *Content-focused coaching: Transforming mathematics lessons.* Portsmouth, ME: Heinemann.

Williams, P. (2003). Analysis of Semiotic Principles in a Constructivist Learning Environment. Retrieved from ERIC database.

Wiske, M. (Ed.). (1998). *Teaching for understanding: Linking research with practice.* San Francisco: Jossey-Bass.

Yatvin, J. (2004). *A room with a differentiated view: How to serve all children as individual learners.* Portsmouth, NH: Heinemann.

Zander, B. (2000). Leading from any chair. In R. S. Zander & B. Zander (Eds.), *The art of possibility* (pp. 66–77). Boston: Harvard Business School Press.

INDEX

A

Accountability, reciprocal, xix, xxi–xxii, 12, 221–230

Accountability through inquiry stance, 237–239, 240

Adjustments (subdimension of assessment for student learning): defined, 25, 40–41, 74; guiding questions on, 96; math lesson analysis noting, 76–78

Adult learning: expertise in, 204–205; support for, 12–15

Algozzine, B., 191

Alvarado, A., 16

Anderson, S., xxii, 226

Assessment (subdimension of assessment for student learning): defined, 25, 37–39, 74; guiding questions on, 95; math lesson analysis noting, 74–76

Asessment for student learning (dimension of 5D framework): description of, 24, 25, 37–41, 46; math lesson analysis using, 74–78

Ashby, P., 193

Authentic engagement, 135

B

Ball, D., xx, 243

Barrera, A., 194

Boatright, B., 190, 192, 197

Bradbury, L., 194

Braley, R., 194

Bransford, J., 4, 9, 12, 28, 32, 33, 37, 38

Brophy, J., 135

Brown, A., 4, 28, 32, 33, 37, 38

Burney, D., 16

C

Calderon, M., 129

Calibration process for learning walkthroughs, 92, 102

Calkins, L., 206

Center for Educational Leadership (CEL): six foundational ideas at, xix–xxiii; two conclusions of, xvii–xviii; Web site, xxiii

Central Office Transformation, Five Dimensions of, 226–229

Change agents, coaches as, 191

City, E., 6, 17, 92

Classroom culture (subdimension of classroom environment and culture): defined, 25, 44–46, 78; guiding questions on, 96; math lesson analysis noting, 82–83; vision of high-quality instruction related to, 46

H

Habits of Thinking for Instructional
Leadership: analysis, 231–232;
conclusions on, 240; discussion
questions on, 240; figure illustrating,
231; inquiry stance and, 230; noticing
and wondering, 4, 92, 97, 230–231;
principal's inquiry cycle, 233–237

Hasbrouck, J., 193

Hawley, W., 204

Hawthorn, T., 204

Haycock, K., xix, 3

Hiebert, J., 35, 38

Hobson, A., 193

Honest conversations and classroom
observations, 129–131

Honig, M., 226, 229

Hord, S., 129

I

Inquiry stance, accountability through,
237–239, 240

Instructional coaching and content
coaching, 197–198

Instructional leadership through-line,
124

Instructional rounds, 17–18

Intellectual work (subdimension of
student engagement): defined, 25,
29–30, 58–59; guiding questions for
evaluating, 94; math lesson analysis
noting, 59–63; vision of high-quality
instruction related to, 30

Interpretations, feedback, and observations, 125–129

Inventory, teacher next steps, 174–177

J

Johnson, S., 130

K

Knapp, M. S., 149, 226

Knight, J., 191

Koballa, T., 194

Kowal, J., 197

L

Leaders as conductors: being a silent
conductor, 151, 152–163; developing leadership in others, 151,
171–173; engaging hearts and
minds, 151, 166–171; four
dimensions of orchestration, 151;
orchestrating professional learning,
173–186; strategizing, 151, 163–166

Learning expertise, 9, 12, 19

Learning target, 27

Learning walkthroughs: background
on, 16–17; calibration and, 92, 102;
district, 102; example, 91–92; letter
to principals regarding, 103–105;
letter to staff regarding, 105–106;
noticing and wondering during, 4,
92, 97, 230–231; purpose of, 89–90;
scripting lessons, 97–102; template
of guiding questions for, 92, 93–96,
theory of action and intended
outcomes and, 90–91

Learning-focused partnerships, 227,
229

Leithwood, K., xxii, 226

Lesson analysis: assessment for
student learning, 74–78; classroom

Student talk (subdimension of student engagement): description of, 25, 29, 32, 33, 59; guiding questions for notes on, 94; math lesson analysis noting, 66–69; vision of high-quality instruction related to, 33

Studio and residency teachers, criteria for, 165

Studio classrooms, 12, 153

Studio-residency example of "silent conductors", 153–163

Supervisory walkthrough, 89, 114–121

T

Talk, student (subdimension of student engagement): description of, 25, 29, 32, 33, 59; guiding questions for notes on, 94; math lesson analysis noting, 66–69; vision of high-quality instruction related to, 33

Taylor, J. E., 191

Teacher expertise: access to, 8–9; in adult professional learning, 204–205; conclusions on, 245–246; in content, 199–202; crisis, 241–245; discussion questions on, 246; expertise to make, 5–15; in instructional practice, 202–204; learner expertise versus, 9, 12, 19; literature on, 4; novice instructional leaders versus, 4–5, 123

Teacher learning, structures and resources for, 180–181

Teacher next steps inventory, 174–177

Teaching: as complex endeavor, xix, xx–xxi; public scrutiny of, xix, xxi, 10–15

Teaching approaches and strategies (subdimension of curriculum and pedagogy): defined, 25, 35, 69; guiding questions on, 95; math lesson analysis noting, 70–72

Teaching licensure, pathways to, 244

Teaching point (subdimension of purpose): defined, 25, 26, 27–29, 52; guiding questions for notes on, 93; math lesson analysis using, 52, 54–58; vision of high-quality instruction related to, 29

Theory-building questions, 209, 211, 212

Theory-forming notes, 208, 210

Through-line, instructional leadership, 124

Tomlinson, P., 193

TOSAs (teachers on special assignment), 14–15

Tung, R., 191

U

Use of physical environment (subdimension of classroom environment and culture): defined, 25, 41–43, 78; guiding questions on, 96; math lesson analysis noting, 78–80

V

Valli, L., 204

Van Lare, M. D., 151, 152, 197

Vision statements that define high-quality instruction, 27, 29, 30, 32, 33, 36, 37, 39, 46

Vygotsky, L. S., 199